PSYCHOLOGY AND POSTMODERNISM

INQUIRIES IN SOCIAL CONSTRUCTION

Series editors
Kenneth J. Gergen and John Shotter

This series is designed to facilitate, across discipline and national boundaries, an emergent dialogue within the social sciences which many believe presages a major shift in the Western intellectual tradition.

Including among its participants sociologists of science, psychologists, management and communications theorists, cyberneticists, ethnomethodologists, literary theorists, feminists and social historians, it is a dialogue which involves profound challenges to many existing ideas about, for example, the person, selfhood, scientific method and the nature of scientific and everyday knowledge.

It has also given voice to a range of new topics, such as the social construction of personal identities; the role of power in the social making of meanings; rhetoric and narrative in establishing sciences; the centrality of everyday activities; remembering and forgetting as socially constituted activities; reflexivity in method and theorizing. The common thread underlying all these topics is a concern with the processes by which human abilities, experiences, common sense and scientific knowledge both are *produced in*, and *reproduce*, human communities.

Inquiries in Social Construction affords a vehicle for exploring this new consciousness, the problems raised and the implications for society.

Also in this series

Collective Remembering
edited by David Middleton and Derek Edwards

Everyday Understanding
Social and Scientific Implications
edited by Gün R. Semin and Kenneth J. Gergen

Research and Reflexivity
edited by Frederick Steier

Constructing Knowledge
Authority and Critique in Social Science
edited by Lorraine Nencel and Peter Pels

Discursive Psychology
Derek Edwards and Jonathan Potter

Therapy as Social Construction
edited by Sheila McNamee and Kenneth J. Gergen

PSYCHOLOGY AND POSTMODERNISM

EDITED BY
STEINAR KVALE

SAGE Publications
London • Newbury Park • New Delhi

First published 1992

 SAGE Publications Ltd
6 Bonhill Street
London EC2A 4PU

SAGE Publications Inc
2455 Teller Road
Newbury Park, California 91320

SAGE Publications India Pvt Ltd
32, M-Block Market
Greater Kailash – I
New Delhi 110 048

British Library Cataloguing in Publication data

Psychology and Postmodernism. –
(Inquiries in Social Construction Series)
   I. Kvale, Steinar   II. Series
   150.1

   ISBN 0–8039–8603–3
   ISBN 0–8039–8604–1 pbk

Library of Congress catalog card number 92–56380

Typeset by Type Study, Scarborough
Printed in Great Britain by
Biddles Ltd, Guildford, Surrey

Contents

Preface   vii

Notes on the Contributors   viii

Introduction: From the Archaeology of the Psyche to the
Architecture of Cultural Landscapes   1
    Steinar Kvale

1   Toward a Postmodern Psychology   17
    Kenneth J. Gergen

2   Postmodern Psychology: A Contradiction in Terms?   31
    Steinar Kvale

3   'Getting in Touch': The Meta-Methodology of a
Postmodern Science of Mental Life   58
    John Shotter

4   Postmodern Subjects: Towards a Transgressive Social
Psychology   74
    Mike Michael

5   Postmodernism and the Human Sciences   88
    Patti Lather

6   An Introduction to Deconstructionist Psychology   110
    Paul Richer

7   Postmodernism and Subjectivity   119
    Lars Løvlie

8   Postmodern Self-Psychology Mirrored in Science and
the Arts   135
    Neil Young

9   Postmodern Epistemology of Practice   146
    Donald E. Polkinghorne

10   The Epic of Disbelief: The Postmodernist Turn in
Contemporary Psychoanalysis   166
    Louis A. Sass

11   From Mod Mascu-linity to Post-Mod Macho:
     A Feminist Re-Play   183
     Mary Gergen

12   From Theory to Practice and Back Again: What does
     Postmodern Philosophy Contribute to Psychological
     Science?   194
     Seth Chaiklin

13   'Postmodernism' and 'Late Capitalism': On Terms and
     Realities   209
     Peter Madsen

Index   224

Preface

This book explores implications of a postmodern culture for psychology. It originated in a symposium on postmodernity and psychology which took place in June 1989 at the Centre for Qualitative Research at the University of Aarhus in Denmark. The presentations by Ken and Mary Gergen, Steinar Kvale, Lars Løvlie and Peter Madsen were later published in a special issue of *The Humanistic Psychologist* on Psychology and Postmodernity, 18 (1), 1990, together with four additional articles by Patti Lather, Paul Richer, John Shotter and Neil Young. We wish to thank *The Humanistic Psychologist* and its editor Chris Aanstoos for permission to reprint these articles.

For the present volume four new chapters were invited – by Seth Chaiklin, Mike Michael, Donald Polkinghorne and Louis Sass – and the earlier articles have been revised. The resulting book then came to represent authors from Denmark, Norway, the United Kingdom and the United States, writing from the perspectives of psychology, education, literary criticism and feminism.

The further origins of this volume may be traced to discussions with students of the Institute of Psychology in Aarhus. From Antonio de Lopes I received a copy of Lyotard's *La condition postmoderne* which he published in Danish in 1982. (The book was then no economic success, and Antonio had to start a Portuguese wine company to help his finances; this soon became so successful that the publication of postmodern texts and study of psychology were left behind.) Discussions with students and colleagues in subsequent seminars on postmodernity and psychology led to my own chapter in this volume, and I am especially grateful to the students Helle Jeppesen, Gerda Kraft, Klaus Nielsen and Birgit Wenzel for their continual inspiration and critical comments. Outside the institute I particularly would like to thank Budd Anderson, San Jose State University, California and Leon Rappoport, University of Kansas, Manhattan, for their critical suggestions and support.

The editing of the present volume has been an unexpectedly easy task, thanks to the co-operation of the contributors and the efficient and pleasant co-ordination of the project by my secretary, Annie Dolmer Kristensen.

Steinar Kvale

Notes on the Contributors

Seth Chaiklin is an Assistant Professor in the Institute of Psychology at the University of Aarhus. He received a PhD in psychology from the University of Pittsburgh. His research areas are subject matter learning of mathematics and science, computer use in community-based settings and formative teaching experiments for cultural minorities. He has recently co-edited *Understanding Practice: Perspectives on Activity and Context* with Jean Lave.

Kenneth J. Gergen is Professor of Psychology at Swarthmore College, Swarthmore, Pennsylvania. He is the author of *Toward Transformation in Social Knowledge* and *The Saturated Self* and co-editor (with John Shotter) of *Texts of Identity*.

Mary Gergen, PhD, is an Associate Professor of Psychology and an Associate of the Women's Studies Program at Pennsylvania State University. She has written extensively on the relationship of feminist theory to psychology, and is editor of *Feminist Thought and the Structure of Knowledge*.

Steinar Kvale is Professor of Educational Psychology at the Institute of Psychology and Director of the Centre for Qualitative Research at the University of Aarhus. He is also adjunct faculty at Saybrook Institute, San Francisco. His work has centred on remembering, on examinations and grading and on the development of the interview as a research method. He is the author of *Prüfung und Herrschaft* and editor of *Issues of Validity in Qualitative Research*.

Patti Lather teaches qualitative research and feminist pedagogy at Ohio State University, where she is part of an effort to offer a Gender and Education doctoral emphasis. She has published *Getting Smart: Feminist Research and Pedagogy with/in the Postmodern* and is currently working on the question, what do you do with validity once you've met poststructuralism?

Lars Løvlie is Professor of Education at the Institute for Educational Research at the University of Oslo. He has written *The Educational*

Argument (in Norwegian) and is currently working on two studies, one on the problem of application in ethics and the other on formation or *Bildung* in the theory of education.

Peter Madsen is Professor of Comparative Literature at the University of Copenhagen. He has worked on critical theory and semiotics as well as projects in literary history, intellectual history and the analysis of literary works and movies. Among his publications are books (in Danish) on semiotics and dialectics, and on socialism and democracy, as well as essays in Scandinavian and international journals. He is currently writing a book on modern culture, *Imagining Modernity*.

Mike Michael is a Lecturer at the School of Independent Studies, University of Lancaster. He has written on poststructuralist approaches in social psychology, discourse analysis and the public understanding of science and technology, and environmental ethics.

Donald E. Polkinghorne is Professor of Counseling Psychology at the University of Southern California and a licensed practising psychologist in California. He received a BD in divinity from Yale University and a PhD in psychology from the Union Institute. He is the author of *Methodology for the Human Sciences* and *Narrative Knowing and the Human Sciences*. His research interests include the use of qualitative procedures to study psychotherapeutic processes.

Paul Richer is an Associate Professor of Psychology at Duquesne University, Pennsylvania. He received a BA in psychology from Bard College, Annandale-on-Hudson, New York, and a PhD in psychology from the New School Graduate Faculty of Political and Social Science, New York. Since then he has been a member of Duquesne University's psychology department, where his research has concentrated on the phenomenology of perception and hallucination, as well as on deconstructionist approaches to psychology.

Louis A. Sass is Associate Professor of Clinical Psychology at Rutgers University in New Jersey. He is interested in the philosophy of psychology, particularly of psychoanalysis, and in phenomenological and hermeneutic approaches to severe psychopathology. He is the author of *Madness and Modernism: Insanity in the Light of Modern Art, Literature, and Thought*, and is completing a second book, a study of psychosis in relation to the philosophy of Ludwig Wittgenstein.

John Shotter is Professor of Interpersonal Relations at the Department of Communication, University of New Hampshire. His long-term concern has been with the social conditions conducive to the development of autonomous personhood, social identities and responsible action. Among his books are *Images of Man in Psychological Research* and *Social Accountability and Selfhood*. He is also the co-editor (with Kenneth J. Gergen) of *Texts of Identity* and (with Ian Parker) of *Deconstructing Social Psychology*.

Neil Young is currently on the graduate faculty of the Existential-Phenomenological Therapeutic Psychology Program at Seattle University. He teaches courses on psychology and art, cross-cultural counselling, birth, death and dying, existential psychotherapy, perspectives of psychotherapy and psychology of spiritual experience.

Introduction
From the Archaeology of the Psyche to the Architecture of Cultural Landscapes

Steinar Kvale

In art, philosophy and the humanities, the current age has been described as postmodern. This book explores the possibilities of a psychological discipline in a postmodern cultural landscape. The chapters contain a variety of positions on psychological knowledge, research and practice, moving within postmodern culture. They go beyond mere critiques of modern psychology as well as a mere legitimation of existing approaches. There is a break with major assumptions about the subject matter of modern psychology, in particular by the decentring of the self, the move from the inside of the psyche to the text of the world, and the emphasis on practical knowledge.

No coherent school of postmodern psychology emerges from the following chapters; indeed, the very concept of a unitary discipline is at odds with postmodern thought. To put it sharply, the issue is whether the modern science of psychology can be developed and enriched by drawing on postmodern knowledge. Or does postmodern thought radically undermine, or transform, the concept of a scientific psychology as developed during the modern age?

In this introduction some meanings of the term 'postmodern' will be presented, followed by an overview of the chapters of this volume. Then some of the diverse positions on postmodernity and on a postmodern psychology in these chapters will be outlined.

Meanings of the 'postmodern'

In the 1950s and 1960s, postmodern themes were discussed within architecture, literary criticism and sociology in the United States. French philosophers addressed postmodernity during the 1970s, and in the 1980s the issue of a postmodern age came to general public attention.

Whether one likes the term 'postmodern' or not, it does seem to point to important issues of the current age. There exists no coherent postmodern philosophy, but a multitude of thinkers who focus on different aspects of a postmodern condition. In France, Lyotard has analysed the status of knowledge in a postmodern age, in particular with respect to legitimation; Foucault has addressed the web of power and knowledge in historical studies; Baudrillard focuses on fascination, seduction and the media's creating of a hyperreality of simulacra; Derrida has addressed language and deconstruction; and Lacan has reinterpreted the psychoanalytic unconscious. In the United States, Jameson has analysed postmodernism as the logic of late capitalism; and Rorty has developed a neopragmatic approach to postmodernity.

The very term 'postmodern' is controversial and ambiguous. It may be helpful to discern at least three meanings: *postmodernity* as referring to a postmodern age; *postmodernism* as referring to the cultural expression of a postmodern age; and *postmodern thought*, or discourse, as referring to philosophical reflection on a postmodern age and culture. (See the discussions of the term by Berg, 1991; Lyotard, 1986; Madsen, this volume.) Although the terms 'post-modernity', 'postmodernism' and 'postmodern thought' are often used indiscriminately in the literature, as well as in the chapters of this volume, it may be useful to discern the three meanings of postmodern which these terms connote.

Postmodernity refers to an age which has lost the Enlightenment belief in emancipation and progress through more knowledge and scientific research. Postmodern society consists less of totalities to be ruled by preconceived models than by decentralization to hetero-geneous local contexts characterized by flexibility and change. There is a change from a mechanical, metallurgic production to an information industry, and from production to consumption as the main focus of the economy. It is an age in which the multiple perspectives of new media tend to dissolve any sharp line between reality and fantasy, undermining belief in an objective reality.

Postmodernism as a cultural expression encompasses art as collage and pastiche, the pop art of Andy Warhol's consumer goods, Las Vegas-style architecture, the media's dissolution of the distinction of reality and image, and the hectic change of perspectives in rock videos. Also focal are the labyrinthine themes of Borges's stories and works like those of the novelist Umberto Eco, who caricatures the interpretation mania of the modern search for meaning.

Postmodern thought replaces a conception of a reality independent of the observer with notions of language as actually constituting the structures of a perspectival social reality. The modern dichotomy of an objective reality distinct from subjective images is breaking down and being replaced by a hyperreality of self-referential signs. There is a critique of the modernist search for foundational forms and belief in a linear progress through more knowledge. The dichotomy of universal social laws and the individual self is replaced by the interaction of local networks. Postmodern thought has involved an expansion of reason, it has gone beyond the cognitive and scientific domains to permeate those of ethics and aesthetics as well; it has analysed the nexus of power and knowledge, in particular the de-individualizing of power into anonymous structures.

These various meanings and aspects of 'modern' and 'postmodern' are more extensively treated in this volume, particularly in the chapters by Ken Gergen, Kvale, Lather, Polkinghorne, Chaiklin and Madsen.

An outline of the chapters

The heterogeneous chapters of this book do not fit into any neat order of categories. Broadly speaking, the first chapters treat general possibilities of a postmodern psychology. The second group of chapters more specifically confronts the issue of the self and subjectivity in a postmodern age and the position of the professional practice of psychology. And in the last chapters, critiques of the concept of postmodernity as well as of a postmodern psychology are raised from feminist, modernist and Marxist perspectives.

The first two chapters converge in their presentations of post-modernity and in their critiques of modern psychology, but diverge on the possibilities of a postmodern psychology. *Ken Gergen* depicts the modernist assumptions of a basic, knowable subject matter of psychology, of universal psychological processes, of method as a truth guarantee and of research as progressive. He outlines the postmodern turn in cultural history, with its perspectivism, its opening of new vistas for study and its development of practical and contextual forms of understanding. The implications of a saturated self vanishing into a state of relatedness are more fully analysed elsewhere (Gergen, 1991). *Steinar Kvale* outlines the entrenchment of modern psychology – behaviourist as well as humanist – in modernity and raises the question whether a postmodern psychology is in fact a contradiction in terms. In contrast to academic psychology, the current theoretical rehabilitation of professional practice is seen as congenial to postmodern thought, focusing, as it does, on situated knowledge of human activity, with an openness to the heterogeneous and qualitative knowledge of the everyday world, and validation through practice. Finally, some scenarios for psychology in a postmodern world are outlined, and the relations of psychology to religion and to consumer culture are pointed out.

The next two chapters treat implications of postmodern thought for cognitive and social psychology. *John Shotter* discusses the possibility of a postmodern science of mental life. This would involve a shift from the detached, theory-testing onlooker to an involved, interpreting participant observer. It elevates the practical embodied knowledge of everyday life over theoretical knowledge. Shotter briefly outlines what happens to individualistically conceived topics such as perception, memory, learning and motivation when they are embedded in the context of a postmodernist practical social research. *Mike Michael* addresses a social psychology of postmodernity; he departs from the epistemological approach of Gergen's social constructionism to focus on subject matter and to map out the social reality of a postmodern world. Michael goes beyond the priority of the linguistic and social, arguing that the natural needs to be integrated into the postmodern project. Drawing upon a sociological study of the interaction of fishermen, researchers and nature, he argues for the grounding of bioregional narratives in geography rather than in an essentialized self, and he advocates environmental ethics and politics.

The political implications of the social sciences are taken up in the next chapters. *Patti Lather* raises the question whether social science must remain a partner in domination and hegemony or whether it can forget itself and become something else. She describes the move from positivism towards an interpretative, value-constituted and value-constituting social science. She dismisses both the modernist reification of the subject and the postmodern 'death-of-the-subject' theories, instead arguing for a decentred subjectivity and multi-sited agency of meaning. *Paul Richer* deconstructs psychological interpretation. He follows Foucault's critique of analyses of power at the level of the conscious intentions of individuals and moves the 'who' of power and of language to anonymous dispersed fields of language structures and webs of power relations. Richer denies an emancipatory potential of psychological interpretation, arguing that today medical and behavioural forms of control are supplemented by more efficient, indirect humanist interpretative techniques of social control.

Deconstructionist approaches to the self are taken up in the following two chapters. *Lars Løvlie* points out that the postmodern 'death of the subject' eliminates a basic presupposition of psychology and education – the idea of an autonomous and intentional agent. The deconstructivist move is to constitute the subject as a text, to describe subjectivity as a linguistic structure of signs and to move human phenomena from the inside of a psyche to the outside of the text. The implications of the deconstruction of the self are then discussed, for the writing of self-biographies, illustrated by Rousseau's *Confessions*. *Neil Young* traces a postmodern self-psychology in art and literature. He outlines history of painting as a retreat along the self–object spectrum towards the subjectivity of the painter, most conspicuous in the art of the Impressionists. In literature, a unified image of the self has become lost in a labyrinth of self-centredness without any 'true self' or 'true centre' as in Ibsen's drama *Peer Gynt*, where man is depicted as a collection of social roles attained and abandoned, of identities discarded or transcended, as an 'onion self'.

Donald Polkinghorne outlines a postmodern epistemology of practice. He depicts academic psychology as a subplot within the history of modernism and argues that the psychology of practice, unlike academic psychology, is configured as a postmodern science. He points to studies which show that psychotherapists rarely find psychological research relevant for practice, and that they have to build up a second body of knowledge. The practitioners' expert knowledge is dynamic and context dependent; and Polkinghorne goes on to argue that this largely oral knowledge of practice is in tune with postmodern ideas of knowledge as without foundations, fragmentary and constructed, as well as with the current neopragmatic shift from metaphors of correctness to those of utility.

The remaining four chapters represent different critical perspectives on the postmodern. *Louis Sass* confronts postmodern trends of relativism, scepticism and fictionalism in contemporary psychoanalysis. He discusses the lived consequences of a philosophy of 'as if' in the psychotherapeutic situation, asking what it means for patients to have their life history aesthetically and relativistically interpreted as merely narratival fictions. He points out how the earlier treatments of these themes by Nietzsche, Musil and Borges also addressed the dark and troubling side of the fictionalized views of reality. *Mary Gergen* takes issue with the postmodern trend of critical unmasking and deconstruction, arguing that feminist sensitivities and priorities can enable the social sciences to move towards a more positive form of postmodernism. She criticizes the masculine biases of academic discourse and departs from the customary forms of 'straight talk'. Her chapter has the form of a stage play, the dialogue of a feminist postmodern critic and a postmodern man who continually play upon, break through and reverse conventional clichés of intellectual discourse.

Seth Chaiklin criticizes meta-theoretical attempts to apply concepts of postmodern philosophy to psychology. In his view the distinctions between a postmodern and a modern psychology that are made in the chapters of this book by Ken Gergen, Kvale and Polkinghorne are overdrawn; and he maintains that more productive paths are available for realizing the goals envisaged in these chapters, in particular within cultural-historical psychology. *Peter Madsen* discusses postmodernism as a late capitalist ideology. Following Jameson he posits postmodernism as an indication of a shift in the public focus from production to consumption, and he depicts architecture as an exemplary field for cultural studies – a place where artistic, cultural and social concerns are obviously bound up with political and economic power. Madsen points out a correspondence between the lack of reference to real foundations in the movements of advanced forms of capital and the absence of the referent at the cultural level. He indicates the possibility of a return from the play of significations and simulations to reality in both the economic and the cultural sphere.

In the following two sections of this introduction a few of the many issues raised in the chapters will be discussed in more detail. Some of the convergent and divergent views will be outlined, first on the concept of the postmodern, and then on the possibilities of a postmodern psychology.

Postmodern issues

It is difficult to present a new mode of thinking without being caught in old categories of thought. Discussions of postmodernism tend to get entangled in modernist dichotomies. This may be due to the failure of writers on postmodernity to get beyond modern polarities of thought, or to the tendency of readers to view postmodern texts through modern binary glasses.

Postmodern discourse is heterogeneous; it emphasizes differences and continual changes of perspectives, and it attempts to avoid dichotomized and reified concepts. A historical example of how to present a new mode of thought without getting entrapped in the conceptualizations criticized is found in Kierkegaard's writings. In his break with the totalizing dialectics of Hegel, Kierkegaard chose an indirect style, full of paradoxes, and through pseudonyms he presented a multitude of perspectives on his topics, thereby avoiding a clear-cut logic and evading the totalizing mode of thought he was criticizing.

The chapters of the present volume follow rather traditional forms of academic 'straight talk' writing. The exception is Mary Gergen, whose style deliberately disorients a modernist reader; her dramatic form and multi-vocal play on language are attempts to break away from a modernist and patriarchal discourse.

Below, some positions will be outlined on the common controversies about the modern vs the postmodern, about objectivism vs relativism and about the political implications of postmodernity.

Postmodern vs modern

Opposing postmodern to modern involves a dichotomy which is contrary to a postmodern move to go beyond binary oppositions and to descriptions of differences and nuances. 'Postmodern' is a descriptive term; it depicts what comes after modernism. The term is not 'anti-modern'; the very concept thus differs from the thrust of the movements of the 1960s and 1970s as anti-authoritarianism, anti-capitalism, etc. A postmodern approach to history is neither a reverence for the past nor a modern erasing of traditions and starting anew from a *tabula rasa*. The approach to history is rather that of re-use and collage, of taking up elements of tradition and recycling them in new contexts, most visible in postmodern architecture and current fashion.

The concept of postmodernity entails the issue of periodization. This raises the question whether postmodernity is so radically new that it depicts a new epoch, or is a transitory phase, or whether it is merely a continuation of issues that originated in the modern epoch and is then more appropriately termed neo-modernism. There are among postmodern writers different views on the relation to modernity; while Baudrillard sees a radical break or rupture, Lyotard depicts postmodern as a new way of knowing (1986). He describes the very idea of chronology as totally modern, the idea that it is possible and necessary to break with tradition. Such a break represents a repressing and a repeating of the past, rather than overcoming it by reflecting it and working it through. Jameson (see Madsen) changes the perspective by regarding both modernism and postmodernism as cultural expressions of different phases of capitalism, reflecting a change from a logic of production to a logic of consumption.

Chaiklin criticizes how several of the present chapters convey a polarized opposition of modernity and postmodernity, neglecting a continuity. Also Michael attempts to transgress the modernist–postmodernist dichotomy, maintaining that modernist positions are perfectly feasible within the postmodern, which he regards as a potential improvement upon the modern.

The use of the term 'postmodern' requires a clarification of what is meant by modern. Thus Ken Gergen characterizes modernity by mechanization and industrialization, while Løvlie focuses on the romanticist writer Rousseau in his analysis of the modern concept of the self, and Kvale includes both the technical rationality and the romanticist reaction as aspects of modernity, tracing the dichotomy into modern psychology. Madsen, following Habermas, points to emancipatory potentials of modernism, which have not yet been fully realized. Aanstoos (1990), referring to Toulmin, emphasizes the rich and open humanism of the Renaissance origin of modernity, which was later replaced by the strict rationality and quest for certainty of the Enlightment.

Perhaps one main effect of the postmodern discourse is a renewed focus upon and clarification of what can be meant by modernity, thus making explicit the main themes of the culture which the present epoch is based upon. And regardless of whether postmodernity is conceived as a rupture with, or a continuation of, modernity, there is in the current discourse a change in the questions asked and the contexts where the answers are sought.

In psychology, a move from an anti-positivist to a postmodern phase is a decisive change. Rather than legitimating developments in psychology with speculations about a mechanist or a relativist science of physics, new approaches in psychology are now placed in a broader historical and cultural context, including the very issue of a transition from a modern to a postmodern culture.

Objectivism and relativism

Perhaps the most frequent critique of postmodern thought is a rampant relativism, leading to nihilism and social anomie. It is maintained that when there are no longer any objective truths or universal values to be pursued; all knowledge and values become equally valid and relative.

The polarization of objectivism vs relativism is again a modern issue. Bernstein (1983) traces it to a 'Cartesian anxiety' formulated as either certitude or moral chaos. He analyses different positions to the dichotomy and argues that both an absolute objectivism and subjectivism are untenable, as arguments for both positions presuppose the more fundamental notion of an intersubjective discourse.

Discussions of objectivism vs relativism tend to take place on a rather general level, abstracted from the culture-specific context of the discourse, and from the practical interests involved. Ken Gergen suggests that a closer historical look at an alleged objective system of thought, based on fundamental and universal laws, may show how this system rests upon a particular perspective which in a given epoch has been made the only possible view. And Gergen (1991) outlines the development of technology and in particular the electronic media as a background for the postmodern multi-perspectival approach to a social reality. Arguing from a feminist perspective, Lather criticizes postmodern nihilistic tendencies of substituting absolutism with relativism. Both positions deny the location, the embodiment and the partial perspective of knowledge and values. It may further be helpful to discern what phenomena a posited relativism pertains to. Shotter thus accepts an epistemic relativity, where all beliefs are socially produced, but he rejects a moral relativity where all beliefs are equally valid, taking the postmodern standpoint that in the forum of scientific judgement questions of justice take an equal place with those of truth.

In a situation where action is demanded, all views are not equally valid. Lather, Polkinghorne and Sass warn against relativism, pointing to its consequences for practice. Lather raises the power context of the objectivism vs relativism issue; relativism appears as a problem for the dominating groups when their ideological hegemony is challenged. Relativist assumptions of a free play of meaning are of little use to women fighting against oppression. And Sass warns against the effects upon patients of relativist and fictionalized interpretations of postmodernist trends in psychoanalysis.

Practice has become a privileged site, where the alternative to relativism is not objectivism, but embodiment in partial perspective. Polkinghorne adopts a neopragmatist approach to clinical work and argues against a relativist position. A belief that there is no differentiation between knowledge claims is untenable in a practical situation. Here it is necessary to decide which actions to choose, and Polkinghorne proposes as a test for pragmatic knowledge whether it functions successfully in guiding human action to fulfil intended purposes.

Postmodernity and politics
With Lyotard's dismissal of global systems of thought, and the meta-narratives of emancipation, postmodern philosophy has become accused of being unpolitical and even neo-conservative. The postmodern endorsement of cultural pluralism has been criticized as allowing for a relativist status quo in politics. The reply has been that the modern emphasis on emancipation and universality has had totalitarian consequences and excluded the discourses of the Third World.

In the present volume Madsen analyses postmodernism as the ideology of consumer capitalism, fostering an ideology of resignation, giving up changing the real world for the play of significations or simulations.

Authors who draw upon Foucault's analyses of the inter-penetration of knowledge and power in the social sciences see the political implications of postmodernism as leading not to apathy, but to activism. Richer thus deconstructs the individualist interpretations of a modern humanistic and therapeutic psychology which he regards as techniques of oppression. These indirect interpretative ap proaches are today more efficient social control techniques than the medical drugs or the shaping techniques of behaviourism. Richer concludes that all psychology is a branch of the police, with psychodynamic and humanistic psychologies as the secret police.

Lather poses the question whether the social sciences must remain a partner in domination or can lead the way to social betterment. Cultural work becomes a battle for the signified – a struggle to fix meaning on behalf of particular power relations and social interests. And following actor-network theory Michael conceives scientists as multi-faceted entrepreneurs, with science becoming politics conducted by other means.

The political implications of postmodernism have in particular been discussed with regard to education. Thus Aronowitz and Giroux (1991) argue that postmodernism must extend and broaden the democratic claims of modernism by providing educators with a more complex and insightful view of the relationships of culture, power and knowledge. This concerns especially the material and ideological conditions that allow multiple, specific and heterogeneous ways of life, allowing for a cultural pluralism.

Implications of postmodernity for psychology

The heterogeneous chapters of this book raise the challenge of the orientation of a psychological science and profession in the landscape of a postmodern culture today. In culture at large, there was a wave of interest in psychology in the 1970s, particularly in psychoanalysis, humanistic psychology and critical emancipatory psychology. In the 1980s, the discipline of psychology virtually disappeared from the main scene of cultural and social debate. Today, there are signs of a disintegration of the scientific foundations of modern psychology. Further, there is a growing boredom with current psychological knowledge, which currently appears to have less to say about the human situation than do the arts and the humanities. And, within the psychological profession, the tensions between the theoretical orientation of academic psychology and professional practice have increased.

A postmodern discourse has long been in focus in the arts and humanities, and recently also in such social sciences as anthropology, education, political science and sociology (see, for instance, Aronowitz and Giroux, 1991; Berg, 1991; Clifford and Marcus, 1986; Featherstone, 1991; Heller and Feher, 1988). In psychology there have been some scattered applications of postmodern philosophy, mainly in relation to radical constructivism in social psychology and systemic therapy, but few discussions among psychologists on the implications of a postmodern culture for the discipline. (See, though, Parker and Shotter, 1990; the special issues of the *Irish Journal of*

Psychology, 1988, on radical constructivism in psychotherapy, and *The Humanistic Psychologist*, 1990, on psychology and post-modernity; and the debate by Gergen, Ash, Luhmann and Bruner in a Festschrift to Graumann, in *Psychologische Rundschau*, 1990.)

The scarcity of discussion of a postmodern culture in psychology may be due to a 'time lag'; it often takes some time before new conceptions of the relation of the human being and world in philosophy and the humanities are taken up by psychologists. The lack of thematization of postmodernity and psychology may, however, also be due to a basic incompatibility of fundamental assumptions of modern psychology and postmodern thought.

Postmodernism may on the other hand come to serve as an external legitimation of marginal views already held or as yet another critique of a mainstream modern psychology. These versions are rather at odds with a postmodern approach, which focuses on new possibilities rather than mere anti-establishment critiques, and rejects a modern legitimation mania of justifying by appeal to some philosophical foundation. The question to pose in relation to the following chapters is whether they lead to new ways of conceiving the relation of the human being and world, and to creative forms of scientific understanding and professional practice.

The chapters of this book diverge on the implications of a postmodern approach to the discipline of psychology:

1 A postmodern discourse leads to a meta-theoretical reconceptualization of the subject matter and opens new vistas for psychology (Ken Gergen, Shotter, Michael and Polkinghorne).
2 A postmodern discourse involves reconceptualizations of psychological topics as the self (Lather, Løvlie and Young) and of therapeutic practice (Polkinghorne).
3 The very conception of a psychological science may be so rooted in modernist assumptions that it becomes difficult to understand men and women in a postmodern culture (Kvale).
4 The concept of a postmodern age is contested, and the alleged implications for psychology are doubtful (Chaiklin).
5 The relativism and fictionalism of postmodernism can be detrimental in a therapeutic relationship (Sass) and serve as an ideological mystification of consumer capitalism (Madsen).

Some more specific implications of postmodern thought which may be drawn from the following chapters are outlined below. They concern knowledge, practice, research, deconstruction, the vanishing subject, humanism and naturalism, and a move from inside to outside.

Knowledge
There is a move from knowledge as abstract, universal and objective to socially useful, local knowledge. More practical forms of knowing are advocated elevating the practical embodied knowledge of everyday life over theoretical knowledge. And there is a move from the knower to the known, from the knowing subject to the subject known, from the psychology of cognitive processes to epistemological investigation of the nature of the knowledge sought. There is an emphasis upon situated, embodied and perspectival knowledge and values (Gergen, Lather, Polkinghorne, Shotter). Chaiklin is largely in agreement with such views but suggests they may better be realized by existing schools in psychology, such as the historical cultural school.

The authors discussing thematical implications of postmodernity for psychology tend to go outside the knowledge developed in academic psychology. Michael's arguments for a postmodern social psychology are drawn from the actor-network theory in sociology of science; Løvlie and Young's deconstruction of the self is based on art and literature; and Richer's contribution hereto draws upon the social historical studies of Foucault. Polkinghorne's discussion of psychotherapeutic practice draws upon philosophy as well as the very knowledge generated from the therapeutic practice.

Other sciences more in line with postmodern thought, as for instance anthropology, literary criticism and media research, provide the more provocative new insights regarding the human situation today. It remains open whether the discipline of psychology will provide new and useful knowledge of the relation of men and women to the cultural world, or whether other disciplines will take over.

Practice
The professional practice of psychologists is today coming to be regarded as an important generator of psychological knowledge. Kvale points to a rehabilitation of professional knowledge, and discusses here the knowledge produced by systemic therapy, by system evaluation, by therapeutic practitioners and by qualitative research as coming close to postmodern conceptions of knowledge. Polkinghorne argues that the psychology of therapeutic practice, although not self-consciously postmodern, demonstrates the effectiveness of a discipline using postmodern principles.

Lather sees practice as an engine of innovation, as a privileged site for emancipatory work, with the legitimacy of knowledge descending from philosophy and theory to the level of practice and becoming immanent in it. A warning against any fetishization of practice is implicit in Sass's critique of the effects upon patients of postmodern interpretations in psychoanalysis

Research

The legitimacy of modern psychology has rested heavily on the application of alleged natural science methods. Ken Gergen rejects method as some kind of truth guarantee, and Polkinghorne takes issue with the modernist epistemology of seeking a method for discovering the truths of the universe, of providing a perspective equivalent to God's view. Through the chapters in this volume there is a changed conception of research – from a method-centredness to a discursive practice. The research process is not a mapping of some objective social reality; research involves a co-constitution of the objects investigated, with a negotiation and interaction with the very objects studied.

A multi-method approach is advocated by several authors, with an emphasis upon qualitative, interactive and involved research. Narrative, hermeneutical and deconstructive approaches are advocated (Kvale, Løvlie, Shotter). With the research process embedded in a concrete and local situation, research becomes a negotiated practice. Polkinghorne points to the value of the knowledge generation reported as case studies in the professional literature and retained in the oral tradition. And Mary Gergen's chapter suggests the stage play as a mode of generating knowledge of the social world.

While most chapters advocate or apply an interpretative approach to research, Lather and Richer, following Foucault, warn against the Big Interpreter, with psychological interpretation as a concealed exertion of power. They are both critical of the interview method as a subjectivist, individualist method, with the interview questions seeking for the labyrinthine intentions of individuals.

Deconstruction

The term 'deconstruction' is a hybrid between 'destruction' and 'construction'; it represents an effort to construct by destruction. Old, obsolete concepts are demolished to erect new ones. Deconstruction focuses on the self-contradictions in a text, on the tensions between what the text means to say and what it is none the less constrained to mean. After having discussed the meaning of deconstruction, Løvlie goes on to apply it to the concept of the self in education and psychology. Young follows up with a deconstruction of the self in literature, and Richer deconstructs psychological interpretation.

The vanishing subject

'The death of the subject' has become a slogan of postmodern thought. Several authors of the present volume take issue with a total deconstruction of the self. They do, though, reject a substantialized conception of the self at the centre of the world, decentring it with a relational concept of subjectivity – the self exists through its relations with others as part of the text of the world. What has died is, according to Lather, the unified, reified and essentialized subject assumed in a humanist and emancipatory discourse. This subject is replaced by a provisional, contingent and constructed subject, a subject whose self-identity is constituted and reconstituted relationally. Lather here warns against a postmodernist tendency to reify a fractured, fragmented and schizoid subject.

Løvlie points out that at face value the postulate 'death of the subject' seems to eliminate the idea of an autonomous and intentional agent; what remains is an anonymous individual submitted to the play of structure and the power of narrativity. More actively the self is seen as the ensemble of stage performances, playing up to the idea of a relative self that knows it is a relative self. The self is the proliferation of roles, the progressive showing of (sur)faces. Løvlie interprets the radical postmodern philosophers as dissolving not the individual as such, but the subject conceived as the centre of the world instead of being part of the text of the world.

Young describes how the solid subject is dissolved in Ibsen's drama *Peer Gynt*; the 'onion self' is a collection of social roles attained and abandoned, of identities discarded or transcended. This Kierkegaard-inspired drama envisages a postmodernist, confused and chaotic experience of the self, and it indicates a reconstruction of the deconstructed self through compassionate and committed relationships with others, a theme further developed in Rollo May's existential analysis of *Peer Gynt* (1991).

Humanism and naturalism

A postmodern approach to the relation of the human being to the world goes beyond a familiar opposition of psychology as a natural or a humanistic science. Postmodern thought is far from the mechanical picture of the natural sciences provided by positivist philosophers. It is closer to the current emphasis on the interpretative, interactive and relative nature of knowledge in the natural sciences, on the catastrophic and the limits of prediction, and in some cases even on the inclusion of the acsthetic and the ethical dimensions of knowledge. The literary and linguistic approach of postmodern thought brings it into the vicinity of a humanistic psychology, whereas the deconstruction of the self dissolves its very subject matter – the self-actualizing humanistic individual.

Kvale argues that the apparent opposites of behaviourist objectivism and humanistic subjectivism are both sides of the same modern coin. Michael goes beyond the social and linguistic to integrate the natural into the postmodern project. Drawing upon actor-network studies of the interaction of scallops, fishermen and scientists in a local community, he posits the impact of the natural in the construction of a postmodern identity. He argues for interweaving the natural and the social, for grounding narratives in geography, nature thereby becoming an important part of identity formation. The decentred subject is part of the text of the world, now understood as the social and linguistic interwoven with the natural.

From inside to outside
In current understanding of human beings there is a move from the inwardness of an individual psyche to being-in-the world with other human beings. The focus of interest is moved from the inside of a psychic container to the outside of the human world.

Løvlie points out how dream interpretation understood as rhetorics involves a move from the 'inside' of the psyche to the 'outside' of the text: the subject becomes part of the text of the world. Arguing from an ecological point of view, Michael likewise goes from an inner essentialized self to grant narrative rights to the objects, to ground bioregional narratives in geography. An ecological consciousness comes to involve the expansion or diffusion of self into nature, proceeding through the narratives and mythologies which are derived from the landscapes and localities themselves.

It remains open whether the science of psychology will leave its selfimposed experimental ghettoization, its unconscious labyrinths and its self cult, and address the relation of human activity to the current natural and cultural world. In contrast to the individualist and intra-psychic terminology of modern psychology, there is a de-individualization and externalization of the person in a postmodern discourse. The age of the self is coming to an end. There is a move from the inside to the outside, from the knower to the known. Concepts of consciousness, the unconscious and the psyche recede into the background; and concepts such as knowledge, language, culture, landscape and myth appear in the foreground. There is a move from the archaeology of the 'psyche' to the architecture of current cultural landscapes.

References

Aanstoos, C. (1990) Preface. *The Humanistic Psychologist*, special issue on psychology and postmodernity, 18: 3–6.
Aronowitz, S. and Giroux, H.A. (1991) *Postmodern Education*. Minneapolis: University of Minnesota Press.

Berg, P.O. (1991) Postmodern management? From facts to fiction in theory and practice. *Scandinavian Journal of Management*, 5: 201–17.

Bernstein, R. (1983) *Beyond Objectivism and Relativism*. Philadelphia: University of Pennsylvania Press.

Clifford, J. and Marcus, E.G. (eds) (1986) *Writing Culture – the Poetics and Politics of Ethnography*. Berkeley: University of California Press.

Featherstone, M. (1991) *Consumer Culture and Postmodernism*. London: Sage.

Gergen, K. (1991) *The Saturated Self*. New York: Basic Books.

Heller, A. and Feher, F. (1988) *The Postmodern Political Condition*. Oxford: Blackwell.

Irish Journal of Psychology (1988) Volume 8, special issue on radical constructivism, autopoesis and psychotherapy.

Lyotard, J.-F. (1986) Defining the postmodern. *Postmodernism ICA Documents*, 4: 6–7.

May, R. (1991) *The Cry for Myth*. New York: Norton.

Parker, I. and Shotter, J. (eds) (1990) *Deconstructing Social Psychology*. London: Routledge.

Psychologische Rundschau (1990) 41.

1

Toward a Postmodern Psychology

Kenneth J. Gergen

For the past forty years or more, psychological study has enjoyed a period of relative tranquility. Research laboratories have sprouted across the world, students have been plentiful and ambitious, research funds have become increasingly available, and international meetings have been marked by the eager exchange of findings, methodological advances and theoretical insights. However, within the more recent past there have been increasingly perceptible indications of an underlying change in temper. There is increasing talk about the problematic values inherent in psychological research. Critical psychologists question the individualistic and exploitative ideology underlying such inquiry; feminists question the androcentric biases inherent in theory and method. There is increasing talk of epistemology. Constructivists raise questions concerning the possibility of a world independent of the observer. Constructionists turn their attentions to the social basis of what we take to be knowledge. There is increasing talk of alternative methodologies. Phenomenologists undertake new forms of qualitative research. Hermeneuticist (or interpretive) psychologists explore the possibilities of dialogic methodology. There is increasing concern with forms of human interdependence. Ecological psychologists search for concepts relating person and environment. Ethogenecists turn their attention from events within the head to the social rituals in which we are enmeshed. Discourse analysts move from the relationship of mind and language to language as a system of social interdependence. There is increasing concern with theoretical as opposed to empirical issues. New, conceptually oriented journals, such as the *Journal for the Theory of Social Behaviour, New Ideas in Psychology, Mind and Behavior, Psychologia Politica, Philosophical Psychology, Feminism and Psychology* and *Theory and Psychology* have now taken wing. The International Society for Theoretical Psychology is now fully established.

In my view these are all related departures, and they are not unique to the discipline of psychology. Essentially they are constituents of a much larger and more profound range of intellectual and cultural transformations. They are constituents of what many now view as the postmodern turn in cultural history.

Much has been said about the dawning of postmodernism within both the intellectual world and society more generally (Connor, 1989; Gergen, 1991; Lawson, 1985; Lyotard, 1984; Rorty, 1983). While the present account will draw from these works, a way of making these developments relevant and apparent for our own discipline is required. My attempt will thus be, first, to render a brief account of what is meant by modernism, and to outline its expression in psychological science. This will allow the subsequent elaboration of the postmodern perspective by way of contrast. After outlining the emergence of postmodernism, and exploring the way in which it undermines modernist psychology, we can turn to the nature of psychology within the new era. Many will initially feel that post-modernism is a bleak and unpromising road. However, it is my view that, in fact, it promises to eclipse anything that psychology has yet known.

Psychology and the age of modernity

In a major sense, modernism in Western culture may be linked to the process of mechanization, and its close association with advances in science and technology.[1] As we moved into the twentieth century, industries made increasingly effective use of steam, electricity and then internal combustion engines. The variety and quantity of available products were increased manifold, with greater profits and greater numbers of jobs. Not only were scientists participating directly in the development of these energy sources, but they were also generating what appeared to be fundamental advances in understanding over a broad spectrum. For example, advances in automotive engineering, aviation technology, electronic circuitry, the control of bacteria and finally the emergence of atomic physics all stood as impressive events. As it appeared, human beings were on the verge of mastering the fundamental order of the universe. With such mastery, one could truly begin to envision the possibility of utopian societies.

Within the intellectual establishment, such developments were largely expressed in a concern with establishing specialized domains of study, each possessing a basic logic of justification. Logical empiricist philosophers were the most ambitious in this case, for they saw the possibility of unifying all scientific endeavors under a single logic. In this case the attempt was to elucidate the rules of procedure by which the important strides in the sciences and technology had been accomplished. These rules of procedure could thereafter be adopted by any discipline that claimed to be generating knowledge. Further, it was believed, if these rules of method were made available to the culture at large, progress of the sort demonstrated in the natural sciences could be achieved across the spectrum of human endeavors.

This concern with foundations was hardly confined to the realm of scientific knowledge. Certainly there are parallels, for example, between the empiricist climate within the scientific establishment and that existing in both modern architecture and modern art. Modern architecture was largely preoccupied with reducing form to function, and modern art with abandoning the merely decorative while searching for essentials of form and color. In effect, both ventures shared in the search for enduring verities. And, it may be ventured, it was largely the belief in underlying fundamentals, or basic essences, that enabled composers to cast aside long-standing conventions and experiment with new tonal ranges, that invited choreographers to abandon classic ballet in search of elemental movements (now modern dance), and challenged literary theorists to replace concerns with literary values in favor of internalist and conceptually based rules of literary criticism (for instance, 'the new criticism'). So the heady and optimistic romance with foundations and essence lies somewhere toward the center of the modernist perspective.

The psychological sciences were, to be sure, enthusiastic and able participants in the modernist romance. In my view, there are four overarching presumptions to which the romance gave rise in psychology.

A basic subject matter

At the core of modernism lies the belief in a knowable world. This belief demands of each discipline that it specify the boundaries of its search, a domain of the knowable world that constitutes its subject matter. Of course, not all psychologists agree on what constitutes the subject matter of the discipline. Many continue to believe that it is the nature of mind (cognition, motivation, emotion, etc.) that is central, while others continue to embrace the notion that observable behavior is the focal concern. However, regardless of the localized conflicts, there is little doubt in the more general premise that there is a basic subject matter to be elucidated.

Universal properties

In addition to presuming a knowable subject, modernist psychology has also fallen heir to a belief in universal properties. That is, it is presumed that there are principles, possibly laws, that may be discovered about the properties of the subject matter. The systematic study of single instances (whether instances of perception, memory, learning or the like) may be generalized to other instances across time, situation and persons. In effect, the discipline is not engaged in the mere documentation of history, but in the development of empirically grounded theoretical networks with capacities for broad prediction.

Empirical method

Following the rational justification of logical empiricist philosophy, modernist psychology has also been committed to a belief in truth through method. In particular, the pervasive belief is that by using empirical methods, and most particularly the controlled experiment, one could derive obdurate truths about the nature of the subject matter and the causal networks in which it is embedded. Further, it is believed, the results of such methodology are impersonal. That is, when properly deployed such methods prohibit the entry of ideology, values or passions into the description and explanation of relevant phenomena.

Research as progressive

Derivative of the preceding assumptions is the final modernist belief, a belief in the progressive nature of research. As empirical methods are applied to the subject matter of psychology, we learn increasingly about its fundamental character. False beliefs can be abandoned, and we move toward the establishment of reliable, value-neutral truths about the various segments of the objective world.

The postmodern turn

To be sure, the vast share of contemporary inquiry in psychology is still conducted within a modernist framework. However, outside the scientific laboratories (insulated as they are from both extraneous stimuli and disagreeable ideas) a new set of intellectual dramas has slowly been unfolding. For many, the critical discussions began within the philosophy of science, that domain to which psychologists looked for rational foundations. Major problems were beginning to develop in empiricist attempts to distinguish between empirical (or synthetic) propositions and definitional or merely analytic statements (Quine, 1951). Nor was there any means of justifying the view that propositions about the world could be derived or induced from observations of the world itself (Popper, 1968). However, it was Kuhn's *The Structure of Scientific Revolutions* (1970) that provided the sharpest attack on foundationalist thought. For, argued Kuhn, what appear to be increments in knowledge (for instance, the transition from Ptolemaic to Copernican astronomy) prove, on closer inspection, to be alterations in viewpoint. We do not improve our knowledge of the world through systematic study, proposed Kuhn, so much as shift our way of seeing the world. To this roundly reverberating attack was then added Feyerabend's *Against Method* (1976), a volume that threw into critical relief the view that knowledge could be derived from the systematic application of research procedures. These and other criticisms shifted the center of gravity in the philosophy of science. Foundationalism went into a retreat, and we entered what many see as a post-empiricist era. The 'problem of knowledge' has not been solved; many now see it as principally insoluble.

In many of these attacks on empiricist foundationalism an important theme also began to recur. As reasoned particularly by Kuhn and Feyerabend, truth seems primarily to be a matter of perspective. For a vocal band of sociologists of knowledge this *sotto*-pitched theme became a robust rhapsody. For, as it was reasoned, perspectives are after all by-products of social interchange. They are built into systems of communication and relationship. Therefore, it followed, what passes as knowledge within the sciences may properly be seen as the result of social processes within the culture of science. These suppositions were then illustrated and vivified in wide-ranging investigations of the culture of science (Barnes, 1974; Bourdieu, 1975; Knorr-Cetina, 1981; Latour and Woolgar, 1979).

The view that factual knowledge is saturated with perspectives – not themselves justified by observation – was also receiving attention in other camps. Even in the 1930s Critical Theorists such as Adorno and Horkheimer had begun to question the claims to value neutrality of social science knowledge. However, it was not until the writings of Habermas (1981) that the implications of such critique became broadly apparent. For, as Habermas argued, questions of value or ideology are systematically transformed by scientists into technical questions. Once this transformation occurs, questions of value are suppressed. Technical solutions triumph, solutions that mystify or obscure the value positions of the technocrats themselves. This line of critique has since been dramatically expanded by feminist scholars. As demonstrated in a multitude of ingenious ways, traditional scientific accounts – long championed for their value neutrality – are saturated with androcentric biases. Such biases are detected in the metaphors scientists use to organize their findings, their interpretation of factual data, their topics of study, the methods selected for research and, indeed, their conception of knowledge (Flax, 1990; Harding, 1986; Keller, 1984). These critiques are especially significant, because they demonstrate that neither rational justification of science nor reliance on empirical methodology enables the scientist to rise above moral, ethical and ideological considerations. All perspectives (whether meta-theoretical or methodological) have consequences, for good or ill, for some cherished way of life.

Still other intellectual developments must be added to the emerging confluence. While initially tangential, developments in literary theory added important new dimensions to the proceedings. During the modernist period, there was great interest in developing foundational standards of literary interpretation. Some interpretations of a text (judicial writ, religious document, or the like) seem obviously superior to others. The quest was thus for a set of rational criteria of interpretation, in effect, foundations of interpretation. However, as the dialogue went on, it became increasingly apparent that such justifications were chimerical. Of particular importance, hermeneuticists such as Gadamer (1960) and literary theorists such as Stanley Fish (1980) argued that readers approach a text with various foreconceptions or styles of reading already intact. Whatever interpretation is made of the text must proceed on the basis of this forestructure. It is not the text that dominates the reader, but the reader who dominates the text.

One must further add to this dialogue the powerful voice of the literary deconstructionists. As theorists such as Jacques Derrida (1976) proposed, when we enter the process of description we invariably rely on conventions of language. We must make use of these conventions or we fail to communicate at all. Yet, these conventions simultaneously govern what can be communicated – or more precisely, the ontological presumptions of a culture. Thus, as the language guides the formation of our accounts, so does it construct an array of putative objects. One may never exit the language (the system of signifiers) to give a true and accurate portrayal of what is the case. Understanding of the world is thus a product not of the world as it is, but of textual history. Other theorists have been quick to see the critical implications of this view. For if our language conventions are, in turn, dependent on social processes, and these processes carry with them various ideological or value biases, then all scientific writing and all our attempts at objectivity are essentially value-saturated products of social agreement.

Consciousness of observer perspective now reverberates across the disciplines. Historians are increasingly concerned with the demands placed on historical writing by conventions of Western narrative or storytelling (White, 1978). If history must be told as a story, and there are certain requirements for proper relating of a narrative, then historical accounts are never objective. History must always be seen through the lens of narrative requirement. Anthropologists became similarly concerned with the objectivity of ethnographic reports. For, as it was reasoned (cf. Clifford, 1983; Marcus, 1982), the reports of the Western anthropologists take place within the writing conventions of the home culture. Not only are the subjects of such reports robbed of voice by such procedures, but the procedures themselves are saturated with Western cultural values. For example, simply to write as an isolated subject independently observing the actions of others is already to carry a Western worldview into the field.

The works of Foucault (1979, 1980) must be given special mention, for as Foucault makes clear, matters of description cannot be separated from issues of power. As perspectives are developed and integrated into society, so are the social arrangements of the society altered. Discourse about sexuality, madness, knowledge, and so on, can thus operate as a fulcrum for social change (or stasis). And it is largely in this context that we now witness a renaissance in the study of rhetoric. For as readily seen by investigators across the sciences and humanities (Ibanez, 1991; Sarbin, 1986; Simons, 1989, 1990; Spence, 1982), academic writing is, after all, a form of rhetoric. Its effects are potentially persuasive, and thus potentially powerful. To understand the rhetorical character of scholarly accounts is thus to comprehend the basis of their power.

This has been an all too rapid scanning of various developments within the postmodern turn. By way of summary, let us briefly return to the modernist presumptions that have centred psychological inquiry for the better part of the century. How are these presumptions challenged by lines of argument within the postmodern sphere?

The vanishing subject matter

In the modernist period psychologists could confidently proclaim that there was a subject matter available for interrogation. Whether mind or behavior, there was a domain to be elucidated. However, in light of postmodern arguments it is no longer easy to occupy such a position. For, as we have seen, postmodernism raises fundamental questions with the assumption that our language about the world operates as a mirror of that world. Rather, discourse about the world operates largely on the basis of social processes, which in turn are crystallized in terms of various rhetorical rules and options (for instance, rules of proper storytelling). Thus, to presume the independent existence of a subject matter, reflected by the discourse, would be to engage in an unwarranted objectification of the discourse. Further, such reification is likely to be fraught with various ideological and valuational biases. Thus, to presume the subject matter is to mystify the valuational basis of one's ontology.

From universal properties to contextual reflection

Within the modernist arena it was possible to launch inquiry into the universal properties of one's subject matter. From the postmodern perspective, such inquiry would not only be to reify one's forestructure of understanding, but again to hide the valuational commitments in which the forestructure is enmeshed. For example, consider the presumption that a major part of psychology's subject matter is cognition, and that cognitive processes operate similarly across time and culture. Such assumptions would not only objectify a peculiarly Western ontology of the person (that is, not all cultures attribute 'cognitive' processes to persons). In addition, such a position would obscure the commitment to an individualistic ideology (that is, viewing the individual as a private decision-maker). Instead, postmodern thought invites the investigator to take account of the historical circumstances of his/her inquiry. What are the roots of the preferred discourse, what are its limits, what patterns of culture does it sustain, what does it discourage? Critical self-reflection is essential for the postmodern scholar.

The marginalization of method

Under modernism, methodology underwent a virtual apotheosis. Methodology was the means to truth and light, and thus to salvation. (Here one should consider the fact that within the typical PhD program in psychology, the number of requirements in research methods and statistics is typically greater than for any subject matter domain. Requirements in historical and philosophical background, and conceptual and/or critical analysis, are a rarity.) Under postmodernism, however, methodology loses its coveted position. Under postmodernism research methods in psychology are viewed, at worst, as misleading justificatory devices. They operate as truth warrants for a priori commitments to particular forms of value-saturated description. Moreover, experimental methodology in particular carries with it a view of human functioning that is subject to critical reflection. Such methodology casts the individual into the role of mechanical automaton whose behavior is a product of environmental inputs, thus denying him/her the possibilities for agency and personal responsibility. Further, such methodology engenders an artificial separation between the scientist-knower and the subject, suggesting that superior knowledge is gained through alienated relationships.

The grand narrative of progress

Within the modernist framework, existential problems of personal significance are solved. The modernist researcher is a soldier in an army where the battles are fraught with difficulty, dedication is valorous, but victory is guaranteed. Each individual scientist makes his/her contribution – great or small – to the annihilation of ignorance and the establishment of truth (often equated with liberty and justice) for all. Yet, for the postmodernist, both the concept of truth and research as a means to truth are impugned. Rather, as Lyotard (1984) suggests, the idea of scientific progress is rendered intelligible by virtue of its literary or narrative character. We can be swayed by such a view precisely because it is one of the 'grand narratives' of Western culture: the long struggle to ultimate victory. In effect, the very idea of scientific progress is a literary achievement.

Psychology in the postmodern era

At this point many psychologists may feel abused and betrayed. What promised to be an interesting intellectual adventure has proved a lethal assault on all that is dear and important. Is this nothing more than nihilism, and if so, need we listen more? Yet, such a rapid exit seems both unwise and unwarranted. It is unwise because postmodernist views, once savored, can scarcely be abandoned. They are, as one young man put it, like a 'sweet poison'. Once tasted, the appetite becomes insatiable. They are an outgrowth of our historical era, and once sophisticated there is no return to virginal purity. The exit is also unwarranted, for, in my view, the postmodern turn begins to offer psychology new ways of conceptualizing itself and its potentials. And, if properly understood, postmodern thought opens vistas of untold significance for the discipline. Let me finally, then, elaborate on four of these potentials.

Technological advance

At the outset, there is nothing about postmodernism that argues against investments in technological inquiry. To be sure, there is widespread skepticism in the narrative of progressive science; however, there is no easy denying that the means by which we now do things called 'curing disease', 'flying to France' or 'generating atomic power' were not available in previous centuries. It is not technology (or 'knowing how') that is called into question by postmodernist thought, but the truth claims placed upon the accompanying descriptions and explanations (the 'knowing that'). In this same sense, psychologists should not be dissuaded by postmodernism from forging ahead with technological developments. The actuarial prediction of performance in schools and occupations, testing for various physiological or psychological deficits, and evaluation research, for example, are all forms of technology. And too, various forms of therapy, skill training and minority education programs serve as useful technologies for various groups.[2] So long as one does not objectify terms such as 'performance', 'deficits', 'evaluation' and 'psychotherapy', but instead remains sensitive and open to the social and valuational implications of such work, then such technologies would be congenial with postmodernism.

To put it in other words, while research attempting to accumulate basic knowledge about 'perception', 'cognition', 'emotion', and the like, is of limited value, there remains an important place for sound prediction and personal skills within various practical settings.

Cultural critique
In my view, while technological innovations have an important place within society, they also lead a precarious life. Patterns of human activity largely revolve around discourse; discourse serves as perhaps the critical medium through which relationships are carried out. And, because discourse exists in an open market, marked by chaotic and broadly diffuse alteration (Shotter, 1985), then patterns of human action will also remain forever unfolding. On the one hand, this means that the efficacy of human technologies is in constant jeopardy. Today's prediction or skill is tomorrow's history. In the case of cultural technologies, the wheel must be constantly reinvented. On the other hand, there is implied a second and very substantial role for psychology. For, in postmodern perspective, we find the culture in constant danger of objectifying its vocabularies of understanding, and thereby closing off options and potentials. Required, then, is a scholarship of critique, a scholarship that continuously sensitizes us to the taken for granted and its imprisoning effects.

Let us consider psychology's role in particular. In Western culture, we no longer question the existence of reason, memory, emotion, motivation, and the like. Such construals of the individual interior are constituents of the taken-for-granted world. Further, as psychologists we are continuously adding constructs to this world: stress, burnout, post-traumatic stress disorder, schizophrenia, and the like. Further, each of these terms is embedded in forms of discourse that favor certain segments of the population or certain patterns of conduct, while disparaging others (for instance, reason is honored;

emotion is anti-rational; men are more rational than women; rationality is needed in positions of responsibility; and so on). With the objectification of such discourse, so occurs the ossification of social pattern.

Required, then, is a form of professional investment in which the scholar attempts to de-objectify the existing realities, to demonstrate their social and historical embeddedness and to explore their implications for social life. Rather than remaining neutral on all questions of value, as in the modernist frame, the psychologist is invited to conjoin the personal, the professional and the political (as feminist scholars have so aptly put it). In some degree, such work is already taking place. It is active within critical, deconstructionist and feminist wings of the discipline (see, for example, M. Gergen, 1988; Hollway, 1989; Parker and Shotter, 1990; Sampson, 1988). It is also being carried out by many attempting to elucidate the taken for granted of daily life – thus furnishing people with options or alternatives. This kind of emancipatory impulse also guides much present work on everyday understanding (Antaki, 1988; Semin and Gergen, 1990), discourse analysis (Potter and Wetherell, 1987), historical psychology (Gergen and Gergen, 1984; Leary, 1990) and social representation (Moscovici, 1984).

The construction of new worlds
There is a final major option for psychological inquiry favored by postmodern thought. Within the modernist era, the scientist was largely a polisher of mirrors. It was essentially his/her task to hold a well-honed mirror to nature. If others wished to use the results for their various pursuits that was their concern. However, for the postmodernist, such a role seems but pale and passive. Postmodernism asks the scientist to join in the hurly-burly of cultural life – to become an active participant in the construction of the culture. For, as we have seen, the primary result of most scholarly inquiry is discourse itself. And, rather than simply recanting the taken-for-granted presumptions of the culture, the psychological scholar is in an optimal role to transform this discourse – and, by implication, the culture itself. Rather than 'telling it like it is' the challenge for the postmodern psychologist is to 'tell it as it may become'. Needed are scholars willing to be audacious, to break the barriers of common sense by offering new forms of theory, of interpretation, of intelligibility. Elsewhere (Gergen, 1982) I have proposed the concept of 'generative theory', or theory designed to unseat conventional thought and thereby to open new alternatives for thought and action. Through such theorizing scholars contribute to the forms of cultural intelligibility, to the symbolic resources available to people to carry

out their lives together. For example, the work of Averill (1982) and others on emotions as cultural performances, Carol Gilligan (1982) and others on a relational orientation to moral decision-making, Middleton and Edwards (1990) and others on collective remembering and Billig (1987) and others on the rhetorical nature of thought strike me as highly generative. Each reconstitutes our conception of human action in ways that open new cultural potentials. In effect, it is through the well-formed word that psychological scholars are positioned to transform culture.

Postmodern consciousness does not thus invite skepticism regarding the potentials for psychological inquiry. Rather, by demystifying the great narrative of modernism, it attempts to bring psychologists and society closer together. Not only is technology placed more directly and openly in the service of values; more important, the psychologist is encouraged to join in forms of valuational advocacy, and to develop new intelligibilities that present new options to the culture. There is no promise of Utopias here. However, the possibility for escaping the pretenses of the past, and more fully integrating academic and cultural pursuits, is one to which I, among others, feel greatly drawn.

Notes

1   For further accounts of cultural and intellectual modernism see Berman, 1982; Frisby, 1985; Gergen, 1991; and Levenson, 1984.
2   Particularly noteworthy are the efforts of organizational psychologists such as Clegg (1990) and Srivastva and Cooperrider (1990), and therapists such as Anderson and Goolishian (1988) and Hoffman (1990), to use various facets of postmodern thought to effect personal and social change.

References

Anderson, H. and Goolishian, H.A. (1988) Human systems as linguistic systems: preliminary and evolving ideas about the implications for clinical theory. *Family Process*, 12: 371–93.
Antaki, C. (ed.) (1988) *Analyzing Lay Explanation: A Casebook of Methods*. London: Sage.
Averill, J. (1982) *Anger and Aggression*. New York: Springer.
Barnes, B. (1974) *Scientific Knowledge and Sociological Theory*. London: Routledge & Kegan Paul.
Berman, M. (1982) *All that's Solid Melts into Air*. New York: Simon & Schuster.
Billig, M. (1987) *Arguing and Thinking: A Rhetorical Approach to Social Psychology*. Cambridge: Cambridge University Press.
Bourdieu, P. (1975) The specificity of the scientific field and the social conditions of the progress of reason. *Social Science Information*, 14: 19–47.

Toward a postmodern psychology   29

Clegg, S.R. (1990) *Modern Organizations: Organization Studies in the Postmodern World*. London: Sage.
Clifford, J. (1983) On ethnographic authority. *Representations*, 4: 118–46.
Connor, S. (1989) *Postmodernist Culture*. Oxford: Blackwell.
Derrida, J. (1976) *Of Grammatology*. Baltimore: Johns Hopkins University Press.
Feyerabend, P. K. (1976) *Against Method*. New York: Humanities Press.
Fish, S. (1980) *Is There a Text in This Class?* Cambridge, MA: Harvard University Press.
Flax, J. (1990) *Thinking Fragments: Psychoanalysis. Feminism, and Postmodernism in the Contemporary West*. Berkeley: University of California Press.
Flick, U. (ed.) (1991) *Alltagswissen über Gesundheit und Krankheit*. Heidelberg, Ansanger.
Foucault, M. (1979) *Discipline and Punish*. New York: Vintage/Random House.
Foucault, M. (1980) *The History of Sexuality*, vol. I. New York: Vintage/Random House.
Frisby, D. (1985) *Fragments of Modernity*. Cambridge: Polity Press.
Gadamer, H.G. (1960) *Truth and Method*. New York: Thomas Crowell.
Gergen, K.J. (1982) *Toward Transformation in Social Knowledge*. New York: Springer.
Gergen, K.J. (1991) *The Saturated Self: Dilemmas of Identity in Contemporary Life*. New York: Basic Books.
Gergen, K.J. and Davis, K.E. (eds) (1985) *The Social Construction of the Person*. New York: Springer.
Gergen, K.J. and Gergen, M. (1984) *Historical Social Psychology*. Hillsdale, NJ: Erlbaum.
Gergen, M. (ed.) (1988) *Feminist Thought and the Structure of Knowledge*. New York: New York University Press.
Gilligan, C. (1982) *In a Different Voice*. Cambridge, MA: Harvard University Press.
Habermas, J. (1981) Modernity vs postmodernity. *New German Critique*, 22.
Harding, S. (1986) *The Science Question in Feminism*. Ithaca, NY: Cornell University Press.
Hoffman, L. (1990) Constructing realities: an art of lenses. *Family Process*, 29: 1–12.
Hollway, W. (1989) *Subjectivity and Method in Psychology*. London: Sage.
Hudson, W. (1986) The question of postmodern philosophy. In W. Hudson and W. van Reijen (eds), *Modern vs Postmodern*. Utrecht: Hes Vitgevers, pp 27–34.
Ibañez, T. (1991) Social psychology and the rhetoric of truth. *Theory and Psychology*, 1: 187–202.
Keller, E.F. (1984) *Reflections on Gender and Science*. New Haven, CT: Yale University Press.
Knorr-Cetina, K.G. (1981) *The Manufacture of Knowledge*. New York: Pergamon Press.
Kuhn, T.S. (1970) *The Structure of Scientific Revolutions*, 2nd edn. Chicago: University of Chicago Press. (Original Publication, 1962.)
Latour, B. and Woolgar, S. (1979) *Laboratory Life: The Social Construction of Scientific Facts*. Beverly Hills, CA: Sage.
Lawson, H. (1985) *Reflexivity, the Postmodern Predicament*. London: Hutchinson.
Leary, D. (ed.) (1990) *Metaphors in the History of Psychology*. Cambridge: Cambridge University Press.
Levenson, M. (1984) *A Genealogy of Modernism*. Cambridge: Cambridge University Press.

Lyotard, J.-F. (1984) *The Postmodern Condition: A Report on Knowledge.* Minneapolis: University of Minnesota Press.

Marcus, G. (1982) Ethnographics as text. *Annual Review of Anthropology*, 11: 25–69.

Middleton, D. and Edwards, D. (1990) *Collective Remembering.* London: Sage.

Moscovici, S. (1984) The phenomenon of social representations. In R.M. Farr and S. Moscovici (eds), *Social Representations.* Cambridge: Cambridge University Press. pp. 14–43.

Murray, K.D. (1985) Life as fiction. *Journal for the Theory of Social Behaviour*, 15: 189–202.

Parker, I. and Shotter, J. (eds) (1990) *Deconstructing Social Psychology.* London: Routledge.

Popper, K.R. (1968) *The Logic of Scientific Discovery.* New York: Harper & Row. (Originally published as *Logik des Forschung.* Vienna: Springer, 1935.)

Potter, J. and Wetherell, M. (1987) *Discourse and Social Psychology.* Beverly Hills, CA: Sage.

Quine, W.V.O (1951) Two dogmas of empiricism. *Philosophical Review*, 60: 20–43.

Rorty, R. (1983) Postmodernist bourgeois liberalism. *Journal of Philosophy*, 80: 585–94.

Sampson, E.E. (1988) The debate on individualism: indigenous psychologies of the individual and their role in personal and societal functioning. *American Psychologist*, 43: 15–22.

Sarbin, T.R. (1986) *Narrative Psychology.* New York: Praeger.

Semin, G.R. and Gergen, K.J. (1990) *Everyday Understanding: Social and Scientific Implications.* London: Sage.

Shotter, J. (1985) Social accountability and self-specification. In K.J. Gergen and K.E. Davis (eds), *The Social Construction of the Person.* New York: Springer. pp. 167–90.

Simons, H.W. (ed.) (1989) *Rhetoric in the Human Sciences.* London: Sage.

Simons, H.W. (ed.) (1990) *The Rhetorical Turn.* Chicago: University of Chicago Press.

Spence, D.P. (1982) *Narrative Truth and Historical Truth.* New York: Norton.

Srivastva, S. and Cooperrider, D.L. (eds) (1990) *Appreciative Management and Leadership.* San Francisco: Jossey-Bass.

White, H. (1978) *Tropics of Discourse.* Baltimore, MD: Johns Hopkins University Press.

2
Postmodern Psychology: A Contradiction in Terms?

Steinar Kvale

In order to understand human activity it is necessary to know the culture, the social and historical situation, in which the activity takes place. In art and philosophy, the current age is described as a postmodern age. Psychology is a project of modernity, coming into use as a term during the Age of Enlightenment and founded as a science in the late nineteenth century. If these two premises are correct – that is, of psychology as a modern project and the current age as postmodern – the science of psychology may be out of touch with the current age. Then the two terms 'psychology' and 'post-modernity' are incompatible, and a postmodern psychology is a contradiction in terms.

The following discussion will attempt to substantiate this postu-late. In the first part, some main themes of a postmodern culture will be described. Then the entrenchment of psychological science in modernity will be outlined, and some developments in professional practice and research will be presented as in line with a postmodern discourse. In conclusion some scenarios for psychology in a post-modern world are outlined, and the relations of psychology to religion and to consumer culture are pointed out.

Postmodern culture

The concept of postmodernity

The term 'postmodernity' came into use in the 1950s and 1960s, within architecture, literary criticism and sociology, and mainly in the United States. French philosophers addressed the postmodern condition in the 1970s, and in the 1980s postmodernism came to general public attention. A comprehensive presentation of post-modern thought has been given by the French philosopher Lyotard in his book *The Postmodern Condition: A Report on Knowledge* (1984). Whereas Lyotard bases his analysis upon philosophy and science,

Baudrillard's writings on postmodernity centre on media, fascination and seduction (1988a).

The term '*post* modernity' indicates what comes after modernity. Modernity may be traced to the Renaissance, developed during the Age of Enlightenment, and coming to full bloom by the time of the French Revolution. Modernity places man in the centre, and sees man as a rational being. There is a basic assumption of emancipation and progress through reason and science. The faith in emancipation through more knowledge dissolved in 1945, if not before then. After Auschwitz and Hiroshima it has become difficult to uphold a belief in general progress of mankind through more rationality and science. Postmodernity indicates a condition after the Utopias are dead, after the modern belief in progress through more knowledge has become difficult to sustain.

It is debatable whether postmodernity is actually a break with modernity, or merely its continuation. Postmodern writers may prefer to write history so that their own ideas appear radically new. Postmodern themes were present in the romanticism of the last century, in Nietzsche's philosophy at the turn of the century, with the surrealists and in literature, for instance in Blixen and Borges. What is new today is the pervasiveness of postmodern themes in culture at large.

'Postmodern' does not designate a systematic theory or a comprehensive philosophy, but rather diverse diagnoses and interpretations of the current culture, a depiction of a multitude of interrelated phenomena. The following exposition is not a philosophical analysis, but sketches some themes of a postmodern culture, seeking for a frame of reference for understanding the present state of psychology.

Themes of postmodernity
Postmodern thought is characterized by a loss of belief in an objective world and an incredulity towards meta-narratives of legitimation. With a delegitimation of global systems of thought, there is no foundation to secure a universal and objective *reality*. There is today a growing public acknowledgement that 'Reality isn't what is used to be' (Anderson, 1990).

In philosophy there is a departure from the belief in one true reality – subjectively copied in our heads by perception or objectively represented in scientific models (Rorty, 1979). There exists no pure, uninterpreted datum; all facts embody theory. In science the notion of an objective reality is an interesting hypothesis, but is not necessary for carrying out scientific work (Maturana, 1988). Knowledge becomes the ability to perform effective actions.

The focus is on the social and linguistic construction of a perspectival reality. In society the development of technology, in particular the electronic media, opens up an increased exposure to a multiplicity of perspectives, undermining any belief in one objective reality (see Gergen, 1991). In a world of media, the contrast between reality and fantasy breaks down and is replaced by a hyperreality, a world of self-referential signs (Baudrillard, 1988a). What remains is signs referring to other signs, texts referring to other texts.

A critique of *legitimation* is central in Lyotard's analysis of the postmodern condition. Legitimacy involves the question of what is valid, what is legal, the issue of whether an action is correct and justifiable. Habermas brought the issue to the fore in his book *Legitimation Crisis* (1975), depicting a general loss of faith in tradition and authority, with a resulting relativity of values.

Lyotard is critical of the modern efforts of legitimation of science through appeal to some grand narratives. He uses 'the term *modern* to designate any science that legitimates itself with reference to a metadiscourse of this kind making an explicit appeal to some grand narrative, such as the dialectics of Spirit, the hermeneutics of meaning, the emancipation of the rational or working subject, or the creation of wealth' (1984: xxiii).

Lyotard identifies '*postmodern* as incredulity towards meta-narratives' (p. xxiv), as a 'paganism', where we pass judgement on truth, beauty and justice without criteria for the judgements. In a comment on the debate between Lyotard and Habermas, Rorty interprets Lyotard as saying that 'the trouble with Habermas is not so much that he provides a narrative of emancipation as that he feels the need to legitimize, that he is not content to let the narratives which hold all culture together do their stuff. He is scratching where it does not itch' (1985: 164). Rather than continuing the Cartesian attempts of 'self-grounding', Rorty advocates a Baconian approach of 'self-assertion'.

Lyotard's own critique of the narratives of legitimation involves a paradox: his book may be read as legitimizing a non-necessity of legitimation. The modern preoccupation with external justification may, in its turn, further a corrosion of legitimation – the more one legitimates, the greater the need for further legitimation. Or, to pursue Rorty's image, scratching may as well intensify the itching as provoke itches where there were previously none. Such a counter-factuality of a modern legitimation mania may be expressed in the folk saying 'Beware when they swear they are telling the truth.'

A further theme of modernity is the dichotomy of the *universal and the individual*, between society and the unique person, whereby the rootedness of human activity and language in a given social and historical context is overlooked. In modernity the person is an object for a universal will, or for general laws of history or nature. Or the person is overburdened; man has become the centre of the world, the individual self-feeling being the cornerstone of modern thought, a self stretched out between what it is and what it ought to be.

If we abstract a human from his or her context, we are trapped between the poles of the universal and the individual – the way out is to study humans in their cultural and social context. With the collapse of the universal meta-narratives, the local narratives come into prominence. The particular, heterogeneous and changing language games replace the global horizon of meaning. With a pervasive decentralization, communal interaction and local knowledge become important in their own right. Even such concepts as nation and tradition are becoming rehabilitated in a postmodern age.

The emphasis upon the local surpasses the modern polarity of the universal and the individual, of the objective and the subjective. The local interaction, the communal network, is the point of departure; universal laws and unique individual selves are seen as abstractions from man's being in the world. Rather than equating universal laws with the objective and the individual with the subjective and relative, valid interpretations of meaning and truth are made by people who share decisions and the consequence of their decisions (Salner, 1989). Instead of a subjective nihilism, we may here talk of a contextual relativism where legitimation of action occurs through linguistic practice and communicative action.

With the collapse of the universal systems of meaning or meta-narratives, a re-narrativization of the culture takes place, emphasizing communication and the impact of a message upon the audience. There is today an interest in *narratives*, on the telling of stories. In contrast to an extrinsic legitimation through appeal to meta-discourses, or Utopia, Lyotard advocates an intrinsic legitimation through a narrative knowledge which 'does not give priority to the question of its own legitimation, and . . . certifies itself in the pragmatics of its own transmission without having recourse to argumentation and proof' (1984: 27). Narratives themselves contain the criteria of competence and illustrate how they ought to be applied; they are legitimated by the simple fact that they do what they do. A narrative is not merely a transmission of information. In the very act of telling a story the position of the storyteller and the listener, and their place in the social order, is constituted; the story creates and maintains social bonds. The narratives of a community contribute to uphold the values and the social order of that community.

Postmodern thought focuses on *heterogeneous* language games, on the non-commensurable, on the instabilities, the breaks and the conflicts. Rather than regarding a conversation as a dialogue between partners, it is seen as a game, a confrontation between adversaries. A universal consensus of meaning is no ideal; the continual effort after meaning is no longer a big deal. The reply to the modern global sense-makers is simply 'just let it be' or 'stop making sense'.

To Lyotard, consensus is merely a stage in a discussion not its end. The alternative here is to think not in either/or dichotomies, or contradictions, but in 'paralogy', emphasizing the open system, the local and an anti-method approach. Linear logic and calculating prediction are no longer paradigmatic of knowledge; rather: 'Post-modern science – by concerning itself with such things as undecid-ables, the limits of precise control, conflicts characterized by incomplete information, "*fracta*", catastrophes, and pragmatic paradoxes – is theorizing its own evolution as discontinuous cata-strophic, nonrectifiable and paradoxical' (Lyotard, 1984: 60).

There exists no standard method for measuring and comparing knowledge within different language games and paradigms; they are incommensurable. A postmodern world is characterized by a con-tinual change of perspectives, with no underlying common frame of reference, but rather a manifold of changing horizons. Rock music videos capture a world of continually changing perspectives and overlapping contexts.

Language and knowledge do not copy reality. Rather, language constitutes reality, each language constructing specific aspects of reality in its own way. The focus is on the linguistic and social construction of reality, on interpretation and negotiation of the meaning of the lived world.

Human language is neither universal nor individual, but each language is rooted in a specific culture, as dialects or as national languages. Current philosophy has undergone a linguistic turn, focusing on language games, speech acts, hermeneutic interpre-tation, textual and linguistic analysis. The language games take place in local communities; they are hetergeneous and incommen-surable. Highly refined expressions in one language, such as poetry, cannot be translated into another language without change of meaning. There exists no universal meta-language, no universal commensurability.

The linguistic and interrelational nature of knowledge was em-phasized by Merleau-Ponty, whose philosophy of perspectivity can be seen as precursor to postmodern thought (Madison, 1990). Merleau-Ponty described the natural intertwining of the meaning of the words, their transfers and exchanges. Language has us and it is not we who have language. His *Phenomenology of Perception* (1945/1962) concludes with a quote from Saint-Exupéry: 'Man is but a network of relations.'

The focus on language implies a decentralization of the subject. The self no longer uses language to express itself; rather the language speaks through the person. The individual self becomes a medium for the culture and its language. The unique self loses prominence; the author is today less an original genius than a gifted craftsman and mediator of the culture through his or her mastery of language.

In postmodern thought there has taken place an *expansion of rationality*. It is not just a 'momentary lapse of reason', but a going beyond the cognitive and scientific domain to include also the ethical and aesthetic domains of life in reason. 'Modern times' involved a restricted concept of rationality, with a dominance of a technical means–ends rationality. There has been an emphasis on plans and programmes, on calculation, prediction and control. Reason and science have been overburdened with visions of Utopia where all human problems would be solved in the long run by the methods of science and technology.

When the presupposed rationality is seldom found in the given reality, another deeper, more essential reality is constructed to account for the disorder we observe in the world around us. The overstressed conception of a rationality has, in its turn, fostered sceptical reactions in the form of romanticist and irrationalist movements.

Postmodern thought goes beyond a Kantian split of modern culture into science, morality and art, and involves a rehabilitation of the ethical and aesthetic domains. The positivists' split of facts and values is no longer axiomatic; science is a value-constituted and value-constituting enterprise. Appeals to formal logic recede before a rehabilitated rhetoric of persuasion. With the loss of general systems of legitimation, when actions are not justified by appeal to some higher system or idea of progress, the values and the ethical responsibility of the interacting persons become central.

Art is not merely an aesthetic experience, but a way of knowing the world. Rationalist thought has abhorred the non-linear, the imprecise, the unpredictable, and has separated art from science. Mathematicians have been more open to an affinity of science and art, emphasizing the elegance and beauty of models as criteria of truth, cf. for instance *The Beauty of Fractals* (Peitgen and Richter, 1986).

Postmodern art is characterized by *pastiche* and collage. Art in a postmodern world does not belong to a unitary frame of reference, nor to a project or a Utopia. The plurality of perspectives leads to a fragmentation of experience, the collage becoming a key artistic technique of our time (see Lund, 1990). Styles from different periods and cultures are put together; in postmodern art high-tech may exist side by side with antique columns and romantic ornamentation, the effects being shocking and fascinating. In contrast to modern architecture, tradition is not rejected; nor is it worshipped as in the new classicism. Elements from other epochs are selected and put together in an often ironical recycling of what is usable as decorum. In literature there are collages of texts put together from other texts; the author's individuality and originality are lost in a pervasive use of and references to other texts. Eco's medieval detective novel *The Name of the Rose*, which may be read as a postmodern caricature of the modern meaning hunters, is thus filled with hidden quotes and allusions to other texts.

The reaction against modern rationality and functionalism was visible at an early stage in *architecture*. There was a protest against the functional, against straight lines and square blocks, against the cold logic and boredom of a modern architecture where function preceded form. Postmodern architecture is a reaction against what the painter Hundertwasser has called 'the tyranny of the straight line'. In the new architecture there is an emphasis on the curvilinear, on the unpredictable, on ornamentation and pastiche and on a non-functional beauty. Reflecting surfaces and labyrinths have become main elements.

On one side there is a return to the medieval village, with its tight-knit community and complex webs of buildings and places. The atriums of the Hyatt Regency Hotels appear as secularized cathedrals with quiet, closed and labyrinthine internal space, with an ornamentation of mixed styles. On the other side there is the Las Vegas trend of architecture, going to the extreme of learning from the most extravagant expressions of current architecture, as expressed in Venturi et al.'s *Learning from Las Vegas* (1972). There is a collage of styles, as in Cesar's Palace with its antique statues and parking valets dressed as Roman legionaries. Here there is dominance of the surface, the immense lighted billboards attracting the customer to the less spectacular interior labyrinths of gambling tables and slot machines.

Postmodern thought focuses on the *surface*, with a refined sensibility to what appears, a differentiation of what is perceived. The relation of sign and signified is breaking down; the reference to a reality beyond the sign recedes. In the media, texts and images refer less to an external world beyond the signs than to a chain of signifiers, to other texts and images. A dichotomy of fantasy and reality breaks down or loses interest. There is an intertextuality where texts mainly point to other texts. The TV series *Miami Vice* may refer less to the vice in Miami than to other TV series, imitating and parodying for example the car chases, playing up to the viewer's expectations of a cops-and-robbers series. The image, the appearance, is everything; the appearance has become the essence.

The interest in surface, in what manifestly appears, is in contrast to a debunking attitude where nothing is what it seems to be. This hermeneutics of suspicion, inherent in much modern thought, was carried to its extremes in some versions of psychoanalytic and Marxist thought. An action may never be what it appears to be; rather it is an expression of some deeper, more real reality, a symptom of more basic sexual or economic forces. There is a continual hunt for the underlying plan or rationale, the hidden plot or curriculum, to explain the vicissitudes and disorder of what manifestly appears.

The modern quest for a unitary meaning, where there may be none, has as its pathological extreme the suspicion of paranoia. The debunking attitude may lead to conspiracy theories seeking for the mastermind plot; or, less extreme, to a continual search for an underlying order, constructing a deeper rationality where none is visible.

A postmodern *attitude* involves a suspicion of suspicion, and a refined sensibility to the surface, an openness to the differences and nuances of what appears. It relates to what is given, rather than what has been or what could be – 'be cool', 'it is no big deal', 'no future'. The fervent critical attitude of the 1960s and 1970s – as anti-authoritarianism and anti-capitalism – has dissolved. The idea of progress and development, be it the progress of mankind or the individual pilgrim's progress towards salvation of his or her soul, is out. An attitude of tolerant indifference has replaced the involvement and engagement in the social movements and the inner journeys of the 1960s and 1970s. What is left is a liberating nihilism, a living with the here and now, a weariness and a playful irony. Fascination may take the place of reflection; seduction may replace argumentation. There is an oscillation of an intense sensuous fascination by the media and a cool, ironical distance to what appears.

To the existentialists, the discovery of a world without meaning was the point of departure; today a loss of unitary meaning is merely accepted; that is just the way the world is. Postmodern man has stopped waiting for Godot. The absurd is not met with despair; rather it is a living with what is, a making the best of it, a relief from the burden of finding yourself as the goal of life; what remains may be a happy nihilism. With the death of the Utopias, the local and personal responsibility for actions here and now becomes crucial.

A final theme of postmodernity to be mentioned here is the intrinsic relation of *power and knowledge*, emphasized by Foucault and Lyotard. Idealistic conceptions of pure speech acts, of a dominance-free dialogue, of a pure search for true knowledge, are becoming difficult to maintain. The modern thinkers were fond of quoting Bacon – knowledge is power. Today, the relationship is reversed – power is knowledge. Socrates' question regarding the relation of power and knowledge is again brought forward: do the philosophers present a given conception of knowledge because it is true, or is the knowledge true because it is presented by the philosophers? Decisions about what knowledge is to be developed are today made through the allocation of economic resources. In discussing the legitimation of scientific knowledge, Lyotard posits that, in the discourse of today's financial backers of research, the only credible goal is power. Scientists are purchased not to find truth, but to augment power. 'The games of scientific language become the games of the rich, in which whoever is wealthiest has the best chance of being right. An equation between wealth, efficiency and truth is thus established' (1984: 45).

The economic basis of a postmodern culture is treated in Jameson's analysis of the cultural logic of late capitalism (1984). To Jameson, the global American postmodern culture is nothing else than the specific ideology of the latest wave of the global American military and economical hegemony. The truth of postmodern thought is its description of consumer capitalism and the new space of multinational capital. Architecture is the form of art which, in its essence, is closest to the capital. The labyrinthine and self-reflecting postmodern space, as in the new hotels, makes it difficult for the body to be oriented in space. This postmodern space may be seen as a symbol of the inability of consciousness to grasp the larger global, multinational and decentralized communication networks of a postmodern society.

A sketch of some themes of postmodern thought has been given here. The presentation has been descriptive, not analytical or prescriptive. The purpose has been to spell out some main themes of a postmodern culture and hereby provide a frame of reference for understanding the present condition of the discipline of psychology.

Psychology in a postmodern age

Psychology is a child of modernity. It was coined as a term in the age of Reformation in the sixteenth century, often, but probably erroneously, attributed to the reformist humanist Philip Melanchthon.

Psychology was developed as a theoretical discipline by Wolff in the eighteenth century, and came to be regarded as a science after Wundt set up his experimental laboratory in 1879. If, a century later, postmodern thinkers are correct in stating that modernity has come to an end, this may also involve the end of psychology as a science.

Man was at the centre of the Age of Enlightenment. The science of psychology was founded on a conception of individual subjects, with internal souls and later internal psychic apparatuses. In a postmodern age, man is decentred; the individual subject is dissolved into linguistic structures and ensembles of relations.

A question arises as to the status of psychology as the science of the individual when the individual has been dethroned from the centre of the world. Except for the theoretical contributions of that marginal school of scientific psychology – psychoanalysis – and the current popularizations in the therapeutic market, psychology has today little to tell other sciences or the public at large. A visit to the psychology shelves of a university bookshop evokes a feeling of boredom. One finds the standard textbooks, the collected works of Freud and Jung, a multitude of therapeutic help-yourself paperbacks and some hardcover cognitive science books. The new provoking insights about man in the current culture are more likely to be found in the shelves for philosophy, literature, art and anthropology.

An epilogue to psychology as a modern science

The lack of relevance of psychology for culture at large is not new. In 1959, Sigmund Koch wrote an 'Epilogue' to *Psychology: A Study of a Science*, a project sponsored by the American Psychological Association and with contributions by major American psychologists from the foregoing decades. Koch described a boredom with the recent history of psychology, a science rendered desperate by the human vacuum in its own content, and a longing for psychology to embrace problems over which it is possible to feel intellectual passion.

Koch's depiction of what he termed the 'Age of Theory' in psychology comes, in our opinion, close to the descriptions of modernity by later postmodern writers. Four common themes are to be mentioned here: extrinsic legitimation; the quest for universality; an abstract rationality; and the idea of commensurability.

The Age of Theory was characterized by a passion for external *legitimation*, most often from some fashionable theory of proper science. The history of psychology became a history of what to emulate in the natural sciences, even regarding the language of physics as the ideal for psychology. Scientific respectability had more glamour than insight – 'psychology was unique in the extent to which its institutionalization preceded its content and its methods preceded its problems' (Koch, 1959: 783).

In the Age of Theory, there was a quest for *universality*, formulating theoretical laws which were potentially adequate to all behaviour, laws of unrestricted generality. The theories of psychology were often based on a rather restricted observation basis, such as the behaviour of white Norwegian rats and white American college students in laboratory settings; still there was a fundamentalist belief in global applicability of the psychological theories.

The Age of Theory involved a formal *rationality*, a scientism of hypothetical-deductive theories and an intervening variable design, correlating linear variables, with prediction and control as the criteria for science. There was a quest for developing a rule for the theoretical process, a hope of discovering a canonical experimental-quantitative method adequate to all problems of psychology.

The Age of Theory emphasized *commensurability*; there was a search for decision procedures for comparing the many heterogeneous theories, a search for rules to decide theoretical controversies. There was the belief in a quantified behaviour theory of comprehensive scope; the ideal was a mathematics of behaviour as precise as the mathematics of machines.

Koch also pointed out some counter-tendencies to the dominant slant of the Age of Theory, which emphasized contextuality and the limits of generality, of formalization and measurement, and today a small ecological movement in psychology may be added. Despite the sweeping and well-documented critique by Koch, there has scarcely been any radical change in the theoretical foundation of psychology since. The development of a humanistic psychology was caught in an opposition to behaviourism; and a cognitive psychology has taken over the hegemony of behaviourism, substituted the grand theories by eclectic models and replaced the white rat with the computer as testing ground for knowledge of human beings.

The more than thirty-year-old epilogue to the Age of Theory in American psychology is not of mere historical or provincial interest. In the opening address of the conference of the International Union of Psychological Science in Mexico in 1984, the president, Friedhart Klix from the German Democratic Republic, advocated the development of psychology as a science in accordance with Galileo's principle: measure what is measurable and make measurable what is not.

Read in a postmodern context, Koch's critique of the Age of Theory in psychology is not merely an epilogue to a study of a science, but an unrecognized epilogue to psychology as the modern science of man.

Behaviourism and humanism as two sides of the modern coin

Psychology has been the privileged mode of modernity for grasping the relation of person and world. Modernity encompasses not only the rationality of the Enlightment, but also the counter-reaction of romanticism. The humanistic psychology which originated at the time of the counter-culture of the 1960s has remained within the structures of modern thought, caught in a polarization to behaviourism. This concerns the quest for external legitimation, the dichotomy of the universal and the individual, the opposing of a technical rationality to a romanticist emotionalism, and the issue of quantitative commensurability vs qualitative uniqueness.

A search for *legitimation* in meta-narratives was prominent in modernity and the Age of Theory in psychology. Also in the new humanistic psychology, the quest for respectability by appeal to external contexts has been strong. Here, philosophies such as phenomenology, existentialism and hermeneutics have often come to serve as external sources of legitimation, rather than as radical new ways of conceiving of the human subject and its relation to the world:

> there are indications that existentialism is tending to be viewed, in some global sense, as an *external source of authority* for whatever ideas the viewer already owns that he feels to be unconventional. There is a marked parallelism here with the tendency of the neobehaviorists to seek support for attitudes which *they* had already embraced by a similarly global appeal to a prestigeful philosophical movement; in that instance, logical postivism. (Koch, 1964: 36)

A legitimatory use of phenomenological and existential philosophy permeates much of humanistic psychology, such as the writings of Rogers and Maslow. It does not pertain to the older German *verstehende Psychologie* after Dilthey, nor to the many scholarly applications of existential and phenomenological philosophy to clinical and general psychology, as for instance by Boss (1963), Giorgi (1970) and May et al. (1958). The present critique of humanistic psychology concerns the popularized versions. Also within behaviourism there are exceptions to Koch's sweeping critique: Skinner thus rejected the main tenets of the Age of Theory. His radical behaviourist 'deconstruction' of mentalistic psychological concepts has even been related to phenomenology (Kvale and Grenness, 1967) and to postmodern thought (Abib, 1991).

Psychology has come to mirror the modern dichotomy between the *universal and the individual*, opposing nomothetic and ideographic methods. Modernity is characterized not only by the quest for objectivity and universality, but also by the other extreme of relativism and individualism. Psychoanalysis encompasses both sides of the universal–individual polarity: Freud's meta-psychology with general structures of consciousness, and the case histories with convincing individual narratives.

Psychology does not merely adapt to social demands; the science of psychology has also contributed to the shaping of the current culture. We live today in a pyschological society, where men and women's understanding of themselves and their relations to others is shaped through psychology (see Leahey, 1987). One consequence of the many behaviourism–humanism debates has been to reinforce the concept of individuals isolated from their culture and history. The earlier religious soul developed with modernity to isolated individual selves and an abstract 'psyche'. Here, humanistic psychology has given support to a cult of the individual subject and its self-actualization.

Not only the subject of the psychological laboratory, but also the humanistic self, is ahistorical and asocial. The ideal self has freed itself from tradition and authority and dissociated itself from the society it inhabits. The promotion of a relativist self-actualization is extensively documented in *Psychology's Sanction for Selfishness* (Wallach and Wallach, 1983). Thus, to Fromm and Maslow, man's individuality became an end in itself that could not be subordinated to purposes of greater dignity. In a humanistic ethics, virtue became responsibility towards one's own existence, and vice irresponsibility towards oneself. The self-actualizing person must be self-contained, true to his or her own nature, ruled by the laws of his of her own character rather than by the rules of society.

Bellah (1987), who criticizes the modern quest for the self, points out how the self is pitted against society where the ideology of self-fulfilment undercuts a commitment to society, leaving an empty self. The notion of a unique isolated individual is a cultural- and historical-specific way of conceiving man, which arose in Europe around the sixteenth century. Sampson (1988) notes that to both anthropologists and historians this self-contained individualism belongs to a specific Western cultural and historical context. He outlines an alternative 'ensembled individualism' with more fluidly drawn self–non-self boundaries, as seen in other cultures and other ages, and also in some trends in current thought. The latter includes feminist theory, which replaces the voice of boundaries and separatedness with connections, relationships and interdependence. The self is here no longer the absolute point of departure; it is not a self-contained entity, but a network or ensemble of relations.

In psychology, behaviourism and humanism became two sides of the same modern coin – the abstraction of man from his specific culture. Both behaviour and consciousness were dissociated from their content, from the intentional object of human activity. The cultural content is then taken as the accidental and local, the psychological processes as the essential and universal (Ratner, 1988). Here appears a double abstraction – the 'psyche' studied by modern psychology is abstracted from its cultural content as well as from its social and historical context.

The behaviourist Age of Theory and the subsequent cognitive computer psychology were extreme in their technical *rationality* and functionalism. This formal rationality is ahistorical: there is one true scientific method, from eternity – the natural science method. Some trends of humanistic psychology became counterparts to an inflated concept of rationality, fostering an irrationality with a romantic counter-culture of creativity, spontaneity, wish fulfilment and individual freedom. Again, psychoanalysis encompasses both trends; the irrational aspects of the psyche were analysed with the aim of developing a rational human being – where id was shall ego be.

The concept of rationality has been restricted to cognition and science, leaving out the ethical and the aesthetic domains of human life. Until a few years ago, ethics was, in psychology, mainly technical rules for treating experimental subjects and patients. Recently the ethical basis and consequences of psychological research and practice have been given more attention. The aesthetic domain of human life still lingers on the border of a psychological science, mainly being addressed by the psychoanalytic tradition, whereas the knowledge of man embedded in art, literature and the new media remains at the periphery of modern psychology.

Commensurability has been a main theme of modern psychology, science sometimes being equated with quantification. The credo of natural science psychology has been: go forth and make all mankind measurable – and commensurable. The antithesis has been a dismissal of methodic procedures and a retreat to the cult of the individual self instead of analysing the contextual rootedness of man's activity in his specific language and culture.

The meaning of human existence got lost between the meaning eliminators in the Ebbinghaus tradition and the meaning constructors of the psychoanalytic schools. Ebbinghaus's invention of the nonsense syllable and the behaviourists' descriptions of nonsense behaviour in physicalist terms were attempts to eliminate meaning from the scientific study of man. At the other extreme, there is the perennial quest for deeper meanings in psychoanalysis. The observed human activity came to be regarded as only surface manifestations of deeper unconscious meanings, of an embedded truth waiting to be uncovered. The psychoanalyst came to be a positivist Sherlock Holmes, intelligently finding the concealed and buried meaning, awaiting discovery. In contrast, the 'detective' of Eco's novel does not find an independent solution to the plot, but is himself part of the game becoming a co-creator of the mystery he seeks to solve.

A borderline psychology
The above discussion suggests that both behaviourism and humanistic psychology have remained outside a postmodern discourse. The latter emphasizes the rootedness of man in a specific historical and cultural situation, with a focus on the interrelations of a local context, on a linguistic and social construction of reality and on the self as a network of relations. Postmodern thought involves a conception of knowledge as open, perspectival and ambiguous, legitimation of knowledge through practice and a multi-method approach to research, including qualitative descriptions of the diversity of men's and women's relation to the world.

The current intellectual status of psychology is somewhat nebulous. When a classical scholar such as Bloom discusses the social sciences in his book *The Closing of the American Mind*, the science of the mind acquires a footnote: 'Psychology is mysteriously disappearing from the social sciences. Its unheard-of success in the real world may have tempted it to give up the theoretical life' (1987: 361). And at the Massachusetts Institute of Technology, the Department of Psychology was recently dissolved, to become integrated into a new department for 'Brain and Cognitive Science'.

One may object that important exceptions to the postulate of an intellectual stagnation of psychology as a science exist. There are, thus, rapid developments in areas as computer simulation, artificial intelligence, neuropsychology, psychogenetics, psycholinguistics and cognitive science. And on the humanities side there is the current focus upon hermeneutics, narratives, scripts, discourse analysis, etc. These active areas are, however, on the borderline of a psychology surviving parasitically on concepts and methods imported from neighbouring disciplines. Apart from psychoanalysis, there has hardly been any major export of psychological knowledge to the neighbouring disciplines. Modern psychology, whether in the naturalist or the humanist version, has become an intellectual second-hand store, displaying a variety of collections from last year's fashions of the neighbouring disciplines – 'you name it, we have it'.

The differences between the modern and the postmodern positions run across the familiar controversy of psychology as a natural or a human science. The affinity of psychoanalysis to both modern and postmodern thought has already been pointed out. Computer simulation of artificial intelligence was previously based on the algorithmic rules of a modern, formal rationality. The more recent parallel distributed processing and neural networks are closer to postmodern conceptions of knowledge; they go beyond a linear logic and copy models of reality and focus upon simultaneous interactions within the network, on contextuality and change. Dreyfus and Dreyfus (1988) have even related the two forms of processing to the difference between Husserl's formal phenomenology of consciousness and Heidegger's existentialism founded in the lived world and in everyday language, a difference which approaches the present distinction of modern and postmodern thought.

There are a few trends within academic psychology which explicitly relate to a postmodern discourse, mainly in social psychology. Parker and Shotter (1990) thus argue for a deconstructive social psychology, with a focus on the deconstruction and rhetorics in texts about man. They follow Derrida, Foucault and Lacan in looking at the internal contradictions of these texts, their social formation, uncovering the power relations at work and bringing forth the voices not expressed, such as in feminist work on the social construction of gender. And Gergen (1991) emphasizes the social construction of personal identities, in particular with the communication technologies leading to a multiplicity of knowledge with a recognition of the perspectival nature of reality, and the transformation of the self into a state of relatedness, to an embeddedness in a multitude of networks.

In several ways the Soviet historical cultural school after Vygotsky and the activity theory of Leontiev and Davidov come close to a social constructionism, in emphasizing the dialectical relation of man and world, and the historical and cultural situatedness of activity. On the other hand there is the adherence to the dialectical materialism of Lenin, positioning one objective reality existing independently of human consciousness. In a review of a work by Davidov, Confrey (1991) argues that Davidov's theory could, by leaving the absolutist position on the nature of knowledge in dialectical materialism, be developed into a position which is more relativist in its construction of reality. This would involve accepting cultural diversity and multiple types of knowledge, which would also necessitate a discussion of the role of power relationships and negotiation of differences in epistemology. It remains rather open today whether Soviet activity theory will be discarded as an ideology of legitimation for the Brezhnev period, or whether it will develop into positions close to social constructionism and postmodern thought.

We may also add a beginning interest in a marginal history of psychology which relates to postmodern conceptions of knowledge.

Wundt not only founded an experimental laboratory in Leipzig in 1879; the major part of his professional life was devoted to cultural psychology. He wrote ten volumes on this *Völkerpsychologie*, focusing on language, myths and customs as products of the collective mind, providing material for inferences about the mental life of individuals. While language, myth and custom presuppose a mental action of individuals, they exceed the scope and abilities of individual consciousness and are not predictable from individual psychology. Wundt's analyses of the relation of language and culture, and of individual consciousness and the cultural heritage, while ignored in modern psychology, have influenced seminal thinkers such as Durkheim, G.H. Mead and Vygotsky. Recently, Wundt's cultural psychology has become interpreted as close to a constructivist and a postmodern psychology (Kroger and Scheiber, 1990).

Vygotsky's development of a cultural historical psychology within a historical materialist context from the 1920s remained at the margins of psychology for nearly half a century. And, from the 1940s, the phenomenological psychology of Merleau-Ponty, a professor of child psychology and later of philosophy in Paris, has been ignored in mainstream psychology. His phenomenological descriptions of behaviour, consciousness and the body, as well as his philosophy of perspectivity, his rejection of the dualism of an inner and outer world and his critique of the prejudice of the objective world (see Kvale and Grenness, 1967) come close to later postmodern conceptions of knowledge.

In conclusion, there exist lines of thought in psychology close to postmodern conceptions of knowledge; but they have been marginalized in the history of psychology and remain today at the periphery of academic psychology. Perhaps one contribution of a postmodern approach will be to open up the history of psychology and recover the knowledge marginalized by modern thought.

The question remains, however, whether the main tasks that Ken Gergen (this volume) envisages for a postmodern psychology – such as cultural critique and the construction of new worlds – may just as well be carried out by other disciplines, such as anthropology, literary criticism, communication and media research. In particular anthropology, despite some functionalist and cognitivist trends, provides an understanding of human beings in a postmodern culture. Anthropology studies the very phenomena which have been discarded by modern psychology: the local context and the situated practices, the material tools and the objects of art; the community, its network of interaction and its historical traditions. The focus is on local knowledge; the culture of the people is essential for understanding their activities; cognition is separated neither from its cultural context nor from its content.

With an inherent affinity of anthropological understanding and central themes of postmodern thought, it is not surprising that today anthropology is becoming the social science of general interest, to philosophers as well as to students in the social sciences. Today anthropology is 'turning inwards', applying the modes of thought developed for understanding alien cultures to the study of the anthropologist's own culture, for instance the behaviour of scientists (Latour and Woolgar, 1979) and the educational situation (Lave and Wenger, 1991; Willis, 1977). And for a provocative account of American culture, see Baudrillard's (1988b) travelogue of driving through the American landscape. He starts with the assumption that all you need to know about American society can be gleaned from an anthropology of its driving behaviour; that behaviour tells you more than all academia could ever tell you.

A rehabilitation of practical knowledge

While the position of a scientific psychology in a postmodern culture remains rather open, there are trends in practical psychology which are close to postmodern conceptions of knowledge. Professional psychology has obtained a strong hold on Western societies; rather than being threatened, psychology is expanding as a profession. Whereas academic psychology is becoming a museum of modern thought, professional psychologists encounter human beings in their current world.

The American Psychological Association has thus been caught in a continual conflict between 'scientific' and 'professional' psychologists, and the association was recently split into a scientific and a professional branch. The issue of legitimation of psychology is one aspect of the gap between theory and practice, between academia and the profession. A hundred years ago, by the founding of a psychological discipline, the appeal to natural science theories and methods served as an external legitimation for a psychological profession breaking away from religion. With the separation from religion and the professionalization of psychology well secured in Western countries today, the appeal to the prestige of natural science loses relevance; the practice is legitimate through its results.

The psychological knowledge taught at the universities, and justified by appeals to alleged theories and methods of the natural sciences, has remained within the abstract, technical rationality of modernity. Psychological laboratory science is today becoming a special case of limited interest, adapted to islands of structure in a world of chaos. Professional practice, on the other hand, has had to cope with the complexities, instabilities and value conflicts of a postmodern world. Recent studies indicate that the technical rationality taught in the universities may be irrelevant, or even detrimental to professional practice (for instance, Hoshmand and Polkinghorne, 1992; Schön, 1983; Scriven, 1986).

We shall here discuss some approaches to the practical knowledge of the everyday world: systemic therapy, system evaluation, practitioners' knowledge and qualitative research. These approaches at the margins of scientific psychology will be related to postmodern conceptions of knowledge, in particular legitimation through practice, local and practical knowledge, and knowledge as heterogeneous, qualitative and linguistic.

The professional field where the implications of a postmodern linguistic shift have been most explicitly taken up is *systemic therapy* (for example, Anderson and Goolishian, 1988). Here there has been a shift from study of the psyche of the individual self to studying the family as a linguistic system. Pathology is no longer seen as residing in consciousness, nor in the unconscious, but in the structures of language. Indeed the very term 'psychotherapist' seems to be inadequate, for the therapists do not attempt to heal some interior 'psyche', but work with language and, as masters of conversation, heal with words.

Research aimed at improving practice, as *system evaluation*, does not pursue knowledge for some universal and eternal audience, but rather seeks to provide knowledge for particular audiences dealing with context-bound issues (House, 1986; Patton, 1980). In system evaluation, which goes beyond the positivist dichotomy of facts and values, the object of study is a local system, for example an educational programme or an institution. The research interest is neither a finding of universal laws of behaviour nor a depth penetration of an individual psyche. The focus of study is the interaction of participants in local contexts; the system as an entity is held responsible and accountable for its results.

There is, in system evaluation, a scepticism towards a rationalistic model presuming an underlying order of the educational system. The everyday world is hardly accessible by the linear logic of traditional scientific rationality, which works with separate variables, well defined and measurable, to be studied by a detached observer in the interests of prediction and control. Today there occurs a rehabilitation of the lived, complex, heterogeneous and conflictual practical world. Scriven is critical of the relevance of the scientific paradigm for the everyday world: 'practical problems are defined by a reference to several parameters concerning which the basic scientist gathers no data and rarely has any competence. These include the not entirely independent parameters of cost, ethicality, political feasibility, the set of practicable alternatives, system lability, and overall practical significance' (1986: 54).

The validity of system evaluation is not linked to the specific methods applied, nor to a theory of truth involving correspondence between what is measured and a postulated objective reality. The focus is here on a communicative and pragmatic evaluation, whether the knowledge produced can be understood, accepted and used by the participants in the evaluated system (Kvale, 1989).

Schön (1983) focuses on *practitioners' knowledge* and reports a study of how professionals think in action, based on studies of how managers, architects, therapists and other professionals go about solving their problems. He describes the knowledge taught at the universities as a 'technical rationality' conceiving of a systematic knowledge base which is specialized, firmly bonded, scientific and standardized. The dichotomized categories of this technical rational knowledge are mismatched to the situations of practice – the 'complexity, uncertainty, instability, uniqueness, and value conflicts which are increasingly perceived as central to the world of professional practice' (1983: 14). The practitioner's 'knowing-in-action' does not rest upon the clear-cut logical categories of a technical rationality, nor need it be explicitly verbalized. Every competent practitioner 'makes innumerable judgments of quality for which he cannot state adequate criteria, and he displays skills for which he cannot state the rules and procedures. Even when he makes conscious use of research-based theories and techniques, he is dependent on tacit recognitions, judgments and skillful performance' (1983: 50).

The professional's reflection and action can proceed in unique situations of uncertainty, instability and value conflicts because they do not depend upon the dichotomies and the linear logic of a technical rationality. Abandoning the cognitivist tyranny of the rule, it may become acceptable that 'knowing that' may occur without necessarily 'knowing why'. The descriptions of the knowledge of professional practice given by Scriven and Schön come close to Lyotard's analysis of postmodern knowledge as incomplete, discontinuous and paradoxical, and where judgements are passed without explicit criteria for the judgements. Professional knowledge is not a mere 'applied knowledge', based on some fundamental scientific laws of behaviour; practice entails an understanding of its own, and is validated through its effects. Polkinghorne (this volume) argues that the knowledge of therapeutic practitioners is in line with postmodern ideas of knowledge as without foundations, fragmentary socially constructed and with pragmatic utility as a criterion of validity.

A rehabilitation of the heterogeneous and non-commensurable contexts of the practical world involves a loss of hegemony for formalized experimental and statistical methods research. The intentional nature of human practices is well captured by *qualitative methods*. There is an acceptance of diverse ways of producing knowledge. A multi-method approach has been strong within system evaluation (Patton, 1980), also encompassing qualitative methods involving interactive and contextual approaches, and including case studies. The current qualitative research interest reflects a linguistic and conversational turn within the philosophy of science. There is a change in emphasis from confrontation with nature to a conversation between persons, from correspondence with an objective reality to negotiation of meaning. Rorty thus points to the 'conversation as the ultimate context within which knowledge is to be understood' (1979: 389). The qualitative research interview is no longer a mere adjunct to the basic scientific methods of observation and experimentation, but provides, through a conversation between persons, privileged access to the cultural world of intersubjective meaning (Kvale, 1983; Mishler, 1986). In several respects, the knowledge produced in an interview comes close to postmodern conceptions of knowledge as conversational, narrative, linguistic, contextual and interrelational (Kvale, 1992).

We have here outlined some areas with a practical orientation to knowledge, such as systemic therapy, systems evaluation, studies of practitioners' knowledge and qualitative research. None of these approaches is specifically postmodern; the knowledge produced by these practices is, however, in line with philosophic analyses of knowledge in a postmodern age – given that they focus on local and narrative knowledge, on acceptance of the openness of practical knowledge, on the study of heterogeneous, linguistic and qualitative knowledge of the everyday world and on validation through practice.

Postmodern thought here appears as a relevant context for the theoretical explication and development of practical knowledge in the psychological professions. This does not imply a practice devoid of theory, but involves a shift in the focus of theorizing in psychology – from the interior of the individual to its relation to society. The accountability of psychologists' work is shifted from meta-narratives of natural science to communities of practice. There is a move from studying the cognitive mechanisms of an internal psychic apparatus or a self-realizing self to examining the implications of practical activity in the world. This includes the generation of knowledge by

professionals and the epistemological, ethical and political implications of this activity. The validity of psychological knowledge
relates to the ethical value of this knowledge. With the focus on the
pragmatic effects of knowledge, the consequences of psychological
practice in relation to the values of the community come into the
foreground, including the contribution of psychology to the constitution of the very values of the community.

Concluding perspectives

The discipline of psychology has been discussed in relation to a
postmodern culture. If the descriptions of postmodernity and of
psychology offered here are adequate, then some trends in the
current status of psychology should become understandable. The
current emptiness and irrelevance of a psychological science to
culture at large may be due to psychology's rootedness in modernity,
in the study of the logic of an abstracted 'psyche', which is out of
touch with a postmodern world. (We leave out here the issue whether
modern psychology was ever adequate for understanding modern
man.)

It follows that the strong tension between academic and professional psychology may be due, at least in part, to the entrenchment
of psychological theory in modernity, whereas professional practice,
on the other hand, has to face human life in a postmodern age. From
a rationalistic concept of science the practical tasks of the profession
are merely the application of principles developed by the aca-
demicians, whereas they appear central to a postmodern understanding.

Scenarios for psychology in a postmodern landscape
The above discussion has given no clear assessment of the possibilities of a psychological science in a postmodern culture. In conclusion,
three scenarios for the development of psychology will be outlined,
each of which derives from somewhat different views on the
relationship between the discipline and the postmodern condition.

First, to take an extreme position, the postmodern death of the
subject may be tantamount to the death of psychology – the modern
science of the subject. If psychology has been the privileged way for
modernity to understand man, a postmodern age may also mean a
post-psychology age.

Less dramatically, the postmodern decentring of the subject could
lead to a decentring of the modern science of the subject. If the
science of psychology has become too centred on individual subjectivity it may dissolve as a separate science. It may then merge with

other disciplines that move more freely in the postmodern landscape, as for example the new cognitive science of computers, neurophysiology and linguistics (in the case of academic psychology), and with the health science movement, investigating and healing the 'biopsychosocial unit' (in the case of professional psychology).

Secondly, at the other extreme, contemporary psychology could be seen as a postmodern conceptual collage – a pastiche of recycled ideas and methods borrowed from other fields and combined according to the most recent consumer demands of a mass culture. With an extreme adaptability and flexibility, psychology does seem able to move – amoeba-like – into whatever niche opens in the markets for therapy and self-realization, as well as for selection and control of personnel.

Thirdly, an alternative psychology moves out of the archaeology of the psyche and into the cultural landscape of the present world, directly entering a postmodern discourse. This would involve facing the rootedness of human existence in specific historical and cultural situations, and being open to the insights into the human condition provided by the arts and the humanities. Main topics of study would include the linguistic and social construction of reality, and the interrelations of a local context and the self in a network of relationships. And this would require accepting the open, perspectival and ambiguous nature of knowledge and validation of knowledge through practice. It would involve a multi-method approach to research, including qualitative descriptions of the diversity of a person's relation to the world and a deconstruction of texts that attempts to describe this relation. The question remains whether such changes are too radical to find their place within a psychological science with strong individualistic and rationalistic roots.

No clear dominance appears among the three scenarios for psychological science in a postmodern age suggested here – a decentred psychology, or psychology as a postmodern conceptual collage, or a radical alternative postmodern psychology. A clarification of these positions would require further reflecting on the historical and cultural situation of psychology. Two aspects of this complex situation should be mentioned in conclusion – the relations of psychology to religion and to the consumer society.

Between the cathedral and the market place

With the death of God, proclaimed by Nietzsche at the turn of the century, man came to be the measure of all things, and psychology became the secularized religion of modernity. In modernity the loss of belief in an absolute God had been succeeded by the modernist declaration of faith: 'I believe in one objective reality.' Religion as a truth guarantee was replaced by the new sciences, the priests as truth mediators were substituted by the scientists. For the sociology Comte founded in the early nineteenth century he explicitly visioned the sociologists as the new positivist high priests preaching the positivist doctrine of the religion of humanity (see Samelson, 1974). And with the current collapse of the modern Utopias of heaven on earth, religion is again becoming revitalized. The history of religion, up to the current controversies of a revivalist fundamentalism and the New Age relativism, is the open book of the many schools of psychology. No psychology for which this book remains closed can become a genuine science.

When religion and the meta-narratives of modernity have eroded, there appear no truths outside of man. In this relativist culture with no fixed and fundamental rules, the moral guide for life is sought in a scientific psychology. The new psychology took over religion's task of providing guidelines for human life. The priests as confessors were replaced by therapists as paid companions. With an economy of production being replaced by an economy of consumption, the Protestant work ethic is gradually replaced by a psychology of need gratification and indulgence. With the erosion of a comprehensive frame of meaning, of traditional values and communal bonds, individual self-realization became the goal of life. 'In the United States, at least, psychology has become a new religion establishing an inner quest for self where before there had been an outer quest for God' (Leahey, 1987: 479). It should be noted that the religious roots of psychology are not confined to the humanistic versions. Thus Watson's scientific behaviourism was almost a literal translation of the Baptist theology that Watson studied while training for the ministry (see Birnbaum, 1964).

The current visual and symbolic landscape is no longer formed by the church; it is dominated by the all-pervasive advertisements and the values of wish gratification and self-realization to be fulfilled by the magic of consumer goods. In contemporary society the consumer industry has replaced the church as a main force in the shaping of cultural values. The new science of psychology became positioned between the cathedral and the market place; its current context is aptly expressed in a book on the culture of consumerism by the chapter 'From salvation to self-realization', subtitled 'Advertising and the therapeutic roots of the consumer culture, 1880–1930' (Jackson Lears, 1983).

A new psychological ethos was promoted by the advertising and therapeutic communities – with spontaneism, wish gratification and self-actualization as ideals to be fulfilled by the purchase of consumer products. 'A quest for self-realization through consumption compensated for a loss of autonomy on the job. Therapeutic ideals converged with advertising and mass amusement to promote new forms of cultural hegemony' (Jackson Lears, 1983: 29). In this context, the career of John Broadus Watson may be seen as symbolic for the new psychology – from aspiring to be a Baptist minister, through founding behaviourism, to become a successful marketing psychologist.

With postmodernism postulated as the ideology of a consumer society, there does remain an issue of whether postmodern discourse, including the few attempts towards a postmodern psychology, merely mirrors consumerism, or whether it entails potentials for a critical reflection upon and a deconstruction of the ruling ideology of a postmodern society.

References

Abib, J. (1991) Some relationships between radical behaviorism and postmodern thinking. Manuscript. Federal University of São Carlos, São Paulo, Brazil.

Anderson, H. and Goolishian, H.A. (1988) Human systems as linguistic systems. *Family Process*, 27: 271–393.

Anderson, W.T. (1990) *Reality Isn't What It Used to Be*. San Francisco: Harper & Row.

Baudrillard, J. (1988a) *Selected Works*. Ed. M. Poster. Cambridge: Polity Press.

Baudrillard, J. (1988b) *America*. London: Verso.

Bellah, R.N. (1987) The quest for the self. In P. Rabinow and M.M. Sullivan (eds), *Interpretative Social Science*. Berkeley: University of California Press. pp. 365–83.

Birnbaum, L. (1964) Behaviorism: John Broadus Watson and American Social Thought, 1913–1933. PhD dissertation. University of California, Berkeley.

Bloom, A. (1987) *The Closing of the American Mind*. New York: Simon & Schuster.

Boss, M. (1963) *Psychoanalysis and Daseinsanalysis*. New York: Basic Books.

Confrey, J. (1991) Steering a course between Vygotsky and Piaget. *Educational Researcher*, November: 28–32.

Dreyfus, H.L. and Dreyfus, S.E. (1988) Making a mind vs modeling a brain: artificial intelligence back at a branchpoint. *Daedalus*, 15–44.

Gergen, K. (1991) *The Saturated Self*. New York: Basic Books.

Giorgi, A. (1970) *Psychology as a Human Science*. New York: Harper & Row.

Habermas, J. (1975) *Legitimation Crisis*. Boston, MA: Beacon Press.

Hoshmand, L.T. and Polkinghorne, D. (1992). Redefining the science–practice relationship and professional training. *American Psychotherapist*, 47: 55–66.

House, E.R. (ed.) (1986) *New Directions in Educational Evaluation*. London: Falmer.

Jackson Lears, T.J. (1983) From salvation to self-realization. In R. Wightman Fox and T.J. Jackson Lears (eds), *The Culture of Consumption*. New York: Pantheon. pp. 1–38.

Jameson, F. (1984) The cultural logic of late capitalism. *New Left Review*, 146: 53–92.

Koch, S. (1959) Epilogue. In S. Koch (ed.), *Psychology: A Study of a Science*, vol. 3. New York: McGraw-Hill. pp. 729–88.

Koch, S. (1964) Psychology and emerging conceptions of knowledge as unitary. In

T.W. Wann (ed.), *Behaviorism and Phenomenology – Contrasting Bases for Modern Psychology*. Chicago: University of Chicago Press.

Kroger, O.R. and Scheiber, K.E. (1990) A reappraisal of Wundt's influence on social psychology. *Canadian Psychology/Psychologie Canadienne*, 31: 220–8.

Kvale, S. (1983) The qualitative research interview – a phenomenological and a hermeneutical mode of understanding. *Journal of Phenomenological Psychology*, 14: 171–96.

Kvale, S. (1989) To validate is to question. In S. Kvale (ed.), *Issues of Validity in Qualitative Research*. Lund: Studentlitteratur. pp. 73–92.

Kvale, S. (1992) Inter views and new views on knowledge – qualitative research in a postmodern context. Manuscript. Aarhus: University of Aarhus.

Kvale, S. and Grenness, C.E. (1967) Skinner and Sartre: towards a radical phenomenology of behavior? *Review of Existential Psychology and Psychiatry*, 7: 128–50.

Latour, B. and Woolgar, S. (1979) *Laboratory Life – the Social Construction of Scientific Facts*. Beverly Hills, CA: Sage.

Lave, J. and Wenger, E. (1991) *Situated Learning: Legitimate Peripheral Participation*. Cambridge: Cambridge University Press.

Leahey, T.H. (1987) *A History of Psychology*. Englewood Cliffs, NJ: Prentice-Hall.

Lund, N.O. (1990) *Collage Architecture*. Berlin: Ernst.

Lyotard, J.-F. (1984) *The Postmodern Condition: A Report on Knowledge*. Manchester: Manchester University Press.

Madison, G.B. (1990) *The Hermeneutics of Postmodernity*. Bloomington: Indiana University Press.

Maturana, H. (1988) Reality: the search for objectivity or the quest for the compelling argument. *Irish Journal of Psychology*, 9: 25–83.

May, R., Angel, E. and Ellenberger, H.F. (eds) (1958) *Existence – A New Dimension in Psychiatry and Psychology*. New York: Basic Books.

Merleau-Ponty, M. (1962) *Phenomenology of Perception*. London: Routledge & Kegan Paul. (Originally published 1945.)

Mishler, E.G. (1986) *Research Interviewing – Context and Narrative*. Cambridge, MA: Harvard University Press.

Parker, I. and Shotter, J. (eds) (1990) *Deconstructing Social Psychology*. London: Routledge.

Patton, M.Q. (1980) *Qualitative Evaluation Methods*. Beverly Hills, CA: Sage.

Peitgen, H.O. and Richter, P.E. (1986) *The Beauty of Fractals*. Berlin: Springer.

Ratner, C. (1988) A lesson from the natives on reconstructing psychology's conception of the individual. Manuscript. Arcata, CA: Humboldt State University.

Rorty, R. (1979) *Philosophy and the Mirror of Nature*. Princeton, NJ: Princeton University Press.

Rorty, R. (1985) Habermas and Lyotard on postmodernity. In R.J. Bernstein (ed.), *Habermas and Modernity*. Oxford: Blackwell. pp. 161–75.

Salner, M. (1989) Validity in human science research. In S. Kvale (ed.), *Issues of Validity in Qualitative Research*. Lund: Studentlitteratur: pp. 47–71.

Samelson, F. (1974) History, origin myth and ideology: Comte's 'discovery' of social psychology. *Journal for the Theory of Social Behaviour*, 4: 217–31.

Sampson, E.E. (1988) Indigenous psychologies of the individual and their role in personal and social functioning. *American Psychologist*, 43: 15–22.

Schön, D. (1983) *The Reflective Practitioner*. New York: Basic Books.

Scriven, M. (1986) Evaluation as a paradigm for educational research. In E.R. House (ed.), *New Directions in Educational Evaluation*. London: Falmer, pp. 53–67.

Venturi, R., Scott Brown, D. and Tzenour, D. (1972) *Learning from Las Vegas*. Cambridge, MA: MIT Press.

Wallach, M. and Wallach, L. (1983) *Psychology's Sanction for Selfishness*. San Francisco: Freeman.

Willis, P.L. (1977) *Learning to Labour*. Farnborough: Saxon House.

3

'Getting in Touch': The Meta-Methodology of a Postmodern Science of Mental Life

John Shotter

Currently, there is a movement away from *modern* toward *postmodern sciences* (Lyotard, 1984; Toulmin, 1982). Among the many changes involved, is a shift in the character of both standpoint and investigatory activity: 1 from the standpoint of the detached, theory-testing onlooker, to the interested, interpretive, procedure-testing participant observer; and 2 from a one-way style of investigation to two-way interactive mode. These shifts open up a wholly new set of research topics to do with what does or can go on between people; and give rise to a noncognitive, nonsystematic, rhetorical, critical social constructionist approach to psychology. Here I want both to critique from a postmodernist perspective the view of modern science implicit in modern psychology, and to outline the nature of a research program for a postmodern science of mental life.

Knowledge 'by looking' and 'by being in touch'

Central to the different perspective I want to formulate is this claim by Rorty (1980: 12) that 'It is pictures rather than propositions, metaphors rather than statements, which determine most of our philosophical convictions.' Thus, instead of the image of (a) 'the mind as a (passive) mirror of Nature', (b) 'knowledge as accuracy of representation' and thus (c) the scientist 'as an external observer', I want to substitute another set of images: the image (a) of the scientist being 'as if one of a community of "blind" persons exploring their surroundings by the use of sticks or through other such instruments'; (b) of the knowledge important to them 'as being to do with them "knowing their way around" in ways communicable between them'; and (c) of 'the mind as actively "making sense" of the *relatively invariant* (Bohm, 1965; Gibson, 1979) features they discover in their instrument-assisted explorations of their surroundings' – a shift from knowing by 'looking at' to knowing by being 'in contact, or in touch with'. Indeed, I want to argue that it is only in terms of activities like these that the kinds of knowledge we possess and make use of in conducting our everyday affairs are possible.

The change in conducting one's investigations from an onlooker standpoint to a position of instrumentally mediated (or prosthetically aided – see below) involvement is central to a postmodern science. But it is not the only change taking place, for this change implies many others. For instance, associated with the adoption of an involved rather than an external, uninvolved *standpoint* are the different attitudes, values, aims, as well as the guidelines, apparatuses and devices that can be used in relation to such standpoints; there are also changes in *starting points* (whether one starts one's investigations when a 'breakdown' occurs, or during the flow of successful activity); in types of *investigative procedure*; in attitudes to language; and especially in modes of *legitimation* (Lyotard, 1984). In detail, there is a shift 1 from a concern with *theories* to *practices*, from theorizing to the provision of practical, instructive *accounts*; 2 from an interest in *things* to an interest in *activities* and the *uses* to which we can put the 'mental tools' or 'psychological instruments' (Shotter, 1989; Vygotsky, 1962) of our own devising; 3 a shift away from what goes on in the heads of individuals to an interest in the (largely social) nature of their surroundings, and what these can (or will) 'allow', 'permit' or 'afford'; 4 a shift from procedures conducted on one's own, to their 'negotiation' with others; 5 from starting points in reflection (when the flow of interaction has ceased), to local starting points embedded in the historical flow of social activity in daily life; 6 from language being primarily for the representation of reality, to it being primarily for the coordination of diverse social action, with its representational function working *from within* a set of linguistically constituted social relations; 7 from a reliance upon our experiences as a basis for understanding our world, to a questioning of the social processes of their 'construction' (Gergen, 1985); and, perhaps most importantly of all, 8 a shift away from investigations *based* in foundations already accepted as authoritative – which thus claim an acceptability for their results ahead of time – toward modes of investigation which allow for error correction 'on the spot', so to speak (Barnes, 1982; Bernstein, 1983; Rorty, 1980), which find their 'warrants' in locally constituted situations or circumstances.

The shift from third person observation to second person 'making sense': from meta-theory to meta-methodology

In the past, in assuming our procedures of inquiry to be secure, and our problems to be located (mainly) in the nature of our subject matter, we have indulged in a great deal of *meta-theoretical* and *epistemological* discussion (for example, Gergen and Morowski, 1980) – we discussed *theories* because we felt accurate theories were the goal of our investigations. In the approach being canvassed here, our supposed objects of study are of less concern to us than the general nature of our investigatory practices. In other words, instead of meta-theory, we become concerned with *meta-methodology*. Primarily, we become interested in the procedures and devices we use both in 'socially constructing' the subject matter of our investigations as well as in how we establish and maintain a contact with it. For the 'hook-up', so to speak, between such devices and our surroundings, determines the nature of the data we can gather *through* their use. We thus move away from the individual, third-person, external, contemplative observer stance, the investigator who collects *fragmented* data from a position socially 'outside' of the activity observed, and who bridges the 'gaps' between the fragments by the imaginative invention of theoretical entities, toward a more interpretive approach; away from the use of *inference* – the *assertion* (on some basis, of course) that essentially unobservable, subjective entities, supposedly 'inside' individuals, nonetheless exist, toward a concern with modes of *hermeneutical* inquiry; away from theoretical toward interests of a more practical kind, concerned with the aids and devices we inevitably make use of in the conduct of all our inquiries. But while we move away from such concerns, we do not – as will be made clear below – turn away from them entirely.

To see the consequences of such a shift, let us examine just one major point of difference between *empirical* and *hermeneutical* methodologies. The devices through which we conduct our hermeneutical investigations, unlike the devices providing us with 'pointer readings' which reside 'on the side of' the world, so to speak, reside 'on our side', that is, they function as *prostheses*, as extensions of ourselves. As such, they do not have any content in themselves; they are transparent – blind people, for instance, do not feel their sticks vibrating in the palms of their hands; nor do they have to infer, as if solving a problem, that the 'data' delivered to them by their sticks mean that the terrain ahead of them is, for instance, rough; they experience it directly as rough, as a result of their stick-assisted way of investigating it 'in' their movement through it. And the knowledge they obtain in such a mode of investigation-in-practice is not fragmentary; it does not require an imaginative filling in of its 'gaps', for simply, any indeterminacies or uncertainties in it (in relation to the information required for the person's movement) can be filled in by further investigation. Hence, in practical hermeneutical investigations, a kind of completeness-for-practical-purposes is available which is unavailable in empirical investigations.

Indeed, the process involved in the development of one's knowledge is quite unlike any so far discussed in the empirical tradition. It is not induction (for it does not depend upon the discovery of regularities), nor is it inference (for the *unique* and *particular* nature of circumstances cannot be understood by assimilating their details to any already established theoretical categories and premises). As each 'part' of the description is supplied, a conceptual 'whole' has to be fashioned to accommodate it. Mentally, we have to 'construct' a context (a world) into which it can fit and play its part – where each new fact 'points to' or 'indicates' a 'world' in which they all have their place or function. And the hermeneutical process continues as each new fact is added to the account; the whole must be progressively transformed and articulated, metamorphosed in fact, in a back-and-forth process, in such a way as to afford all the parts of the whole an undistorted accommodation.

In the hermeneutical account of knowing, then, a process of 'making' or construction is at work. Indeed, even the seeing of objects involves an active psychological process of construction involving socially derived knowledge – doesn't it? Yet currently, we feel the opposite is the case: that in our 'experience', outer 'objective' events cause inner 'subjective' effects. And we make use of this in our theories about the nature of knowledge and modes of inquiry. We feel some claims to truth are *certain*, not because of the arguments given for them, but because in some way they are caused in us or imposed upon us by the outer, objective nature of the world. These truths can be used as 'foundations' upon which to base our further inquiries. Deconstructive analyses such as Rorty's (1980), however, show such beliefs to be an illusion. To build knowledge upon foundations constructed upon an analogy between perceiving and knowing is to see *certainty* as a matter of the world 'outside' our human world imposing something upon us, rather than as something we achieve both in interaction with it and in conversation between ourselves, isn't it?

Well, yes (to a degree) and no (to a degree); and in fact, in my view, both are true – they are both moments in the two-way, interactive mode of investigation I mentioned above. What such a deconstructive analysis means, I think, is that we must finally face up to the lack of any pre-established orders in the world: 1 that instead of thinking of our task as that of finding such an order, ready made, we must consider activities which begin with vague but not wholly unspecified 'tendencies' which are then open to, or which permit a degree of, actual further specification; *and also* 2 instead of thinking it possible for special individuals trained in special methods simply to make 'discoveries', any further specifications of states of affairs, if

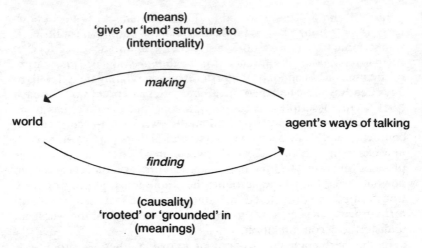

Figure 3.1

they are to be considered *intelligible and legitimate* to those around us, must be negotiated in a back-and-forth process with them. In other words, we must now think in terms of processes of investigation involving both 'finding' *and* 'making'.

I have tried to include the main aspects of this two-way process in Figure 3.1. To adapt the useful 'direction of fit' terminology introduced by Searle (1983), what this shows (bottom limb) is that in the world-to-agent *direction of fit*, as in classical empiricist approaches, we *could say* (that is, the facts will 'afford' us saying) that our ways of talking depend upon the world; they are 'rooted' or 'grounded' in its nature. To that extent our talk is about what we 'find' to be there. But on the other hand (top limb), in line with *hermeneutical* or interpretive views, in the agent-to-world *direction of fit*, it is equally true to say that what we take the nature of the world to be *depends* upon our ways of talking about it. To the extent that they 'give' or 'lend' its otherwise open nature a determinate (and legitimate) structure and significance, its significance for us 'is' as we 'make' it to be.

Thus the fact is, not only *can* one make both of these claims, but one *must* assert that both are true. Indeed, as Derrida (1976) would point out, they owe their distinct existences to their *interdependency*; one claim is an *absent-presence* in 'lending' intelligibility to the other. Thus although one should say only what the facts will permit, the nature of the facts here is such that, although they draw upon different *systematic discourses* for their representation, two equal and opposite truths can, and must, be asserted. And this, of course, is

precisely what Billig (1987) is now arguing in relation to the importance of rhetoric and the two-sidedness of human thinking generally.

However, more analysis of the detailed nature of such two-way,
investigatory processes is required than I have space to enter into
here. Suffice it to say that many of the analyses already conducted by
phenomenologists, such as Merleau-Ponty – whose influence is implicitly present in the formulation above – seem to me of central
importance. For instance, in a section entitled 'The theory of the
body is already a theory of perception' (Merleau-Ponty, 1962: 203),
he discusses the case in which we draw together all the different,
successive views of an object as we walk around it, as views *all of the
same thing*, for instance, all of them *as* 'a three-dimensional cube':

> As I move around it, I see the front face, hitherto a square, change its
> shape, then disappear, while the other sides come into view and one by
> one become squares. But the successive stages of this experience are for
> me merely the *opportunity* of conceiving the whole cube with its six equal
> and simultaneous faces, the *intelligible structure* which provides the expla-
> nation of it. (1962: 203; my emphases)

Thus, it is on the basis of the 'opportunities' the object affords me in
my tour around it (as well as on the basis of my sense of my own
bodily movements) that 'I am able to interpret perceptual appearance and *construct* the cube as it truly is' (my emphasis).

Currently however, we find such two-way or two-sided accounts
very difficult to accept. For all kinds of reasons, not just in the history
of philosophy (see, for example, Cassirer, 1951), but also because of
our socialization into the official communicative practices of academic life, we are still committed to an Enlightenment image of
knowledge as being both *systematic* and *unitary*, that is, a hierarchical
structure of one-way dependencies. What other form could it have?
Institutionally, only certain forms of investigation and argumentation can (morally) 'make sense'. We *must* talk in terms of such
systems of one-way dependencies, in terms of relations of dominance. We cannot build two-sided truths into an atemporal system.
Of the two equal and opposite claims – about which is or should be
the *dominant* dependency relation – we feel that it is impossible for
both claims to be true. Failing to give any place to time, or to
'moments' in a process in our current ways of thinking, we claim such
two-sided truths to be unthinkable.

Grammatical illusions, the *ex-post-facto* facts fallacy and entrapment

Why is it so difficult for us to recognize the nature of our own
involvement in such temporally constituted, constructive processes?

Why are we continually *tempted* to espouse what are essentially philosophical 'assumptions' (and are initially presented as such) as undeniable 'givens' in our investigations?

As I said above, our major 'prosthetic device' – through which we can gain a grasp of the nature of the 'others' around us – is *language*; and it is the nature of the social conditions required for its proper, communicative usage which is of interest to us in our meta-methodological inquiries. But if, instead of thinking of language as being used in this way – to 'make contact' with those around us – we still insist upon thinking of our sentences as *pictures*, in which we can *see* the structure of the sentence the 'things' they represent, then we can mislead ourselves in fundamental ways. Committed to a 'picture' theory of linguistic function, as Wittgenstein (1953: no. 114) says (still using a visual idiom, but now ironically): 'One thinks that one is tracing the outline of the thing's nature over and over again, and one is merely tracing round the frame through which we look at it.' In other words, as he (Wittgenstein) also says elsewhere, a way of speaking is what prevents us from seeing the facts (that is, our practices and procedures of usage) without prejudice. And it is overcoming our own misconceptions about our own use of language (and the temptations to misinterpret its nature that it itself offers us) which is one of our main aims in our meta-methodological investigations.

But we mislead ourselves in other more complex ways than simply by such 'grammatical illusions'; there are other kinds of ways in which we can 'entrap' ourselves within linguistic worlds of our own making. Stolzenberg (1978) describes such traps as 'a closed system of attitudes, beliefs, and habits of thought for which one can give an objective demonstration that certain of the beliefs are incorrect and that certain of the attitudes and habits of thought prevent this from being recognized' (p. 224). This gives rise, Stolzenberg says, to 'methodological errors' which are 'those failures to take into account considerations of standpoint that have the effect of *maintaining* the system' (p. 224). These, whatever the nature of the system in question, function to undermine the proper processes of rational argumentation and debate, and to bias its outcome always in favour of the status quo. They are errors *in method* because, of course, the fundamental nature of all scientific methods of investigation *ought* to be such that they are always open to the correction of error; this, however, is not the case when one is 'entrapped'; objections to the system of thought are either rendered unintelligible or assimilated to it in some way. One only has to call to mind one's own attempts to argue with Piagetians, Freudians, Skinnerians or cognitivists to understand what Stolzenberg means by such 'closed' systems of thought.

The 'fall' into such a trap comes about as follows:

1 First, a statement is formulated as a description of a state of affairs which, although we may not realize it at the time, is *open* to a number of possible interpretations.
2 We are then tempted to accept the statement as true.
3 By its very nature the statement then 'affords' or 'permits' the making of further statements, now of a more well articulated *and systematic* nature.
4 The initial interpretation (already accepted as true) is now perceived *retrospectively* as owing its now quite definite character to its place 'within' the now well-specified context produced by the later statements – it has been 'given' or 'lent' a determinate character in their terms which it did not, in its original *openness*, actually have.

This is how it comes about that something which was at first merely an *assumption* takes on the appearance of a *definition*; and what had a social *history* of its production appears as an atemporal, ahistorical system of natural necessities.

Someone who has studied its nature in relation to scientific developments is Fleck (1979). He comments upon the general nature of the process as follows:

> once a statement is published it constitutes part of the social forces which form concepts and create habits of thought. Together with all other statements it determines 'what cannot be thought of in any other way'. Even if a particular statement is contested, we grow up with its uncertainty which, circulating in society, reinforces its social effect. It becomes a self-evident reality which, in turn, conditions our further acts of cognition. There emerges a closed, harmonious system within which the logical origin of individual elements can no longer be traced. (Fleck, 1979: 37)

In attempting retrospectively to understand the origins and development (and the current movement) of our thought, we describe their nature within our to an extent now finished and systematic schematisms. But the trouble is, once 'inside' such systems, it is extremely difficult to escape from them.

What Stolzenberg and Fleck show, then, is how a system of thought and expression can work to disconnect itself from its own social and historical origins, and also (seemingly) from its rooting or grounding in the social practices which maintain its appearance of autonomy, and creates the illusion of it being about 'a world of things' existing independently of it and external to it. Indeed, the process Stolzenberg describes is entirely general. Ossorio (1981) calls it the '*ex-post-facto* facts paradox'.

The difference between a genuinely scientific approach and an approach within an entrapping system of beliefs lies in their respective methodologies. In genuine science, one can *ironicize* one's experience (Pollner, 1975), whereas in a *system* of belief, all acts of observation, judgment, etc., are performed solely from the particular standpoint of the system itself: 'Specifically, the ironicizing of experience occurs when one experience, tacitly claiming to have comprehended the world objectively, is examined from the point of view of another experience which is honoured as the definitive version of the world intended by the first' (p. 412). The irony resides in the subsequent appreciation that the initial experience no longer possesses the objective nature it was originally felt to have. Entrapping systems possess a methodology which prevents the ironicizing of experience in Pollner's sense; by their very nature, they rule out of court criticisms not intelligible within the terms decreed by their system's methodology – there are many such approaches with such a character in psychology.

A research program for a postmodern science of mind

The switch from a detached, theoretical, individualistic standpoint to a practical, socially involved (interactionist and constructionist) stance for the conduct of socio-psychological inquiries, besides opening up a whole new set of topics for investigation and questions about them, also suggests new methods of inquiry and means for validating their results (for an account of some of these issues, see Billig, 1987; Gergen, 1982, 1985; Harré, 1979, 1983; Shotter, 1984). And in a moment, I will turn to a listing of what happens to the traditional topics of psychological research – thinking, motivation, emotion, memory, learning, perception, language, social behavior, etc., normally considered as *individualistic* phenomena – when embedded in the context of a postmodernist, practical-social, approach. But it is the social activity of *narration* which must be considered first, for it emerges as a central (and primary) topic when we turn to such investigations. Why?

We can mention at least the following reasons: because the game of inquiry can only proceed when it has been decided (a) what the fundamental entities are under investigation; (b) how they interact with each other and with the senses; and (c) what questions may be legitimately asked about them and what techniques employed in seeking solutions (Kuhn, 1962). Just as in a court of law, where a witness's 'story' can, if told appropriately, work to specify quite precisely the evidence required to corroborate or refute it, so in science: narratives function to construct the requirements in terms of which the reality they specify can be checked out. In other words, the narrative form not only 'lends' itself to, but it can 'provide a unifying context for', a great variety of language games, and thus it promotes rational inquiry.

But it is not just in science that narratives are important; they also have a number of important parts to play in everyday life, in the transmission of knowledge, as well as being to do with how a society both remembers its past and presents itself to itself in the present (Lyotard, 1984). A 'narrative tradition' is, says Lyotard, 'the tradition of the criteria defining a three-fold competence – "know-how," "knowing-how-to-speak," and "knowing-how-to-hear" – through which the community's relation to itself is played out. What is transmitted through these narratives is the set of pragmatic rules that constitutes the social bond' (p. 21). This affects all our other concerns, all the traditional psychological topics listed above. For we now see them all as structured or informed, if not in a grand narrative, at least by one or another *local* narrative; for primarily, what matters to us at any one moment is our *social identity*, that is, how we are 'placed' in relation to those around us, and who (and what) we take our placement there (in terms of some sense-making narrative) as permitting us to be. For our placing has to do with our *situation* and our *position* in it, with the rights and duties, the privileges and obligations, the invitations and barriers to practical action 'afforded' us by our surroundings. And this means in general, in the context of practical, postmodern, daily social life, that all our traditional topics of research in psychology must be seen in a new light:

First, *thinking* becomes, not a matter of computational processes, but *argumentative*: the image of thinking provided by information-processing and rule-following models 'curiously demeans the nature of thought itself, for it describes processes which are principally thoughtless. Rules do not exist only to be followed: they also have to be created, interpreted and challenged' (Billig, 1986: 11; 1987). The whole new *rhetoric of inquiry* movement is explicitly a postmodernist enterprise (McCloskey, 1983; Nelson and Megill, 1986).

Secondly, talk of *motives* becomes talk of reasons for action, that is, justifications offered to others (and perhaps to oneself) in rendering one's actions reasonable or appropriate in their context of occurrence (Mills, 1940; Peters, 1958) – while the study of practical action in a context becomes a *prospective* enterprise (see below).

Thirdly, studies of *emotion* too become more concerned with 'movements' in one's position in relation to those around one; they can be viewed as 'transitory social roles' (Averill, 1980), and accounted for in terms of one's (moral) relations to others (Harré, 1986).

Fourthly, studies of *memory* cease to be about the nature of 'storage' and 'retrieval' (of a present record of past events) and become (as Bartlett, 1932, originally formulated the problem) studies of collective remembering (Middleton and Edwards, 1990), or of socially constructed memories (Bransford et al., 1977; Meacham, 1977), and indeed, of socially constructed amnesias also (Jacoby, 1975). Remembering in a social group clearly raises matters of authority, and the right to formulate what is to count as the group's memory, as well as what should be taken as the relevant materials for the formulation.

Fifthly, *learning* ceases to be the sole process for the gaining of knowledge; and knowledge ceases to be solely an epistemological matter; it becomes an ontological one also. For only those who are already constituted as *socially* competent within a particular setting can go out and gather 'information' about the nature of that setting in a wholly individualistic way; but they cannot gain their social competence in that setting in the same way. That involves a different kind of 'learning' altogether; it involves 'instruction' by another person, an interactive process – indeed, it involves acquiring the knowledge of how to collaborate effectively in institutions of learning (Shotter, 1984; Vygotsky, 1962).

Sixthly, being instructed in how 'to be' in different particular settings is to be instructed in the accepted ways (procedures) of making sense of the 'affordances' (to use a Gibsonian term) available to one in that setting. *Perception* thus takes on a noncognitive, ontological aspect; and studies of perception become concerned with (a) what there is available to be perceived in one's surroundings; (b) the strategies or procedures required to 'pick up' the information available; and (c) the nature of the social conditions required for their development – much of this work is now being pursued by those taking an 'ecological' approach to perception (Gibson, 1979).

Finally, *language* is no longer seen as serving solely a representative function, but as also being *formative*, that is, rather than being of use merely to refer to circumstances within a situation, it functions to formulate the situations in which we are involved *as* situations *as* states of affairs, to formulate them as common 'places' in terms of which we can relate ourselves to one another, to 'lend' them a form which they 'afford' or 'permit' but which they would not, in themselves, otherwise have (Harris, 1981; Mills, 1940; Wittgenstein, 1953).

These reorientations in attitude toward the major topics of psychological investigation outlined above are merely general. Rather than settling their nature, they all become in Gallie's (1955–6) terms 'essentially contested' concepts, that is, concepts 'the proper use of which involves endless disputes about their proper usage on the part of their users' (p. 169). But what is clear is that their effective investigation will not be a matter of 'proving a theory true', but a matter of exploring the scope and limits of a *practical procedure* informed by an image or paradigm (the intersubjective 'feelings' against which the adequacy of a theory's formulation is judged) shared among the members of a research community (McGuire, 1973; Smedslund, 1980). The empirical content of a science can then be judged, not in terms of its possession of true theories, but in terms of the number of interpretive standpoints which have won a place within it (Toulmin, 1982), that is, the degree of systematic (or disciplined) pluralism it affords.

In such circumstances, the 'essentially contested' nature of concepts becomes the norm. This does not mean that such concepts are therefore unusable; it simply means that their usage becomes itself a research topic – the science must possess the resources to ironicize its own claims. It also means that the very hurly-burly of social life, as an ecology of interdependent, local, *heterogeneous* regions and moments of self-reproducing orderliness, suspended in a more chaotic (but 'nutrient' medium), requires study (Prigogine and Stengers, 1984). But, not now as if from a position on another planet, but from within the finitude of our own situation, from how we find ourselves historically placed – our current 'placement' being itself a contested topic of research.

Concluding comments

What is utterly strange to us at the moment – because, whenever we attempt to engage in rational discussion of its nature, we mystify ourselves by routinely adopting a decontextualized, theoretical stance – is our ordinary world of everyday social life. A postmodernist approach to its understanding requires us, first and foremost, to abandon the 'grand narrative' of a theoretical unity of knowledge, and to be content with more local and practical aims. This means abandoning one of the deepest assumptions (and hopes) of Enlightenment thought: that what is 'really' available for perception 'out there' is an orderly and systematic world, (potentially) the same for all of us – such that, if we really persist in our investigations and arguments, we will ultimately secure universal agreement about its nature. But we also should note that although no such unity as yet exists, and experts continue to argue as to what might lead to its discovery, everyday social life still continues in spite of its disorderliness. Our failure to understand how this is possible is an important failure; we continue to treat what is probably a unity of *heterogeneity* (that is, a system of differences) as if it is a unity of *homogeneity* (that is, a system of similarities).

In other words, our failure stems not just from the atomistic individualism implicit in modernism – which has it that people can be treated for the purposes of science as the indistinguishable atoms of physics – but also from us committing what Bhaskar (1989) calls 'the epistemic fallacy' – our reformulation of (ontological) questions of *being* in terms of our *knowledge* of being. Although I am not in agreement with Bhaskar about the precise character of the ontological dimension he proposes, in separating ontological from epistemological questions, I am in total agreement about the necessity for their separation. Indeed, my arguments above have mostly been 'conditions of possibility' arguments in the ontological sphere, that is, analyses of what something *must be like* for it to be able to produce what we already know of and take to be a real part of our existence. This also, I might add, is what gives a social constructionist approach a *critical* dimension; for the formulation of an ontological discourse separate from epistemological forms of talk provides us with a means for confronting claims to knowledge with the question, could it be otherwise? Thus, as Bhaskar (1989: 21–2) points out:

> It entails the acceptance of (i) the principle of *epistemic relativity*, which states that all beliefs are socially produced, so that all knowledge is transient, and neither truth-values nor criteria of rationality exist outside historical time. But it entails the rejection of (ii) the doctrine of *judgemental* [or moral: J.S.] *relativity*, which maintains that all beliefs are equally valid, in the sense that there can be no rational grounds for preferring one to another.

Indeed, as I see it, the parties to an argument *must* (rationally) accept the necessary existence of certain socio-psychological conditions, if argumentation is to be possible at all. Justifying one's claims to knowledge comes to an end, not by them being linked to supposed self-evident propositions, but by their 'placement' within a way of being and acting, a tradition or, in Wittgenstein's (1953) terms, particular *forms of life*. In other words, a complex relation between people's identities and their 'hook-up' to their surroundings is involved (Shotter, 1990), a relation which a postmodern psychology must explore.

Without exploring it any further here, we can still draw the following conclusions: that although the postmodern *self* may be something of a mosaic, no self is completely an island. In postmodern everyday life, as well as in postmodern science, one occupies a multiplicity of standpoints, each within at least a local community; and within such communities there are standards, ways of judging, to which one must conform if one is be accounted a member. This does not mean, however, that it is only the standards within one's own 'clan' which count. For along with one's own ways of judging, one can ask, could they be otherwise, and what other ways of judging might be possible? And it would be intellectually irresponsible (as well as being rude, unjust, illegal, libelous, partisan, discriminatory, etc.) to ignore those who judge their lives in other ways, and not to treat their claims seriously too. As Toulmin (1982) points out, from the postmodern standpoint questions of *justice* take an equal place in the forum of scientific judgment with those of *truth*. Indeed, we may find that on different occasions, for different purposes, we have *good reasons* for switching from one standpoint to another, for taking up a position within a different community of inquiry. But none (of our reasons) will have the absolute 'knockdown' certainty we crave, because there are no universally accepted systems of knowledge to which to appeal. So, although we can find reasons for preferring some ways of life to others, no single way of life is obviously best – and that is, perhaps, just as well!

References

Averill, J. (1980) A constructivist view of emotion. In R. Plutick and H. Kellerman (eds), *Theories of Emotion*. New York: Academic Press.

Barnes, B. (1982) *T.S. Kuhn and Social Science*. London: Macmillan.

Bartlett, Sir F.C. (1932) *Remembering: A Study in Experimental Psychology*. London: Cambridge University Press.

Bernstein, R.J. (1983) *Beyond Objectivism and Relativism*. Oxford: Blackwell.

Bhaskar, R. (1989) *Reclaiming Reality: A Critical Introduction to Modern Philosophy*. London: Verso.

Billig, M. (1986) *Thinking and Arguing: An Inaugural Lecture*. Loughborough: University of Loughborough.

Billig, M. (1987) *Arguing and Thinking: A Rhetorical Approach to Social Psychology*. London: Cambridge University Press.

Bohm, D. (1965) Appendix: physics and perception. In *The Special Theory of Relativity*. New York: Benjamin.

Bransford, J.D., Franks, J.J., McCarrell, N.S. and Nitsch, K.E. (1977) Toward unexplaining memory. In R. Shaw and J. Bransford (eds), *Perceiving, Acting, and Knowing: Toward an Ecological Psychology*. Hillsdale, NJ: Erlbaum.

Cassirer, E. (1951) *The Philosophy of the Enlightenment*. Princeton, NJ: Princeton University Press.

Derrida, J. (1976) *Of Grammatology*. Baltimore, MD: Johns Hopkins University Press.

Fleck, L. (1979) *The Genesis and Development of a Scientific Fact*. Chicago: University of Chicago Press.

Gallie, W.B. (1955–6) Essentially contested concepts. *Proceedings of the Aristotelian Society*, 56: 167–98.

Gergen, K.J. (1982) *Toward Transformation in Social Knowledge*. New York: Springer.

Gergen, K.J. (1985) The social constructionist movement in modern psychology. *American Psychologist*, 40: 266–75.

Gergen, K.J. and Morowski, J.G. (1980) An alternative metatheory for social psychology. In L. Wheeler (ed.), *Review of Personality and Social Psychology*. Beverly Hills, CA: Sage.

Gibson, J.J. (1979) *The Ecological Approach to Visual Perception*. London: Houghton Mifflin.

Goffman, E. (1972) *Relations in Public*. Harmondsworth: Penguin.

Harré, R. (1979) *Social Being: A Theory for Social Psychology*. Oxford: Blackwell.

Harré, R. (1983) *Personal Being: A Theory for Individual Psychology*. Oxford: Blackwell.

Harré, R. (1986) The social construction of selves. In K. Yardley and T. Honess (eds), *Self and Identity*. Chichester: Wiley.

Harris, R. (1981) *The Language Myth*. London: Duckworth.

Jacoby, R. (1975) *Social Amnesia: A Critique of Conformist Psychology from Adler to R.D. Laing*. Sussex: Harvestser.

Kuhn, T.S. (1962) *The Structure of Scientific Revolutions*. Chicago: University of Chicago Press.

Lyotard, J.-F. (1984) *The Postmodern Condition: A Report on Knowledge*. Manchester: Manchester University Press.

McCloskey, D.M. (1983) The rhetoric of economics. *Journal of Economic Literature*, 21: 481–516.

McGuire, W.J. (1973) The yin and yang of progress in social psychology. *Journal of Personal and Social Psychology*, 26: 446–56.

Meacham, J.A. (1977) A transactional model of remembering. In N. Datan and H.W. Reese (eds), *Lifespan Developmental Psychology: Perspectives on Experimental Research*. New York: Academic Press.

Merleau-Ponty, M. (1962) *Phenomenology of Perception*. London: Routledge & Kegan Paul.

Middleton, D. and Edwards, D. (1990) *Collective Remembering*. London: Sage.

Mills, C.W. (1940) Situated actions and vocabularies of motive. *American Sociological Review*, 5: 904–13.

Nelson, J.S. and Megill, A. (1986) Rhetoric of inquiry: projects and problems. *Quarterly Journal of Speech*, 72: 20–37.

Ossorio, P.G. (1981) Ex post facto: the source of intractable origin problems and their resolution. Boulder, CO: Linguistic Research Institute report No. 28.

Peters, R.S. (1958) *The Concept of Motivation*. London: Routledge & Kegan Paul.

Pollner, M. (1974) Mundane reasoning. *Philosophy of Social Science*, 4: 35–54.

Pollner, M. (1975) 'The very coinage of your brain': the anatomy of reality junctures. *Philosophy of Social Science*, 5: 411–30.

Prigogine, I. and Stengers, I. (1984) *Order Out of Chaos: Man's New Dialogue with Nature*. New York: Bantam.

Rorty, R. (1980) *Philosophy and the Mirror of Nature*. Oxford: Blackwell.

Searle, J. (1983) *Intentionality: An Essay in the Philosophy of Mind*. Cambridge: Cambridge University Press.

Shotter, J. (1984) *Social Accountability and Selfhood*. Oxford: Blackwell.

Shotter, J. (1989) Vygotsky's psychology: joint activity in a developmental zone. *New Ideas in Psychology*, 7: 185–204.

Shotter, J. (1990) Wittgenstein and psychology: on our 'hook up' to reality. In A. Phillips-Griffiths (ed.), *The Wittgenstein Centenary Lectures*. Cambridge: Cambridge University Press.

Smedslund, J. (1980) Analysing the primary code. In D. Olson (ed.), *The Social Foundations of Language: Essays in Honor of J.S. Bruner*. New York: Norton.

Stolzenberg, G. (1978) Can an inquiry into the foundations of mathematics tell us anything interesting about mind? In G.A. Miller and E. Lenneberg (eds), *Psychology and Biology of Language and Thought: Essays in Honor of Eric Lenneberg*. New York: Academic Press.

Toulmin, S. (1979) The inwardness of mental life. *Critical Inquiry*, 6: 1–16.

Toulmin, S. (1982) The construal of reality: criticism in modern and postmodern science. *Critical Inquiry*, 9: 93–111.

Vygotsky, L.S. (1962) *Thought and Language*, ed. and trans. E. Hanfmann and G. Vakar. Cambridge, MA: MIT Press.

Winch, P. (1958) *The Idea of a Social Science and its Relations to Philosophy*. London: Routledge and Kegan Paul.

Wittgenstein, L. (1953) *Philosophical Investigations*. Oxford: Blackwell.

4

Postmodern Subjects: Towards a Transgressive Social Psychology

Mike Michael

The fraught problematic of the 'postmodern' seems to have finally reached that sometimes shallow social science backwater, social psychology. Whether the impact of the postmodern takes the form of ripples or whirlpools, this arrival marks a range of potential trajectories for the future of social psychology. Ken Gergen (this volume) has outlined one such possibility. The present chapter sketches another. Elsewhere, I have examined the conceptual axes that, in spite of appearances, seem to be shared by postmodern (social constructionist) and modernist (cognitive) paradigms in social psychology (Michael, 1991). However, in the present chapter, I will argue that once we take up a postmodern 'posture', whether that be as a reader of texts or as a social psychological practitioner, then we have available to us multiple readings/interpretations, including modified modernist ones. I illustrate this in relation to the type of subject position projected by ostensibly postmodern texts. If, from within the postmodern, it becomes possible to transgress the postmodernist/modernist dichotomy, then it also becomes feasible to transcend the prioritization of the social. Drawing upon actor-network theory, I will suggest that rather than confining itself to the study of the 'social construction' of identity, a transgressive post-modern social psychology will also need to engage with the role of both the 'real' and the 'natural'.

Postmodern social psychologies

Gergen (this volume) has outlined the parameters of a postmodern (social) psychology. If modernist psychology adheres to a commit-ment to a knowable world of mind or behaviour, the investigation of universal properties, the empirical method and a notion of research as progressive and knowledge as cumulative, with the postmodern turn, we find the focus upon linguistic resources and conventions, context, method as rhetoric and value-laden change. The immediate pay-offs for social psychology include according to Gergen a 'professional investment in which the scholar attempts to de-objectify the existing realities, to demonstrate their social and historical embeddedness and to explore their implications for social life' (p. 27). As a corollary, 'the psychologist is invited to conjoin the personal, the professional and the political' (p. 27). Examples of this are found in feminist psychology, social constructionist psychology, discourse analysis and rhetoric studies, and social representations.

Within its own social constructionist terms of reference, we can interpret Gergen's programmatic outline as the forging of an, albeit decentred, identity for the discipline. However, this stands in partial contrast to other treatments of the postmodern, especially in sociology. There we find, in addition to a concern with epistemology and methodology, a parallel effort to map out the *reality* of the postmodern in relation to a range of social and theoretical issues. (This same contrast is articulated by Featherstone, 1991, in terms of a postmodern sociology versus a sociology of postmodernism.) Thus, we have a series of volumes and collections that have considered in detail, for example, the relations between modernity and postmodernity, transitions in patterns of consumption and production and the phenomenological facets of the postmodern epoch such as the experience of time and space (for instance, Featherstone, 1991; Harvey, 1989; Lash and Urry, 1987; B. Turner, 1990). In all this, there is increasing attention given to the empirical basis of this change – witness Featherstone's (1991) complaint that theorizations of the postmodern experience characteristically focus upon postmodern texts and artefacts, while their 'reception' by putative postmoderns has been neglected (even if it has proved analytically amenable).

Indeed, if social psychologists were to seek out more energetically concrete instances of the postmodern, then I can see no reason why an altogether different 'postmodern social psychology' should not emerge. Thus, if Gergen's projected enterprise focuses upon epistemology and methodology, we can envisage another postmodern social psychology, or rather, a social psychology of postmodernism, which focuses upon subject matter. For example, the traditional experimental methods of intergroup and social identity theory, attribution theory, social cognition, and the like, can be used to examine the social identity formation, classification, lay epistemics and attribution of causality that reflect and mediate the supposed postmodern social individual. For example, one might ask, what actor/observer attributional patterns might we find when postmodern subjects are decentred? Would we expect postmoderns to be more readily capable of taking up the perspective of the 'other' in the actor/observer paradigm? How would the fragmented individual – say, a member of the new class factions (Lash and Urry, 1987), part of whose identity is tied up with the systematic denial of group membership, self-categorize? What minimal intergroup experimental results would we find for a sample of postmoderns whose main self-category is that they belong to no category or that they are constantly shifting/transgressing categories?

As we have seen above, one of the defining parameters of the postmodern turn in social psychology is the import assigned to language as the medium by which typically 'social psychological' phenomena are realized (for instance, Parker, 1989; Parker and Shotter, 1989; Potter and Wetherell, 1987; Shotter and Gergen, 1989). This has been aligned with the overt political purpose of changing prevailing conceptions of the human being and the social world. The constructive potency of language and this explicit generative intent (Gergen, 1982) suggest an important tension within postmodern social psychology. Now, postmodern social psychology, as with all 'sciences', produces texts (for instance, Latour and Woolgar, 1979) which have particular performative impact and constructive ramifications. More specifically, such texts can be said to project particular subject positions (for instance, Fairclough, 1989; Henriques et al., 1984) for the reader. If this is the case, what exactly is the subject position so projected, and how appropriate is it to the social, cultural and political aspirations of postmodern social psychology?

It is the stated aim of some theorists in social psychology to promote some alternative 'self' to the prevailing Western, modernist, self-contained individualized identity (for instance, Sampson, 1988; Shotter and Gergen, 1989). If the exact social route by which this strategic intervention by social psychologists might remain somewhat obscure, there nevertheless remains the use of the texts of postmodern social psychology. Despite their select audience, these writings can attempt to project a subject position that lies at some remove from the 'centrality and sovereignty of the individual' (Shotter and Gergen, 1989: ix).

One candidate for this contra-individualist alternative self can be derived from the analyses of several writers who, though they span a variety of disciplines and epochs, share a perception of the 'self' as altogether more dispersed and decentred. The following list of dichotomies reflects not only the range of terms and metaphors deployed to 'capture' or, more properly, construct this dichotomy; it also suggests a narrative resource by which a postmodern alternative might be realized. As such, the array of oppositions can be seen as both descriptive, in that it maps out individualist/anti-individualist dichotomies, and prescriptive, in that it begins to promote the move from the modernist to the postmodernist self. The terms on the left are individualist and modernist; the terms on the right are anti-individualist and postmodern: Apollonian/Dionysian (Benedict, 1935; Nietzsche, 1956); Discursive/Figural (Lash, 1988; Lyotard, 1971); Contemplative/Ecstatic (Baudrillard, 1983; Lash and Urry, 1987); Terminus/Communitas (Liminality) (Martin, 1981; Turner, 1969); molar (sedentary, root-ish)/molecular (nomadic, rhizomic) (Deleuze and Guattari, 1984, 1987).

Though it is no doubt intellectually suspect to gather all these writers together within the space of half a paragraph, such close proximity none the less facilitates the derivation, with all due caution, of an aggregated contrast. The 'modernist' individual is 'self–controlled', unitary, discrete, orderly, oriented towards thought, language and representation. The postmodern is 'uncontrolled' decentred, multiplicitous, transgressive, oriented towards affect, image and simulation.[1]

In light of the political intent of postmodern social psychological texts, the question that arises is, to what extent do these writings not so much clarify the divide as actively project a postmodern subject position?

Projecting a postmodern subject position

Examples of writing strategies that project a postmodern subject position can be found in, for example, the Sociology of Scientific Knowledge (SSK). Woolgar (1988a) has directly problematized the 'ethos' of representation that infuses SSK. In his view, SSK needs to reflect upon its own status as a research programme that represents and socially constructs the processes of representation and the social construction of scientific facts and artefacts. To this end, effort is directed at developing modes of writing that can reflect upon themselves and that admit of their own status as representations by effectively deconstructing the textual means by which representation is achieved. The consequent relativism is not seen as a reason for lamentation, but as the cause of celebration – SSK texts should playfully explore their own constructed constitution. Examples of this reflexive strategy have included the development of various novel textual forms such as multiple voices intervening in the text, plays, strange loops and encyclopaedias (Ashmore, 1989; Mulkay, 1985; Woolgar, 1988a, 1988b; however, also see Doran, 1989; Fuhrman and Oehler, 1986).

Such SSK reflexivity might offend the political sensibility that can attach to postmodern social psychology in so far as the explicit programme of postmodern betterment is side-stepped. To the extent that reflexivity is privileged, then it seems to be a perfectly legitimate strategy to eschew ethics and take on the role of epistemological border guards endlessly patrolling the rhetorical and constructed parameters of knowledge and knowledge about knowledge. However, such reflexive texts can be viewed as evoking a postmodern subject position by virtue of their problematizations of representation and the unitary author, and by their deployment of a multiplicity of voices, their vertiginous, transgressive and playful use of parody and irony which undermine any simple or single reading. In the present context, it is interesting to compare the chapters by K. Gergen and M. Gergen in the present volume. In the former, the modernist subject position is retained; the chapter is eminently rationalist in its form. In contrast, M. Gergen's chapter deploys just the sort of techniques which 'disorient' the modernist reader, indeed, which project a postmodern subject position (while simultaneously raising major reservations about the political efficacy of the postmodern turn, especially for women).

However, the above comparison is too facile; the projected postmodern audience of M. Gergen's text does not preclude a modernist reading. Indeed, if the postmodern penchant for irony and parody is being 'inculcated' in some way, then an ironic reading can be made of a postmodern text which renders it modernist. Thus, the 'real meaning' behind the overt textual and formal pyrotechnics is that parody, irony and transgression are 'good' things, or that 'anti-representation' can be profoundly addressed, not to say represented (Latour, 1988b). The point of this is that within the postmodern, modernist positions are perfectly feasible. It is a question of what is prioritized among the array of characteristics that delimits the postmodern. If the emphasis falls primarily upon the linguistic turn, then the suggested interpenetration of the modern and the postmodern is highly problematic; the modern is bracketed by virtue of its neglect of the linguistic turn and its abiding foundationalism. If, however, transgression (irony, parody, heterogeneity, etc.) is highlighted, the interweaving of postmodern and modern seems a legitimate and perhaps inevitable development. In the following sections, I will explore the implications of this latter 'dialectic' for the (social) construction of identity.

Transgressing the postmodern

To continue to engage critically with the postmodern project as articulated above, what is needed is a transgression of disciplinary boundaries that is generalized beyond the humanities, arts and social sciences; there should be a venturing into the natural sciences. In other words, the 'natural' needs to be integrated into the postmodern project.

Certainly this re-evaluation of the status of the natural has become increasingly evident in the social sciences. Thus, we witness attempts to problematize the division between human and social sciences. For example, Horigan (1988) has shown how the 'natural' was variously differentiated from the 'social' in an attempt by social anthropologists to separate anthropology from its parent disciplines of biology and natural philosophy. The long-term result, according to Horigan, is that there has been a privileging of social factors to the extent that the influence of natural factors upon human social behaviour and structures, by and large, has been bracketed (also cf. Ingold, 1989). Even more recently, Benton (1991) has attempted to identify some of the pressures placed upon the social/biological divide and the dichotomies that characterize it (mind/body, culture/nature, society/ biology, meaning/cause, human/animal) by contemporary social movements such as feminism and environmentalism.

What this suggests, in the present context, is an increasing consideration of the role social and biological sciences might play in the sort of generative and political intent that Gergen associates with postmodern social psychology. One concrete example of such transgressive strategy can be found in the works of Bruno Latour, Michel Callon and their associates on actor- (or actant-) network theory in SSK (for instance, Callon, 1986a, 1986b, 1987; Callon and Latour, 1981; Latour, 1986, 1987, 1988a, 1988b; Law, 1987).

In their approach, scientists are treated not simply as scientists *per se* but as multi-faceted entrepreneurs who, with due discrimination, engage in political, sociological and and economic activities as well as those practices traditionally assigned the label 'scientific'. Thus they are viewed as harnessing a multiplicity of materials and techniques to extend their influence beyond the laboratory; science is politics conducted by other means.

However, Callon and Latour are also intent on granting sociological or, perhaps more accurately, narrative rights to objects (going onto the side of the known, as Latour, 1988b, puts it). In the following, I cannot hope to do full justice to actor-network theory; therefore I will simply outline how Callon and Latour go about investing 'the known' with its own imperative.

The actor-network perspective rests on three tenets: generalized agnosticism – analytic impartiality as to whatever actors are involved in controversy; generalized symmetry – the use of a vocabulary to understand and explain the conflicting viewpoints of actors; free association – the repudiation of a priori distinctions between the social and the natural.[2] Within this meta-theoretical framework, scientists are regarded as ceaselessly concerned with enlarging, beyond the confines of the laboratory, their spheres of influence, or rather their networks. To do this they must *enrol* others. Actor-network theory has evolved a variety of terms with which to conceptualize this process. At the most general and inaugural level is *intéressement* – 'actions by which an entity attempts to impose and stabilize the identity of other actors it defines through its problematization' (Callon, 1986a: 207–8). This broad term encompasses a variety of strategies and mechanisms by which one entity – whether that be an individual like Pasteur, a small group like the three marine biologists of St Brieuc Bay, or an institution like Electricité de France – attempts to 'corner' and enrol other entities such as scientists, publics, institutions, scallops, electrons. This is achieved by interposing oneself between the target entity and its pre-existing associations with other entities that contribute to the formulation of its identity. Only with the successful disconnection from these other associations can enrolment be said to have, albeit temporarily, succeeded.

However, enrolment is not a unilateral process of imposition; it entails both the 'capturing' of the other and the other's 'yielding'. It is a multilateral process. For Latour, power is not a possession, but an arrangement of assent: 'Power is always the illusion people get when they are obeyed . . .[they] discover what their power is really made of when they start to lose it . . . it was "made of" the wills of all the others . . . power [is] a consequence and not a cause of collective action' (Latour, 1986: 173). Enrolment has been fleshed out through a consideration of a variety of other concepts which examine how it is that some entities are in the thrall of others. Translation is the means by which one entity gives a role to others, from the macro-sociological to the subatomic. In the process, the translator sets itself up as their spokesperson. If these identities are to take hold, then also necessary is the invention of a geography of 'obligatory points of passage'; for those elements and entities that wish to continue to exist and develop and which the enrolling entity wishes to enrol, such points then constitute unavoidable conduits through which they must pass in order to articulate their identity and realize their *raison d'être*. Another mode of translation is displacement; this refers to the ways in which entities organize and structure, and the movement of materials, resources and information. By the organization of meetings, the making and maintaining of contacts, the carrying out of experiments, entities can accumulate just those materials that render their actor-network (or more accurately actor-world) more durable.

And yet the whole network is inherently unstable. In Callon's (1986b) terms the actor-world can convert or revert to an actor-network. That is to say, particular, seemingly unitary entities can suddenly become problematized (un-black-boxed). The roles and identities assigned by one entity to another may suddenly be challenged, undermined or shattered. Where once the 'enrolling' actor organized the obligatory points of passage for others, it finds itself forced, in order to survive, to traverse the obligatory points of passages that are 'dictated' by others. And it is not only social others who intervene; the heterogeneity of the networks means that any entity can begin to step out of semiotic character within the network – including electrons, microbes, scallops, the Atlantic.

This thumb-nail sketch of actor-network theory has aimed to outline how it might be that nature (the 'known') can be integrated into the analytic narrative of an SSK text. The deprivileging of the social is thus used to show how the unity and identity of actors and entities within the network are affected by the 'natural' – by the *resistance* that the 'natural' puts up to the efforts of human and institutional actors to enrol it into their particular networks (Latour, 1988b). This differs from the textual perspective on identity (for instance, Gergen and Davis, 1985; Harré, 1987; Shotter and Gergen, 1989) in so far as, in addition to the social and textual contingency of identity, actor-network theory places the use of those texts in the context of the intractability of nature. Nature is thus seen as having its own autonomous 'plans' which, though obscure, nevertheless shape the practices, discourses and identities of human actors. In what follows I will elaborate on this point and examine the way that 'nature' might serve as a resource not only in the construction of identity *per se*, but also in the construction of the 'postmodern self'.

Resources of the self in 'nature'

The questions that we are faced with can be phrased in the following way: how might nature intervene in the construction of identity in general and of the postmodern identity in particular? How might this new form of personhood (decentred, ensembled, molecular, etc.) be generated in relation to the natural world? While the transgression of the social science/natural science border can contribute to the answers to these questions, in the present instance I will focus upon the way that the 'natural' serves to enrol human actors, and how its resistance – a resistance that is always already historically contingent – begins to shape the construction of a distinctively postmodern identity.

In regard to the role of the 'natural' in the constitution of non-postmodern identity, we can draw upon Callon's classic study of the scallops, researchers and fishing community of St Brieuc Bay (1986a). This we can reinterpret in terms of the production of identity that was partially shaped by the intransigence of both social and natural entities. In the early 1970s, three scientists attempted to develop techniques for cultivating the scallop, *Pecten maximus*, in order to restock St Brieuc Bay. In the process, they constructed an actor-network in which they narrated the roles of the component actants. Thus, the local fishermen were represented as fundamentally interested in the restocking; the scallops were represented through the various techniques of science as potentially cultivatable; and the relevant scientific community was represented as an assenting constituency. The influence of the three researchers derived from the fact that they headed these three heterogeneous populations. In effect, their constructed identity was constituted across these three domains each of which apparently supported their self-narration as experts, representatives, scientists, advisers, and so on. However, this complex of identity could only survive as long as each of the actors in the researcher's network played their allotted part. When the fishermen betrayed the scientists by, contrary to their supposed long-term aims, fishing to the point of decimating the scallop beds, then it was no longer feasible for the three scientists to claim to represent the interests of the fishermen. Likewise, when the scallop larvae levels became hopelessly low, the stories the researchers could tell about themselves as scientists and cultivators became subverted. In sum, their identity, dispersed and decentred across the network as it was, became suspect – their texts of identity were effectively exploded.

Turning to the possible impact of the 'natural' in the construction of a postmodern identity which is arguably 'better' than its modernist counterparts, we can explore one recent trend in the burgeoning field of environmental ethics.[3] Much of the intellectual effort expended in environmental ethics seeks to find a philosophical (for instance, Heideggerian, aesthetic, phenomenological) or theological (for instance, Christian, American Indian) basis for 'ecological con-sciousness' (cf. Rodman, 1983).[4] In this, Jim Cheney's (1989) work stands out as particularly pertinent. Cheney attempts to theorize how what he perceives to be the urgent need for an environmental ethics and an ecological consciousness might embody the postmodern decentred self. This project becomes workable when we take 'ecological consciousness' to be the loss, expansion or diffusion of self in(to) nature: an immersion of the I in nature in which the I is 'transcended' in some way. Here, the 'centrality and sovereignty of the individual' is clearly dispensed with. Rather, what takes ethical priority is a self–other, human–nature, I–thou confluence (Evernden, 1985; Harrison, 1986; Mabey, 1981, 1984).

Cheney's attempt to articulate such a consciousness in relation to the postmodern individual rests upon a notion of the 'bioregional narrative'. If Cheney is fundamentally concerned with the postmodern project of avoiding the essentialization of the self, his 'solution' is to ground these bioregional narratives in geography. 'Narrative is the key then, but it is narrative grounded in geography rather than in a linear, essentialized narrative self. . . . .Totalizing masculine discourse (and essentializing feminist discourse) give way to a contextualized discourse of place' (1989: 126). Thus 'Within the geography of the human landscape the contextual voice can emerge in clarity and health only through a "constant recontextualizing" which prevents the oppressive and distorting overlays of cultural institutions . . . from gathering false, distorting and unhealthy identities of "the positive desire for unity, for Oneness"' (p. 128).

Clearly Cheney is fully aware of the danger of a recourse to an essentializing discourse. His partial answer is to

> expand the notion of a contextualizing narrative of place so as to include nature – nature as one more player in the construction of community . . .[he proposes] that we extend these notions of context and narrative outwards so as to include not just the human community, but also the land, one's community in a larger sense. (1989: 128)

The medium through which this could be achieved is, according to Cheney, myth. If 'bioregionalism can "ground" the construction of self and community' (1989: 134), it will proceed through the narratives and metaphors of mythology which are derived from the landscapes and the localities themselves. This begs a lot of questions as to how such a process of derivation might come about; however, this does not mean that practical measures are impossible. Common Ground (a British organization engaged in fostering the new environmental sensibility), for example, have been experimenting with various techniques which might root ecological consciousness in people's locality and commonplace. Thus, in their Parish Maps project, groups and individuals were encouraged to explore their relation to their local environment in all its biological, social and historical complexity through the making of maps.[5]

In sum, in terms of actor-network theory, nature, *qua* bioregional locality, is an actant – but it is an actant that is not given the coherence of a unitary entity. Rather, its very diversity and richness serve to disaggregate the texts of identity of its human inhabitants. Again, in terms of actor-network theory, we might say that it has enrolled human actors, who begin to formulate, that is to say, narrate themselves in like fashion – they are dispersed and decentred – in short, they are postmoderns. The obligatory point of passage is one in which the core texts of identity are those of fracture, of the forgoing of 'coherence, continuity and consistency' (Cheney, 1989: 126). In the process, the power of nature does indeed take the form of an association in which the human actants give up their stories of unitary self if they wish to 'carry on'. For Cheney, this 'carrying on' is crucially attached to ecological survival. Moreover, it is, as Cheney notes, a human achievement.

To reiterate, many issues remain to be considered in relation to this interweaving of the natural and the social, the postmodern and the ethical. For example, there are grave dangers to any simplistic adoption of this localized, bioregional ethics. Harvey (1989; also cf. Bourdieu, 1991) has pointed out in relation to Heidegger that any such concoction of ethics, nature and identity can lead to an espousal of the sort of 'blood-and-soil' morality that characterized Nazism. Indeed as Anna Bramwell (1989) has documented, albeit contentiously, the Nazis were in some ways good ecologists; perhaps the most discomfiting example that she provides is that of Himmler's establishment of SS organic farms at Dachau.

Nevertheless, in Cheney's environmental ethics (and also in Common Ground's practice) we see the potential for the development of a non-essentialized view of both the 'natural' and the 'social', with the concomitant postmodern problematization of the 'centrality and sovereignty of the individual'. It is not altogether inconceivable that this signals the glimmer of a postmodern *rapprochement* between the social and natural that takes into full account the contingent and constructed character of both while giving due narrative and ethical weight to each.

Concluding remarks

To construct postmodern social psychology by contrasting it against modernist social psychology is effectively to position the former as part of a definitive epistemological and political break. What I have tried to suggest in this chapter is that postmodern social psychology, by virtue of its transgressive potential, has a number of intellectual and practical options available to it, some of which can incorporate a modulated version of modernism in a sort of *Aufhebung*. Along these lines, I have attempted to set out and illustrate the case that the critical political dynamic of which postmodern social psychology is a part can be thought in terms of a complex, transgressive interweaving of the social and the natural (and of the social and natural sciences). In addition, formulations of identity in general and postmodern identity in particular can move beyond social constructionism to encompass the 'natural' as well as the conventional and the discursive.

If the present brief and tentative consideration of identity has deprioritized the social and the linguistic, it is nevertheless hoped that a return to the stale nature/nurture dichotomies of the recent past is avoided. Rather, identity should be seen as the product of a heterogeneous network of actors, both 'social' and 'natural', which reflects the postmodern turn turned upon itself.

Notes

The author would like to thank Gavin Kendall, Susan Condor and Vicky Singleton for their helpful comments on previous drafts of this chapter.

1 This version of the 'postmodern' is treated here as a potential improvement upon the the 'modern'. Clearly this is contentious, and numerous authors have bemoaned the rise of the postmodern not so much as a mode of resistance to hegemonic discourses and practices, but as another twist in the logic of capitalism (see, for example, Featherstone, 1991; Jameson, 1984; Lash and Urry, 1987).

2 As the principles of actor-network theory find partial expression in a vocabulary that transcends social/natural dichotomies, the terms 'actor', 'actant' and 'entity' will be used interchangeably. Unfortunately, as a result, the outline presented here is somewhat abstract, though the case studies presented by Callon, Latour and Law are satisfyingly concrete.

3 Of course, environments which destabilize identity by virtue of their significatory over-abundance need not be 'natural'. Urban spaces are no less able to furnish just this surfeit of signifiers. Indeed, in certain accounts, the city is assigned pride of place as the site of significatory transgression and vertiginous turnover (see Berman, 1982; Featherstone, 1991; Harvey, 1989).

4 See especially the journal *Environmental Ethics* for a selection of these and other 'syntheses'.

5 Some of the activities and programmes of Common Ground are set out in their pamphlet *An Introduction to the Deeds and Thoughts of Common Ground* (1990).

References

Ashmore, M. (1989) *The Reflexive Thesis: Wrighting Sociology of Scientific Knowledge*. Chicago: University of Chicago Press.

Baudrillard, J. (1983) The ecstasy of communication. In H. Foster (ed.), *The Anti-Aesthetic: Essays in Postmodern Culture*. Port Townsend, WA: Bay Press. pp. 126–34.

Benedict, R. (1935) *Patterns of Culture*. London: Routledge.

Benton, T. (1991) Biology and social science: why the return of the repressed should be given a (cautious) welcome. *Sociology*, 25: 1–29.

Berman, M. (1982) *All that Is Solid Melts into Air*. London: Verso.

Bourdieu, P. (1984) *Distinction: A Social Critique of the Judgement of Taste*. London: Routledge & Kegan Paul.

Bourdieu, P. (1991) *The Political Ontology of Martin Heidegger*. Cambridge: Polity Press.

Bramwell, A. (1989) *Ecology in the 20th Century: A History*. New Haven, CT: Yale University Press.

Callon, M. (1986a) Some elements in a sociology of translation: domestication of the scallops and fisherman of St Brieuc Bay. In J. Law (ed.), *Power, Action and Belief*. London: Routledge & Kegan Paul. pp. 196–233.

Callon, M. (1986b) The sociology of an actor-network: the case of the electric vehicle. In M. Callon, J. Law and A. Rip (eds), *Mapping the Dynamics of Science and Technology*. London: Macmillan. pp. 19–34.

Callon, M. (1987) Society in the making: the study of technology as a tool for sociological analysis. In W.E. Bijker, T.P. Hughes and T. Pinch (eds), *The Social Construction of Technological Systems*. Cambridge, MA: MIT Press. pp. 83–103.

Callon, M. and Latour, B. (1981) Unscrewing the big Leviathan. In K.D. Knorr-Cetina and M. Mulkay (eds), *Advances in Social Theory and Methodology*. London: Routledge & Kegan Paul. pp. 277–303.

Cheney, J. (1989) Postmodern environmental ethics: ethics as bioregional narrative. *Environmental Ethics*, 11: 117–34.

Common Ground (1990) *An Introduction to the Deeds and Thoughts of Common Ground*. London: Common Ground.

Deleuze G. and Guattari, F. (1984) *Anti-Oedipus: Capitalism and Schizophrenia*. London: Athlone Press.

Deleuze, G. and Guattari, F. (1987) *A Thousand Plateaus: Capitalism and Schizophrenia*. London: Athlone Press.

Doran, C. (1989) Jumping frames: reflexivity and recursion in the sociology of science. *Social Studies of Science*, 19: 515–31.

Evernden, N. (1985) *The Natural Alien: Humankind and Environment*. Toronto: Toronto University Press.

Fairclough, N. (1989) *Language and Power*. London: Longman.

Featherstone, M. (1991) *Consumer Culture and Postmodernism*. London: Sage.

Fuhrman, E.R. and Oehler, K. (1986) Discourse analysis and reflexivity. *Social Studies of Science*, 16: 293–307.

Gergen, K.J. (1982) *Toward Transformation in Social Knowledge*. New York: Springer Verlag.

Gergen, K.J. and Davis, K.E. (eds) (1985) *The Social Construction of the Person*. New York: Springer.

Harré, R. (1987) Social construction of selves. In K. Yardley and T. Honess (eds), *Self and Identity*. Chichester: Wiley. pp. 41–52.

Harrison, F. (1986) *The Living Landscape*. London: Pluto Press.

Harvey, D. (1989) *The Condition of Postmodernity*. Oxford: Blackwell.

Henriques, J., Hollway, W., Unwin, C., Venn, C. and Walkerdine, V. (1984) *Changing the Subject: Psychology, Social Regulation and Subjectivity*. London: Methuen.

Horigan, S. (1988) *Nature and Culture in Western Discourses*. London: Routledge & Kegan Paul.

Ingold, T. (ed.) (1989) *What Is an Animal?* London: Unwin Hyman.

Jameson, F. (1984) Postmodernism or the cultural logic of late capitalism. *New Left Review*, 146: 53–92.

Lash, S. (1988) Discourse or figure? Postmodernism as a 'regime of signification'. *Theory, Culture and Society*, 5: 311–36.

Lash, S. and Urry, J. (1987) *The End of Organized Capitalism*. Cambridge: Polity Press.

Latour, B. (1986) The powers of association. In J. Law (ed.), *Power, Action and Belief*. London: Routledge & Kegan Paul. pp. 264–80.

Latour, B. (1987) *Science in Action: How to Follow Engineers in Society*. Milton Keynes: Open University Press.

Latour, B. (1988a) *The Pasteurization of France*. Cambridge, MA: Harvard University Press.

Latour, B. (1988b) The politics of explanation – an alternative. In S. Woolgar (ed.), *Knowledge and Reflexivity: New Frontiers in the Sociology of Knowledge*. London: Sage. pp. 155–76.

Latour, B. and Woolgar, S. (1979) *Laboratory Life: The Construction of Scientific Facts*. London: Sage.

Law, J. (1987) Technology and heterogeneous engineering: the case of Portugese expansion. In W.E. Bijker, T.P. Hughes and T. Pinch (eds), *The Social Construction of Technological Systems*. Cambridge, MA: MIT Press. pp. 111–34.

Lyotard, J.-F. (1971) *Discours, Figure*. Paris: Klincksieck.

Mabey, R. (1981) *The Common Ground*. London: Arrow/Nature Conservancy Council.

Mabey, R. (ed.) (1984) *Second Nature*. London: Cape.

Martin, B. (1981) *A Sociology of Contemporary Cultural Change*. Oxford: Blackwell.

Michael, M. (1991) Some postmodern reflections on social psychology. *Theory and Psychology*, 1: 203–21.

Mulkay, M. (1985) *The Word and the World*. London: Allen & Unwin.

Nietzsche, F.W. (1956) *Birth of Tragedy, and the Genealogy of Morals*. New York: Doubleday.

Parker, I. (1989) *The Crisis in Modern Social Psychology – and How to End It*. London: Routledge & Kegan Paul.

Parker, I. and Shotter, J. (eds) (1989) *Deconstructing Social Psychology*. London: Methuen.

Potter, J. and Wetherell, M. (1987) *Discourse and Social Psychology: Beyond Attitudes and Behaviour*. London: Sage.

Rodman, J. (1983) Four forms of ecological consciousness reconsidered. In D. Scherer and T. Attig (eds), *Ethics and the Environment*. Englewood Cliffs, NJ: Prentice-Hall. pp. 82–92.

Sampson, E.E. (1988) Indigenous psychologies of the individual and their role in personal and social functioning. *American Psychologist*, 43: 15–22.

Shotter, J. and Gergen, K.J. (eds) (1989) *Texts of Identity*. London: Sage.

Turner, B. (ed.) (1990) *Theories of Modernity and Postmodernity*. London: Sage.

Turner, V.W. (1969) *The Ritual Process*. London: Routledge & Kegan Paul.

Woolgar, S. (1988a) *Science: The Very Idea*. Chichester: Ellis Horwood.

Woolgar, S. (ed.) (1988b) *Knowledge and Reflexivity: New Frontiers in the Sociology of Knowledge*. London: Sage.

5

Postmodernism and the Human Sciences

Patti Lather

[Is it possible for social science] to be different, that is, to forget itself and to become something else . . . [or must it] remain as a partner in domination and hegemony? (Said, 1989: 225)

These are the days of disenchantment, of questions that cut to the bone about what it means to do empirical work in the human sciences. The erosion of the assumptions that support social inquiry is part of the relentless undermining of the Enlightenment code of values which increasingly appears the key Western intellectual project of the late twentieth century. Those choosing to encourage rather than resist this movement are using it to stretch the boundaries that currently define what we do in the name of science. A behavioral science governed by adherence to methods and standards developed in the natural sciences is being displaced by what Harland (1987: 92) calls 'a science for philosophers'. A 'narrative, semiotic, particularist, self-aware' science is emerging from those who work 'to reorient and redirect theoretical, methodological and empirical aims and practices' across the human sciences (Van Maanen, 1988: 125). Turning away from the enormous pretensions of positivism, their project is the development of a human science much more varied and reflexive about its limitations.

Rooted in such work, this chapter interrogates the values underlying the cultural practices we construct in the name of the human sciences. I begin by playing with the question, what is science? Next, I construct three possible framings of research in the human sciences in terms of ideology and methodological attitude. I then look at two key issues in what it means to reinscribe science, to do science otherwise in a post-foundational context: the issue of relativism, and the continued lack of an adequate poststructuralist theory of the subject. Both are surveyed by probing the varied moves in feminist receptions of postmodernism.

What is science?

The sciences of man . . . which have so delighted our 'humanity' for over a century, have their technical matrix in the petty, malicious minutiae of the disciplines and their investigations. These investigations are perhaps to psychology, psychiatry, pedagogy, criminology, and so many other strange sciences, what the terrible power of investigation was to the calm knowledge of the animals, the plants or the earth. Another power, another knowledge. (Foucault, 1979: 226)

The world that made science, and that science made, has disappeared, and scientific thought is now an archaic mode of consciousness surviving for a while yet in degraded form. (Tyler, 1987: 200)

Ethnology almost met a paradoxical death that day in 1971 when the Philippine government decided to return to their primitive state the few dozen Tasaday discovered deep in the jungle, where they had lived for eight centuries undisturbed by the rest of mankind, out of reach of colonists, tourists, and ethnologists. This was at the initiative of the anthropologists themselves, who saw the natives decompose immediately on contact, like a mummy in the open air. For ethnology to live, its object must die. But the latter revenges itself by dying for having been 'discovered,' and defies by its death the science that wants to take hold of it. (Baudrillard, 1984: 257)

These passages from poststructuralist discourse evoke my puzzlement regarding how far to go with the anti-science position so evident in Foucault and Tyler's words. And what is one to make of Baudrillard, the 'wild man' of postmodernism whose 'hyperdeconstuctions' of the basic premises of Western thought map hysterical forms of 'panic' analysis as a strategy for unseating logocentrism? As Nelson et al. (1987) point out, one does not need to accept *all* of what the poststructuralists say in order to learn from them. My present position is neither an anti-science nor a post-science one. By deconstructing assumptions of a knowing subject, a known object and an unambiguous, complete knowledge outside of the unsaid and the unsayable, the embedded force-structures of understanding, I will present science as one among many truth games. Rather than Althusser's movement from ideology to science, my argument is part of Foucault's movement of a succession of different ideologies, some of which consider themselves 'scientific' (Harland, 1987: 102). In this movement, truth is viewed as at least as rhetorical as it is procedural (Nelson et al., 1987), and science is, according to my present favorite definition, 'a much contested cultural space, a site of the surfacing of what it has historically repressed' (Hutcheon, 1988: 74).

Legitimating itself in opposition to theology and aristocracy, science's claim to authority has been premised on its appeal to experience mediated by a purportedly value-neutral, logical-empirical method which promised the growth of rational control over ourselves and our worlds (Popkewitz, 1984). In this post-positivist era, it is easy to not see that what Comte termed 'positivism' was part of the liberatory impetus of the Enlightenment project. This was recently underscored for me by learning that it was the British feminist Harriet Martineau who, in 1853, translated Comte's first lectures on the possibilities of a positive social science capable of leading the way to social betterment (Riley, 1988: 49).

But the intentions of science to liberate reason from the dictates of kings and priests were inscribed into practices of control and prediction. These practices were rooted in a binary logic of hermetic subjects and objects and a linear, teleological rationality; the innocence of both observable facts and transparent language was assumed. Quantum physics has problematized such concepts in the natural sciences and it, along with the human sciences, is still reeling from the aftershocks. Binary either/or positions are being replaced by a both/and logic that deconstructs the ground of both reductionist objectivism and transcendental dialectics (Derrida, 1978). Linearity and teleology are being supplanted by chaos models of nonlinearity (Gleick, 1987) and an emphasis on historical contingency (Foucault, 1980). Power is assumed to permeate all aspects of our efforts to know (Habermas, 1971; Nicholson, 1990), and language is theorized as constitutive rather than representational, a matrix of enabling and constraining boundaries rather than a mirror (Rorty, 1979; Tyler, 1987).

Within this poststructural context, the value-neutral claim at the heart of positivist authority is untenable. Foregrounded as an ideological ruse, the claim to value neutrality is held to delimit our concept of science and obscure and occlude its own particularity and interest. Truth, objectivity and reason are reinscribed as what Foucault calls 'effects of power', and the subject–object opposition implodes. Transhistorical assertions of value are seen as based not on an innocent reason or logic but on an alliance with power. Objectivity 'creates its object to be objective about' (Harland, 1987: 104). Facts are not given but constructed by the questions we ask of events. All researchers construct their object of inquiry out of the materials their culture provides, and values play a central role in this linguistically, ideologically and historically embedded project that we call science.

Contesting the suppression of values in the production and legitimation of knowledge has been led by the 'ex-centrics' (Hutcheon, 1988) who, in turn, have had their way paved by the sociology of knowledge, broad intellectual traditions in social theory (for instance, Marx, Nietzsche, Freud) and attention to the actual practices of science itself. While the critique of scientism antedates Kuhn, he was the first to show historically how infused with the social and the arbitrary were the allegedly neutral and empirical observations of science. Such work has propelled the surge away from positivism and toward an interpretive, value-searching conception of the human sciences (Inglis, 1988). Neutrality, objectivity, observable facts, transparent description, clean separation of the interpreter and the interpreted – all of these concepts basic to positivist ways of knowing are called into question. Science as codified by conventional methods which marginalize value issues is being reformulated in a way that foregrounds science as a value-constituted and value-constituting enterprise.

The discourses of the human sciences

Frame 1: the discourse of paradigm shifts

> Scientists firmly believe that as long they are not *conscious* of any bias or political agenda, they are neutral and objective, when in fact they are only unconscious. (Namenwirth, 1986: 29)

Thomas Kuhn's *The Structure of Scientific Revolutions* (1962/1970) has been appropriated by post-positivist philosophers of science as a canonical text. The concept of paradigm shift has permeated discourse across the disciplines now for over two decades. With positivist hegemony broken, many see this as a time for exploring ways of knowing more appropriate for a complex world of interacting, reflexive subjects rather than for the mute objects upon which is turned the gaze of methods developed in the natural sciences (Bakhtin, 1981). Kuhn wrote: 'rather than a single group conversion, what occurs [with paradigm shift] is an increasing shift in the distribution of professional allegiances' as practitioners of the new paradigm 'improve it, explore its possibilities, and show what it would be like to belong to the community guided by it' (1970: 157–8).

Kuhn's model of scientific change is rooted in the history of the natural sciences. In his view, the social sciences are a pre-paradigmatic hodgepodge of techniques largely borrowed from the natural sciences, too unformed to support productive normal sciences (1970: 160). This aspect of Kuhn's thought has not been much noted, however, by those in the human sciences who have appropriated his language of successive paradigms, anomalies, revolutions and competing modes of scientific activity.

Within the Kuhnian argument, the central tension that causes a paradigm shift is internal to the discipline, technical breakdown brought on by the inability of the dominant paradigm to explain empirical anomalies: 'Change comes from within and is formed by the limitations of what is already known. It is a closed system, constrained by the limited knowledge of the trained practitioners who are admitted to the club' (Gonzalvez, 1986: 9). The interspersal of periods of normal and revolutionary science is assumed via an orderly succession of paradigmatic shifts.

Within such frameworks, method serves to provide some standards of logic and evidence and is seen as emergent but capable of increasing systematization (for instance, Bogdan and Biklen, 1982; Lincoln and Guba, 1985; Miles and Huberman, 1984). Methodological variety is presented as assumedly politically neutral choices, all of which seek to capture, via language, the closest possible representation of what is 'really going on'. Ideology is framed either as a depoliticized sort of worldview that shapes paradigmatic choice, or as bias to be controlled for in the name of objectivity. The descriptive adequacy of language as a transparent representation of the world is assumed.

By assuming the descriptive adequacy of language as a mirror of the world, such work remains positioned in a representational logic. Seeking to capture the object of our investigation as it 'really' is, independent of our representational apparatus, such logic denies the productivity of language in the construction of the objects of investigation. Additionally, by deemphasizing the political content of theories and methodologies, Kuhnian work sidesteps how politics pervades science. As Cherryholmes (1988: 183) points out: 'policing some methodological rules to the exclusion of other sets of rules is a political as well as scientific activity' (see also Eisner, 1988). 'Truth' is still procedural, methods still objectifying, values still to be controlled for and minimized in the effort toward precise, unbiased results.

In terms of the relationship between researcher and researched, what Dreyfus and Rabinow (1983) term 'The Great Interpreter who has privileged access to meaning' (p. 180) plays the role of adjudicator of what is 'really' going on, while insisting that the truths uncovered lie outside of the sphere of power. Willis (1980) terms this claim of privileged externality, this assumedly political neutral position, a 'covert positivism' (p. 90) in its tendencies toward objectification, unitary analysis and distanced relationships between subject and object. In Foucault's words, 'Knowable man [becomes] the object-effect of this analytic-investment, of this domination-observation' (quoted in Dreyfus and Rabinow, 1983: 160).

Kuhnian frameworks deemphasize the political content of theories and methodologies and deny the dissolving of the world as structured by referential notions of language. They also diminish the play of multiple emergent knowledges vying for legitimacy.[1] Caught up in a representational logic, they search for codifications and standards instead of asking if something more fundamental than a 'paradigm shift' in the academy might be going on.

Caputo's (1987) term 'post-paradigmatic diaspora' (p. 262) prob-
lematizes the concept of paradigm shift so central to contemporary
discourse in the human sciences. The central argument is that
'paradigm' may be a useful transitional concept to help us move
toward a more adequate human science, but that 'to still pose one
paradigm against the other is to miss the essential character of the
moment as an exhaustion with a paradigmatic style of discourse
altogether' (Marcus and Fischer, 1986: x). Atkinson et al. (1988: 233)
outline 'the dangers of paradigms', 'the dangers of Kuhnian rhetoric':
the presentation of ideas as novel and distinctive that are better
framed as historically rooted and relationally shaped by concepts that
precede and parallel as well as interrupt them. They also note the
'intolerance, fruitless polemic, and the hypercriticism' that accompany paradigmatic allegiances.

Caputo's 'post-paradigmatic diaspora' creates a liminal moment in
the human sciences that escapes, exceeds and complicates Kuhnian
structures. While we need conceptual frames for purposes of understanding, 'classifying research and researchers into neatly segregated
"paradigms" or "traditions" does not reflect the untidy realities of
real scholars . . . and may become an end in itself. . . . "Traditions"
must be treated not as clearly defined, real entities but only as loose
frameworks for dividing research' (Atkinson et al., 1988: 243).

I will deal later with the poststructuralist argument that we must
abandon efforts to represent the object of our investigation as it
'really' is, independent of our representational apparatus, for a
reflexive focus on how we construct what we are investigating. I turn
now to those concerned with the ways in which ideas about science
serve particular political or economic interests, the discourse of
feminists and neo-Marxists who raise the question, 'in whose
interest, by sex, race and class, has knowledge been generated?'
(Gonzalvez, 1986: 16).

Frame 2: Discourse toward a critical social science

> What counts is the further scientific development at such a theoretical and
> methodological level, and in terms of such problem constellations, that
> the distance of science from politics becomes unacceptable by its own
> standards. (Dubiel, 1985: 187)

> There is no social practice outside of ideology. (Hall, 1985: 103)

Efforts toward a critical social science raise questions about the
political nature of social research, about what it means to do
empirical inquiry in an unjust world. Based on Habermas's (1971)
thesis in *Knowledge and Human Interests* that claims to value-free
knowledge obscure the human interests inherent in all knowledge,

critical theorists hold that there is no end to ideology, no part of culture where ideology does not permeate. This most certainly includes the university and the production of social knowledge. Grounded in the reemergence of the Frankfurt School and its concern with questions of domination and resistance at the level of subjectivity, 'Action science as a form of praxis' aspires to paradigmatic status as a major alternative to other forms of social research (Peters and Robinson, 1984). A primary concern of discourse toward a critical social science is how to generate knowledge in ways that turn critical thought into emancipatory action.

As part of the post-Althusserean rejection of economism and determinism, consciousness and subjectivity rise to the fore in critical inquiry as the juncture between human agency and structural constraint takes on theoretical urgency. The goal is a critical social science which alleviates oppression by spurring 'the emergence of people who know who they are and are conscious of themselves as active and deciding beings, who bear responsibility for their choices and who are able to explain them in terms of their own freely adopted purposes and ideals' (Fay, 1987: 74).

The subject of such a science is theorized as living in a crisis of legitimacy (Habermas, 1975); this crisis provides a material base for the hope that subordinated groups will arise to construct more democratic social forms. The ability of the oppressed to comprehend a reality that is 'out there' waiting for representation by social inquirers is assumed (Fay, 1987; Flax, 1987), as in the central role to be played by 'transformative intellectuals' (Aronowitz and Giroux, 1985), who will serve as catalysts for the necessary empowering dialogue. Much of this goes on under the rubric of 'critical ethnography' (Simon and Dippo, 1986) where neo-Marxist ideology critique (for example, Repo, 1987) is being supplanted by more linguistically informed ethnography. This emergent body of work combines phenomenology and semiotics to focus on the relationship between the conscious and unconscious dynamics embedded in social relations and cultural forms (for example, Simon, 1987).[2]

Within the context of a critical social science, methodology is viewed as inherently political, as inescapably tied to issues of power and legitimacy. Methods are assumed to be permeated with what Gouldner (1970) terms 'ideologically resonant assumptions about what the social world is, who the sociologist is, and what the nature of the relation between them is' (p. 51). Methods, then, are politically charged 'as they define, control, evaluate, manipulate and report' (Gouldner, 1970: 50). The point is that 'the role of ideology does not diminish as rigor increases and error is dissipated' (Lecourt, 1975: 200). Such a stance provides the grounds for an 'openly ideological' approach to critical inquiry (Lather, 1986) where the central issue is how to bring together scholarship and advocacy in order to generate new ways of knowing that interrupt power imbalances. The line between emancipatory inquiry and pedagogy blurs as critical researchers focus on developing interactive approaches to research. In addition, there is growing concern with the dangers of researchers with liberatory intentions imposing meanings on situations, rather than constructing meaning through negotiation with research participants (for instance, Acker et al., 1983; Berlak, 1986; Miller, 1990).

Science could develop into a progressive moment within the consciousness of the society it both studies and shapes, but it is not enough to be oriented toward the interests of underprivileged social groups. An emancipatory, critical social science will develop out of the social relations of the research process itself, out of the enactment of what in the Frankfurt School was only incipient: implementation in research praxis (Dubiel, 1985: 185). Fay (1987) argues that such a critical social science must be limited in aspiration and see itself as a way that intellectual effort might help improve the political situation, as opposed to seeing itself as 'the key to redeeming our social and political life' (p. ix).

As we shall see in the next section, however, poststructuralism argues that no discourse is innocent of the Nietzschean will to power. Spivak (1987: 88) cautions that 'the desire to "understand" and "change" are as much symptomatic as they are revolutionary'. Whether the goal of one's work is prediction, understanding or emancipation, all are, for Foucault, ways of 'disciplining the body, normalizing behavior, administering the life of populations' (Rajchman, 1985: 82). All forms of knowledge and discourse that we have invented about ourselves – all define, categorize and classify us. All elicit the Foucauldian question, how do practices to discover the truth about ourselves impact on our lives?

Frame 3: Poststructuralism – discourse on discourse

> A good proportion of our intellectual effort now consists in casting suspicion on any statement by trying to uncover the disposition of its different levels. That disposition is infinite, and the abyss that we try to open up in every word, this madness of language [is an] abyss that has to be opened up first, and for tactical reasons: in order to break down the self-infatuation in our statements and to destroy the arrogance of our sciences. (Barthes, quoted in Smith, 1988: 99)

The recent linguistic turn in social theory focuses on the power of language to organize our thought and experience. Language is seen as both carrier and creator of a culture's epistemological codes. The ways we speak and write are held to influence our conceptual boundaries and to create areas of silence as language organizes meaning in terms of preestablished categories. Poststructuralism displaces both the post-Kuhnian view of language as transparent, and critical theorists' view of language as ideological struggle waged on the playing field of dialectics. Raising both the dangers of objectification and the inadequacies of dialectics, poststructuralism demands radical reflection on our interpretive frames as we enter the Foucauldian shift from *paradigm* to *discourse*, from a focus on researcher ontology and epistemology in the shaping of paradigmatic choice, to a focus on the productivity of language in the construction of the objects of investigation.

Poststructuralism holds that there is no final knowledge; 'the contingency and historical moment of all readings' means that, whatever the object of our gaze it 'is contested, temporal and emergent' (Clifford and Marcus, 1986: 18–19). Whether the reign of paradigms is over or merely suspended for a time, the argument is that 'the play of ideas free of authoritative paradigms' (Marcus and Fischer, 1986: 80–1) will move us further into some new way of producing and legitimating knowledge. Van Maanen (1988) cautions: 'Confident possession of some grail-like paradigm is at best a passing fancy or at worst a power play', but 'the paradigm myth . . . dies more slowly than the post-paradigm reality' (p. xiv).

From a poststructuralist perspective, ideology remains a much disputed term. While orthodox Marxists define it as false consciousness and oppose it to the 'true' knowledge of scientific Marxism, Foucault argues for the concept of power/knowledge to replace the reductionist Marxian usage of ideology, finding it too embedded in assumptions of 'false consciousness' and a human essence awaiting freedom from constraints (Sholle, 1988). Others view ideology as a constitutive component of reality: 'The production of meaning, the positioning of the subject and the manufacture of desire' (McLaren, 1986: 303). Within this neo-Gramscian view, there is no meaning making outside of ideology (Gramsci, 1971). There is no false consciousness, for such a concept assumes a true consciousness accessible via 'correct' theory and practice (Hall, 1985). The postmodern feminist cultural critic Teresa Ebert (1988: 23) defines ideology as the following:

> not false consciousness or distorted perception [but rather] the organization of material signifying practices that constitute subjectivities and produce the lived relations by which subjects are connected – whether in hegemonic or oppositional ways – to the dominant relations of production and distribution of power . . . in a specific social formation at a given historical moment.

Poststructuralism views research as an enactment of power relations; the focus is on the development of a mutual, dialogic production of a multi-voice, multi-centered discourse. Research practices are viewed as much more inscriptions of legitimation than procedures that help us get closer to some 'truth' capturable via language (Cherryholmes, 1988). Attention turns away from efforts to represent what is 'really' there and shifts, instead, toward the productivity of language within what Bakhtin (1981: 358) has termed 'the framing authorial context'. Objectivity, for example, is seen as textual construction more fruitfully displaced by a deconstructive emphasis on writing as an enactment of the social relations that produce the research itself. Rather than 'objectivity', questions such as the following rise to the fore:

- How do we address questions of narrative authority raised by poststructuralism in our empirical work?
- How do we *frame* meaning possibilities rather than *close* them in working with empirical data?
- How do we create multi-voiced, multi-centered texts from such data?
- How do we deconstruct the ways our own desires as emancipatory inquiries shape the texts we create?
- Why do we do our research: to use our privileges as academics to give voice to what Foucault terms 'subjugated knowledges'? As another version of writing the self?
- What are the race, class and gender relations that produce the research itself.[3]

Within poststructuralism, a relational focus on how method patterns findings replaces the objectifying and dialectical methods of post-Kuhnian and critical approaches. For example, the following deconstructs what an interview is:

> As a mode of knowing, the interview technique is an exemplary strategy of traditional humanism since such a device inscribes fundamental humanist values (that is, liberal pluralism, unmediated knowledge, participatory democracy, consensus among free subjects) in the very practices it claims to be studying. . . . The focus of the interviews (unitary, sovereign subjects) reaffirms the belief that people contain knowledge (they are self-present subjects) and all that one has to do to have access to that knowledge is to engage in 'free' and 'unconstrained' discussions. . . . The interview technique is, of course, an exemplary instance of what Derrida has called the desire for presence, which is an affect of the dominant logocentrism in the academy. (Zavarzadeh and Morton, 1986–7: 16)

What is sought is a reflexive process that focuses on our too easy use of 'imposed and provided forms' (Corrigan, 1987: 33) and that might lead us toward a science capable of continually demystifying the realities it serves to create.

To conclude this section on reinscribing otherwise the cultural practices we call science, what we are talking about, in Yvonna Lincoln's (1989) wonderful word play, 'is NOT your father's paradigm'. It is an altogether different approach to doing empirical inquiry. This approach, paradoxically, both calls into question 'the dream of scientificity' (Barthes, quoted in Merquior, 1986: 148) and advocates for the creation of a 'more hesitant and partial scholarship' capable of helping us 'to tell a better story' (Grossberg, 1988: 17) in a world marked by the elusiveness with which it greets our efforts to know it.

Just say no to nihilism: relativism as a god trick

> Feminist theory is neither subjective nor objective, neither relativist nor absolutist: it occupies the *middle ground* excluded by oppositional categories. . . . Absolutism and relativism both ignore the concrete functioning of power relations and the necessity of occupying a *position*.
> (Grosz, 1988: 100)

Postmodern theories of language, subjectivity and power profoundly challenge the discourse of emancipation on several fronts. The assumption of a potentially fully conscious human agent will be dealt with later. What I want to address here are the contradictions involved in post-foundational intellectual work committed to social justice. I will focus specifically on the age-old issue of relativism as foregrounded in Bernstein's (1983) question: Does the move away from foundationalist or absolutist epistemologies entail embracing 'the spectre of relativism' as our inevitable companion?

Surveying the reception of postmodernist in the academy, postmodernism evokes criticism from all sites in the political spectrum. Both 'neo-conservatives' and 'progressives' reject the postmodern questioning of the 'grand narratives of legitimation' (Lyotard, 1984) as a 'French fad' which, by advocating the loss of foundational standards, propels us into irrationalism. Some lament the loss of 'classical' standards and fear anarchy and cultural disintegration (for instance, Bloom, 1987). Others see a slide into relativism that is dangerous for the dispossessed in its undercutting of the grounds for social justice struggle and its feeding of nihilism and quietude (Dews, 1987; Hartsock, 1987; West, 1987).

Nancy Hartsock (1987), for example, joins race, class and sex into a deconstruction of the intellectual moves that shape how postmodern issues get framed. Attempting to come to grips with the social and historical changes of the middle to late twentieth century, postmodern theorizers have 'set the rules of the discussion in a way inappropriate to those of us who have been marginalized' (p. 200). The retreat from historical agency and action, the lack of foundational grounding, the debunking of anything other than local, contingent theory, the insistence upon a fragmented, decentered self – these may be useful strategies 'for the inheritor of the voice of the transcendental ego' (p. 201), but they pose dangers for any appropriation of postmodernism on the part of the marginalized.

Hartsock's concerns are echoed in Longino's (1988) worries that a denial of objective value takes away the ground of feminist claims. Like Grosz's words which began this section by positioning concerns with relativism as within a binary logic, the feminist philosopher of science Sandra Harding (1987: 10) turns such fears of relativism upside-down by arguing that we must 'relativize relativism itself':

> Historically, relativism appears as an intellectual possibility, and as a 'problem,' only for dominating groups at the point where the hegemony of their views is being challenged. . . . The point here is that relativism is not a problem originating in, or justifiable in terms of, women's experiences or feminist agendas. It is fundamentally a sexist response that attempts to preserve the legitimacy of androcentric claims in the face of contrary evidence.

Caputo (1987) asks, 'How many of our questions arise from foundational compulsions, Cartesian anxieties?' (p. 262). To see relativism as a Cartesian obsession is to argue that it is an issue only within the context of foundationalist epistemologies which search for a privileged standpoint as the guarantee of certainty. Regardless of political positioning, the concept of relativism assumes a foundational structure, an Archimedean standpoint outside of flux and human interest. In Cherryholmes's (1988: 186) words:

> Relativism is an issue for structuralists because they propose structures that set standards. Relativism is an issue if a foundational structure *exists* that is ignored. . . . A Derridian might argue, however, that the issue is *différance*, where meanings are dispersed and deferred. If dispersion and deferral are the order of the day, what is relative under structuralism is difference under deconstruction. If there is no foundation, there is no structure against which other positions can be 'objectively' judged.

If the focus is on the procedures which take us as objects and involve us in systems of categories and procedures of self-construction, relativism becomes a nonissue. If the focus is on how power relations shape knowledge production and legitimation, relativism is a concept from another discourse, a discourse of foundations that posits grounds for certainty outside of context, some neutral, disinterested, stable point of reference. 'Relativism is the perfect mirror twin of totalization in the ideologies of objectivity;

both deny the stakes in location, embodiment, and partial perspective; both make it impossible to see well' (Haraway, 1988: 584).

All thought is not equally arbitrary, Bakhtin (1984) argued over fifty years ago; positionality weighs heavily in what knowledge comes to count as legitimate in historically specific times and places. The world is spoken from many sites which are differently positioned regarding access to power and resources. Relativism foregrounds the shifting sands of context, but occludes the play of power in the shaping of changing structures and circumstances. As such, it is what Haraway (1988: 584) calls 'a god trick . . . a way of being nowhere while claiming to be everywhere equally'. In sum, fears of relativism and its seeming attendant, nihilism or Nietzschean anger, seem to me an implosion of Western, white male, class-privileged arrogance – if we cannot know everything, then we can know nothing.

Relativistic assumptions of a free play of meaning that denies power relations are of little use for those struggling to free themselves from normalizing boundaries and categories. Fraser and Nicholson (1988: 92) point out the practical political interests of feminism that have saved it from some of the hand-wringing of other leftists: 'women whose theorizing was to serve the struggle against sexism were not about to abandon powerful political tools merely as a result of intramural debates in professional philosophy'. The point is that while oppositional critical work remains to be developed in the wake of postmodernism, 'in periods when fields are without secure foundations, practice becomes the engine of innovation' (Marcus and Fischer, 1986: 166).

With practice as a privileged site for working out what it means to do emancipatory work within a post-foundational context, 'The alternative to relativism is partial, locatable, critical knowledges' (Haraway, 1988: 584). Legitimacy is plural, local and context-specific: 'instead of hovering above, legitimacy descends to the level of practice and becomes immanent in it' (Fraser and Nicholson, 1988: 87). Interventions are situationally and participatorily defined. Cultural work becomes 'a battle for the signified – a struggle to fix meaning temporarily on behalf of particular power relations and social interests' (Weedon, 1987: 98). Ellsworth (1987: 14), for example, asks 'how have we closed down the process of analysis and self-reflection long enough to take a stand, and what or who have we had to put on hold or bracket in order to do that?'

As Fekete (1987) notes, it is 'strategically desirable to move people to think about the life beyond the horizons of the more nihilistic and paralyzing aspects of postmodernism'. Fears of relativism are displaced by explicit interventions that collapse the boundaries between scholarship and politics. Absolute knowledge was never possible, anyway. Archimedean standpoints have always been shaped in the crucible of the power/knowledge nexus. We just thought otherwise, believing in gods and kings and, more recently, the 'objectivity' of scientists.

All of this argues that something new is emerging, something embryonic, liminal, not yet in place. The objective, the apolitical and the value neutral have been foundational in scientific claims to authority. Relativity has been put forth as the great bugbear against which we must commit to some foundational absolute if anarchy and chaos are not to descend upon us. It has been the primary intent of this section to argue that such claims are cultural dominants which masquerade as natural, rational, necessary, but which are a fact less of nature than of human production. They are, in spite of their denial, embedded in what Foucault (1980) terms 'regimes of truth', the power/knowledge nexus which provides the constraints and possibilities of discourse.

Subject-ed subjects[4] and identity politics

Fictions of the subject

A post-humanist theory of the subject combines Derrida's critique of the metaphysics of presence with a post-Althusserean focus on human agency. The result is a shift in cultural theory to seeing subjectivity both as socially produced in language, at conscious and unconscious levels, and as a site of struggle and potential change. In poststructuralist theories of the subject, identity does not follow unproblematically from experience. We are seen to live in webs of multiple representations of class, race, gender, language and social relations; meanings vary even within one individual. Self-identity 'is constituted and reconstituted relationally, its boundaries repeatedly remapped and renegotiated' (Scott, 1987: 17). This focus on the fundamentally relational nature of identity results in the historically constituted and shifting self versus the static and essentialized self inherent in the concept of the free and self-determining individual.

Identities are continually displaced/replaced. The subject is neither unified nor fixed. We occupy conflicting subject positions where language is understood as competing discourses. Poststructuralism theorizes the subject 'as a site of disarray and conflict, central to the process of political change and to preserving the status quo' (Weedon, 1987: 21). In the discursive struggle for our subjectivity, we are 'active but not sovereign' (Weedon, 1987: 41). Within this decentering of the subject, the key Enlightenment equation of knowing, naming and emancipation becomes problematic. The self becomes an 'empirical contingency' (Flax, 1987: 626), both site and subject, produced by diffuse forms of power. The subject is constantly figured and refigured within a context of bombardment by conflicting messages, a 'semiotic glut' (Collins, 1987: 25), spawned by the intensified sign production of consumer society.

Johnson's (1986–7: 69) 'post-post-structuralist account of subjectivity' and Grossberg's (1987: 39) rejection of postmodernism's tendency to reify a fractured, fragmented, schizoid subject illustrate the continued lack of an adequate poststructuralist theory of subjectivity. While we are not the authors of the ways we understand our lives, while we are subjected to regimes of meaning, we are involved in discursive self-production where we attempt to produce some coherence and continuity. We need a theory of the subject that recognizes both of these moments, a theory grounded in the 'hunkering down on detail' so important in what Marcus and Fischer (1986: 118) note as 'the ethnographic task' of reconstructing dominant macro-frameworks 'from the bottom up, from the problem of description . . . back to general theory which has grown out of touch with the world on which it seeks to comment'.

The subject of fictions

At the center of deconstruction is the fiction of the self-determining subject of modern political, legal, social and aesthetic discourse. Neither feminist nor neo-Marxist theorizing has escaped what Fay (1987) calls 'a metaphysics of human agency' (p. 26), 'an inflated conception of the powers of human reason and will' (p. 9). While competing conceptions of the subject have long haunted Marxism and forced it to reexamine its notion of the revolutionary subject, the subjects of critical activity have never been properly identified. Marxism's premise of the constructedness of human nature has, however, saved it from some of the essentialism that reveals how much of feminist thought is embedded in the very assumptions it is critiquing. Postmodernism provides a critical analysis of the very discourse of liberation and revolution, of both the 'ideological self-righteousness of the Marxist critic' (Rajchman, 1985: 80) and the essentialism that haunts contemporary feminist theory (Eisenstein, 1983; Haraway, 1985; Harding, 1986).

While we cannot but be engulfed by the categories of our times, self-reflexivity teaches that our discourse is the meaning of our longing. Derrida's 'the always already' means that how we speak and write tells us more about our own inscribed selves, about the way that language writes us, than about the 'object' of our gaze. The trick is to see the will to power in our work as clearly as we see the will to truth. One example of a key concept that needs to be deconstructed is that of false consciousness. In trouble since Althusser, the concept of false consciousness 'is a moment of extreme ideological closure' (Hall, 1985: 105) which frames the issue in terms of a true consciousness, a totality. Given that 'there is no experiencing *outside* of the categories of representation of ideology', understanding people's complicity in their own oppression becomes a matter of developing a nonreductive problematic that focuses on the relationship between conscious understanding and the unconscious dynamics embedded in social relations and cultural forms. This requires a poststructuralist theory of subjectivity where ideology is seen not as false consciousness but as an effort to make sense in a world of contradictory information, radical contingency and indeterminacies, 'a way of holding at bay a randomness incongruent with consciousness' (Spivak, 1987: 78). From this perspective, ideology becomes a strategy of containment for beings who, in spite of David Byrne's advice, cannot 'stop making sense'.[5]

Identity politics

> My project . . . is an attempt to dis-cern the 'subject', and to argue that the human agent exceeds the 'subject' as it is constructed in and by much poststructuralist theory as well as by those discourses against which poststructuralist theory claims to pose itself. (Smith, 1988: xxx)

Marxism's long-running search for the revolutionary subject has focused much attention on the notion of the 'death of the subject' promulgated by postmodernism. What has 'died' is the unified, monolithic, reified, essentialized subject capable of fully conscious, fully rational action, a subject assumed in most liberal and emancipatory discourse. Such a subject is replaced by a provisional, contingent, strategic, constructed subject which, while intelligible, is not essentialized. To quote Foster (1985: 136):

> Here, then, we begin to see what is at stake in this so-called dispersal of the subject. For what is this subject that, threatened by loss, is so bemoaned? Bourgeois perhaps, but patriarchal and phallocentric certainly. For some, for many, this may indeed be a great loss, a loss which leads to narcissitic laments and hysterical disavowals of the end of art, of culture, of the west. But for others, precisely for Others, it is no great loss at all.

Decentering is not so much the elimination of the subject as it is the multi-centeredness of action, a reconceptualization of agency from *subject-centered agency to the plurality and agency of meaning*. The demise of foundationalist philosophy, the epistemological subject and the traditional objectivist ideas of knowledge and truth create many problems for the emancipatory convictions of post-Marxist discourse on the Other. Ross (1988) asks in whose interest it is to abandon universals and answers that the very idea of interests must be problematized as interests can no longer be universalized and identities are not already *there* (p. xvii).

For example, Hall (1985) writes of how his sense of racial identity, his 'blackness', has shifted over time and place. Pratt (1984) explores the same ground of meaning as the locus of action, but from the perspective of white privilege. (For an incandescent critique of Pratt, see Martin and Mohanty, 1986.) Additionally, while class and gendered self-conceptions seem widely variable across and within individual biographies, sexual orientation seems especially shifting in terms of identity politics. While Lugones (1987) celebrates that 'the construction of "lesbian" is purposefully and healthfully still up in the air, in the process of becoming' (p. 10), Lerner (1987) raises cautions regarding how we treat our historical foremothers in terms of interpreting their sexuality. As Weedon (1987) writes 'the meaning of lesbianism changes with historical shifts in the discursive construction of female sexuality' (p. 159).

What all of this means strategically, how one builds a politics on a postmodern questioning of the unified, stable subject, is only beginning to be articulated (Epstein, 1987; Harasym, 1988; Laclau and Mouffe, 1985; Penley, 1986: 142–4; Smith, 1988; Weedon, 1987). I find Riley (1988) and Ellsworth (1989) especially evocative on this rethinking of agency within a context of the unknowable. Both stress West's point that in contemporary identity politics, totalizing categories like 'women' and 'blacks' and 'third world women' are most usefully conceptualized as heuristic rather than ontological categories (interview with Stephanson, 1988: 270). To quote Riley (1988: 113–14): 'Of course, this means that feminism must "speak women," while at the same time, an acute awareness of its vagaries is imperative . . . while it's impossible to thoroughly be a woman, it's also impossible never to be one. On such shifting sands feminism must stand and sway.'

Conclusion

Preceded, paralleled and interrupted by critical 'ex-centric' discourses and global struggles for social justice, postmodernism is a process of retheorizing the objects and experiences of everyday life in the twilight of modernity, an epochal turning point in how the world and the possibilities of human agency are conceived. It is a shift from the conjunction of liberal humanism with positivistic science to a conjunction of decentered subjectivity and multi-sited agency within a post-paradigmatic diaspora. The resultant opening up of legitimate ways to produce and legitimate knowledge has profound implications for reinscribing otherwise the cultural practices we construct in the name of the human sciences.

Notes

1 The work of Guba and Lincoln, 1981, and Lincoln and Guba, 1985, was problematic in its collapsing of all alternative paradigms into one, the 'naturalistic'. They have rethought this position, as evidenced by the framing of Egon Guba (ed.), *The Paradigm Dialog* (1990), the proceedings from the Alternative Paradigms for Inquiry Conference, sponsored by Phi Delta Kappa and Indiana University, San Francisco, 25–6 March 1989, which includes an earlier version of this chapter.
2 Livingstone et al., 1987, combines both types of neo-Marxist inquiry, the more self-righteous ideology critique and the more self-reflexive work influenced by the linguistic turn in social theory.
3 These questions grow out of my fruitful collaboration over the last few years with Ann Berlak and Janet Miller.
4 Coward and Ellis, 1977, coined the phrase 'the subject-ed subject'.
5 David Byrne, Talking Heads rock impresario, is oftentimes referred to as a 'postmodern' artist. *Stop Making Sense* is both an album and a critically acclaimed rock concert movie.

References

Acker, J., Barry, K. and Essevold, J. (1983) Objectivity and truth: problems in doing feminist research. *Women's Studies Forum*, 6: 423–35.
Aronowitz, S. and Giroux, H. (1985) Radical education and transformative intellectuals. *Canadian Journal of Political and Social Theory*, 9 (3): 48–63.
Atkinson, P., Delamont, S. and Hammersley, M. (1988) Qualitative research traditions: a British response to Jacob. *Review of Educational Research*, 58 (2): 231–50.
Bakhtin, M. (1981) *The Dialogic Imagination: Four Essays*, trans. C. Emerson and M. Holquist. Austin: University of Texas Press.
Bakhtin, M. (1984) *Problems of Dostoevsky's Poetics*, ed. and trans. C. Emerson. Minneapolis: University of Minnesota Press.
Baudrillard, J. (1984) The precession of simulacra. In B. Wallis (ed.), *Art after Modernism: Rethinking Representation*. Boston, MA: Godine. pp. 235–81.
Berlak, A. (1986) Teaching for liberation and empowerment in the liberal arts: towards the development of a pedagogy that overcomes resistance. Paper presented at the Curriculum Theorizing Conference, Dayton, OH, October.
Bernstein, R. (1983) *Beyond Objectivism and Relativism: Science, Hermeneutics, and Praxis*. Philadelphia: University of Pennsylvania Press.
Bloom, A. (1987) *The Closing of the American Mind: How Higher Education Has Failed Democracy and Impoverished the Souls of Today's Students*. New York: Simon & Schuster.
Bogdan, R. and Biklen, S. (1982) *Qualitative Research for Education: An Introduction to Theory and Methods*. Boston, MA: Allyn & Bacon.

Caputo, J. (1987) *Radical Hermeneutics: Repetition, Deconstruction and the Hermeneutic Project*. Bloomington: University of Indiana Press.

Cherryholmes, C. (1988) *Power and Criticism: Poststructural Investigations in Education*. New York: Teachers' College Press.

Clifford, J. and Marcus, G. (1986) *Writing Culture: The Poetics and Politics of Ethnography*. Berkeley: University of California Press.

Collins, J. (1987) Postmodernism and cultural practice: refining the parameters. *Screen*, 28 (2): 11–26.

Corrigan, P. (1987) In/forming schooling. In D. Livingstone (ed.), *Critical Pedagogy and Cultural Power*. South Hadley, MA: Bergin & Garvey. pp. 17–40.

Coward, R. and Ellis, J. (1977) *Language and Materialism: Development in Semiology and the Theory of the Subject*. London: Routledge & Kegan Paul.

Deleuze, G. (1988) *Foucault*. Minneapolis: University of Minnesota Press.

Derrida, J. (1978) Structure, sign and play in the discourse of the human sciences. In *Writing and Difference*, trans. A. Bass. Chicago: University of Chicago Press. pp. 278–93.

Dews, P. (1987) *The Logic of Disintegration: Poststructuralist Thought and Claims of Critical Theory*. London: Verso.

Dreyfus, H. and Rabinow, P. (1983) *Michel Foucault: Beyond Structuralism and Hermeneutics*, 2nd edn. Chicago: University of Chicago Press.

Dubiel, H. (1985) *Theory and Politics: Studies in the Development of Critical Theory*, trans. B. Gregg. Cambridge, MA: MIT Press.

Ebert, T. (1988) The romance of patriarchy: ideology, subjectivity, and postmodern feminist cultural theory. *Cultural Critique*, 10: 19–57.

Eisenstein, H. (1983) *Contemporary Feminist Thought*. Boston, MA: G.K. Hall.

Eisner, E. (1988) The primacy of experience and the politics of method. *Educational Researcher*, 17 (5): 15–20.

Ellsworth, E. (1987) The place of video in social change: at the edge of making sense. Manuscript.

Ellsworth, E. (1989) Why doesn't this feel empowering? Working through the repressive myths of critical pedagogy. *Harvard Educational Review*, 59 (3): 297–324.

Epstein, S. (1987) Gay politics, ethnic identity: the limits of social constructionism. *Socialist Review*, 92–3, 17 (3, 4): 9–54.

Fay, B. (1987) *Critical Social Science*. Ithaca, NY: Cornell University Press.

Fekete, J. (ed.) (1987) *Life after Postmodernism: Essays on Value and Culture*. New York: St Martin's Press.

Flax, J. (1987) Postmodernism and gender relations in feminist theory. *Signs*, 12 (4): 621–43.

Foster, H. (1985) *Recodings: Art, Spectacle, Cultural Politics*. Post Townsend, WA: Bay Press.

Foucault, M. (1979) *Discipline and Punish*. New York: Vintage Books.

Foucault, M. (1980) *Power/Knowledge: Selected Interviews and Other Writings, 1972–1977*, ed. and trans. C. Gordon. New York: Pantheon.

Fraser, N. and Nicholson, L. (1988) Social criticism without philosophy: an encounter between feminism and postmodernism. In A. Ross (ed.), *Universal Abandon: The Politics of Postmodernism*. Minneapolis: University of Minnesota Press.

Gleick, J. (1987) *Chaos*. New York: Viking.

Gonzalvez, L. (1986) The new feminist scholarship: epistemological issues for teacher education. Manuscript.

Gouldner, A. (1970) *The Coming Crisis of Western Sociology*. New York: Basic Books.

Gramsci, A. (1971) *Selections from the Prison Notebooks of Antonio Gramsci*, ed. and trans. Q. Hoare and G. Smith. New York: International Publishers.

Grossberg, L. (1987) The in-difference of television or, mapping TV's popular economy. *Screen*, 28 (2): 28–47.

Grossberg, L. (1988) Rockin' with Reagan, or the mainstreaming of postmodernity. *Cultural Critique*, 10: 123–49.

Grosz, E. (1988) The in(ter)vention of feminist knowledges. In B. Caine, E. Grosz and M. de Lepcruanche (eds), *Crossing Boundaries: Feminism and the Creation of Knowledges*. Sydney: Allen & Unwin. pp. 92–104.

Guba, E. (ed.) (1990) *The Paradigm Dialog: Options for Social Science Inquiry*. Newbury Park: Sage.

Guba, E. and Lincoln, Y. (1981) *Effective Evaluation*. San Francisco: Jossey-Bass.

Habermas, J. (1971) *Knowledge and Human Interests*, trans. J. J. Shapiro. Boston, MA: Beacon Press.

Habermas, J. (1975) *Legitimation Crisis*. Boston, MA: Beacon Press.

Habermas, J. (1981) Modernity versus postmodernity. *New German Critique*, 22: 3–14.

Hall, S. (1985) Signification, representation, ideology: Althusser and the post-structuralist debates. *Critical Studies in Mass Communication*, 2 (2): 91–114.

Harasym, S. (1988) Practical politics of the open end: an interview with Gayatri Spivak. *Canadian Journal of Political Theory*, 12 (1, 2): 51–69.

Haraway, D. (1985) A manifesto for cyborgs: science, technology and socialist feminism in the 1980's. *Socialist Review*, 80: 65–107.

Haraway, D. (1988) Situated knowledges: the science question in feminism and the privilege of partial perspective. *Feminist Studies*, 14 (3): 575–99.

Harding, S. (1986) *The Science Question in Feminism*. Ithaca, NY: Cornell University Press.

Harding, S. (ed.) (1987) *Feminism and Methodology*. Bloomington: Indiana University Press.

Harland, R. (1987) *Superstructuralism: The Philosophy of Structuralism and Post-Structuralism*. New York: Methuen.

Hartsock, N. (1987) Rethinking modernism: minority vs majority theories. *Cultural Critique*, 7: 187–206.

Hutcheon, L. (1988) *A Poetics of Postmodernism: History, Theory, Fiction*. New York: Routledge.

Inglis, F. (1988) *Popular Culture and Political Power*. New York: Harvester Wheatsheaf.

Johnson, R. (1986–7) What is cultural studies anyway? *Social Text*, 16: 38–80.

Kuhn, T. (1970) *The Structure of Scientific Revolutions*. Chicago: University of Chicago Press. (Originally published in 1962.)

Laclau, E. and Mouffe, C. (1985) *Hegemony and Socialist Strategy: Towards a Radical Democratic Politics*, trans. W. Moore and P. Cammack. London: Verso.

Lather, P. (1986) Issues of validity in openly ideological research: between a rock and a soft place. *Interchange*, 17 (4): 63–84.

Lecourt, D. (1975) *Marxism and Epistemology*. London: New Left Books.

Lerner, G. (1987) Where biographers fear to tread. *Women's Review of Books*, 4 (12): 11–12.

Lincoln, Y. (1989) The making of a constructivist: a remembrance of transformations past. Paper presented at the Alternative Paradigms for Inquiry Conference, San Francisco, March.

Lincoln, Y. and Guba, E. (1985) *Naturalistic Inquiry*. Beverly Hills, CA: Sage.

Livingstone, D. (ed.) (1987) *Critical Pedagogy and Cultural Power*. South Hadley, MA: Bergin & Garvey.

Longino, H. (1988) Science, objectivity, and feminist values. *Feminist Studies*, 14 (3): 561–74.

Lyotard, J.-F. (1984) *The Postmodern Condition: A Report on Knowledge*, trans. G. Bennington and B. Massumi. Minneapolis: University of Minnesota Press.

Lugones, M. (1987) Playfulness 'world'-travelling, and loving perception. *Hypatia*, 2 (2): 3–19.

McLaren, P. (1986) Postmodernity and the death of politics: a Brazilian reprieve. *Educational Theory*, 36 (4): 389–401.

Marcus, G. and Fischer, R. (1986) *Anthropology as Cultural Critique: An Experimental Moment in the Human Sciences*. Chicago: University of Chicago Press.

Martin, B. and Mohanty, C.T. (1986) Feminist politics: what's home got to do with it? In T. de Lauretis (ed.), *Feminist Studies/Critical Studies*. Bloomington: Indiana University Press. pp. 191–212.

Merquior, J.G. (1986) *A Critique of Structuralist and Poststructuralist Thought*. London: Verso.

Miles, M. and Huberman, M. (1984) *Qualitative Data Analysis: A Sourcebook of New Methods*. Beverly Hills, CA: Sage.

Miller, J. (1990) *Creating Spaces and Finding Voices: Teachers Collaborating for Empowerment*. Albany, NY: State University of New York Press.

Namenwirth, M. (1986) Science through a feminist prism. In R. Bleir (ed.), *Feminist Approaches to Science*. New York: Pergamon Press. pp. 18–41.

Nelson, J.S., Megill, A. and McClosky, D.N. (eds) (1987) *The Rhetoric of the Human Sciences: Language and Argument in Scholarship and Public Affairs*. Madison: University of Wisconsin Press.

Nicholson, L. (1986) *Gender and History: The Limits of Social Theory in the Age of the Family*. New York: Columbia University Press.

Nicholson, L. (ed.) (1990) *Feminism/Postmodernism*. New York: Routledge.

Penley, C. (1986) Teaching in your sleep: feminism and psychoanalysis. In C. Nelson (ed.), *Theory in the Classroom*. Urbana: University of Illinois Press. pp. 129–48.

Peters, M. and Robinson, V. (1984) The origins and status of action research. *Journal of Applied Behavioral Sciences*, 20 (2): 113–24.

Popkewitz, T. (1984) *Paradigm and Ideology in Educational Research: The Social Functions of the Intellectual*. New York: Falmer Press.

Pratt, M.B. (1984) Identity: skin, blood, heart. In E. Burkin, M.B. Pratt, and B. Smith (eds), *Yours in Struggle: Three Feminist Perspectives on Anti-Semitism and Racism*. Brooklyn, NY: Long Haul Press. pp. 11–63.

Rajchman, J. (1985) *Michel Foucault: The Freedom of Philosophy*. New York: Columbia University Press.

Repo, S. (1987) Consciousness and popular media. In D. Livingstone (ed.), *Critical Pedagogy and Cultural Power*. South Hadley, MA: Bergin & Garvey. pp. 77–98.

Riley, D. (1988) *'Am I That Name?' Feminism and the Category of 'Women' in History*. Minneapolis: University of Minnesota Press.

Roberts, H. (ed.) (1981) *Doing Feminist Research*. London: Routledge & Kegan Paul.

Rorty, R. (1979) *Philosophy and the Mirror of Nature*. Princeton, NJ: Princeton University Press.

Ross, A. (ed.) (1988) *Universal Abandon: The Politics of Postmodernism*. Minneapolis: University of Minnesota Press.

Said, E. (1989) Representing the colonized: anthropology's interlocutors. *Cultural Inquiry*, 15, 205–25.

Scott, J. (1987) Critical tensions. (Review of Teresa de Lauretis, *Feminist Studies/Critical Studies*.) *Women's Review of Books* 5 (1), October: 17–18.

Sholle, J. (1988) Critical studies: from the theory of ideology to power/knowledge. *Critical Studies in Mass Communication*, 5: 16–41.

Simon, R. (1987) Work experience. In D. Livingstone (ed.), *Critical Pedagogy and Cultural Power*. South Hadley, MA: Bergin & Garvey. pp. 155–78.

Simon, R. and Dippo, D. (1986) On critical ethnographic work. *Anthropology and Education Quarterly*, 17 (4): 195–202.

Smith, P. (1988) *Discerning the Subject*. Minneapolis: University of Minnesota Press.

Spivak, G. (1987) *In Other Words: Essays in Cultural Politics*. New York: Methuen.

Stephanson, A. (1988) Interview with Cornel West. In A. Ross (ed.), *Universal Abandon*. Minneapolis: University of Minnesota Press. pp. 269–86.

Tyler, S. (1987) *The Unspeakable: Discourse, Dialogue, and Rhetoric in the Postmodern World*. Madison: University of Wisconsin Press.

Van Maanen, J. (1988) *Tales of the Field: On Writing Ethnography*. Chicago: University of Chicago Press.

Weedon, C. (1987) *Feminist Practice and Poststructuralist theory*. Oxford: Blackwell.

West, C. (1987) Postmodernism and black America. *Zeta Magazine*, 1 (6): 27–9.

Willis, P. (1980) Notes on method. In S. Hall, D. Hobson, A. Lowe and P. Willis (eds), *Culture, Media, Language*. London: Hutchinson. pp. 88–95.

Zavarzadeh, M. and Morton, D. (1986–7) Theory pedagogy politics: the crisis of 'the subject' in the humanities. *Boundary*, 2, 15 (1, 2): 1–21.

6

An Introduction to Deconstructionist Psychology

Paul Richer

Through a critique of humanistic and psychodynamic psychology, this chapter presents an introduction to deconstructionist psychology, a movement that has yet to reach the American continent in any significant way. America knows deconstructionism mostly as a branch of literary criticism, somewhat elitist and inspired by figures such as Derrida and de Man. The anarchist tendency of deconstructionism has, on this continent, been aimed at texts more than social situations. In Europe, however, small groups of social activists in psychology have formed, largely inspired by Foucault's textual and nontextual work. This chapter will review Foucault's positions pertinent to psychology, along with those of some of his French colleagues. We should point out that in addition to the French position presented here, there are important deconstructionist positions asserted elsewhere in Europe, especially in Britain and in Italy (where a number of concrete reforms have been accomplished along deconstructionist lines in the mental health services).

Until Foucault's upsurge, most political criticism of psychology focused on the border zones between psychology and other fields, especially medical and legal. It was said that border zone infiltrations have tainted psychological theory, infected it with inappropriate medical models or questionable quasi-juridical responsibilities. Szasz and Laing, for example, have argued that way, pointing to a possible future when psychology can clean up its act by enforcing stricter border regulations, imagining a virginal psychology that could resist the penetrations of power mechanisms. Foucault taught us to be skeptical. He could not imagine any production of knowledge as a virgin birth, and he illustrated in a number of academic fields how power dynamics are intrinsic to both their theoretical and practical functioning. Psychology is a prime example, and one of Foucault's favorites. *Madness and Civilization* (1973b), *History of Sexuality*, Vol. I (1978) and *Discipline and Punish* (1979) take up psychology specifically; *The Order of Things* (1973a), *The Archeology of*

Knowledge (1972) and *Power/Knowledge* (1980) look more broadly at the human sciences at large.

Foucault detected extra-psychological power structures – structures of domination – in the production, categorization, distribution and utilization of psychological knowledge all along the spread of its field. Those domination structures are political, economic, ideological, religious or any combination of these. The multiplicity of power structures, according to Foucault, is overlooked in the economic reductionism of classical Marxism, as Althusser first pointed out, but also in the newer sexist reductionism of contemporary feminism. (Marxist and feminist tensions operate to continue the intra-deconstructionist dialogue.)

What is interesting is the blanket nature of Foucault's assertion regarding the power–knowledge doublet. It is less like a marriage, more like two sides of the same coin. From *Discipline and Punish*: 'Power and knowledge directly imply one another; there is not any power relation without the correlative constitution of some field of knowledge, nor any knowledge that does not presuppose and constitute at the same time power relations.' This general stance can be taken as an operating principle for suspicion – those psychological movements that most insist on their own social-political purity are most assuredly duplicitous, although this is not to say that the psychologist is himself intending the duplicity, it is true. Poor Chomsky, a socially aware and activist psychologist if ever there was one, yet, I suppose blind with regard to the social consequences of his 'purely theoretical' research on syntactical development. Just discovering the natural stages of syntactical development, it would seem, but soon enough we have a new set of objectivized and scientized concepts to apply to deficits in minority children, the retarded, schizophrenics. New academic hyper-words to make our judgments sound more believable.

The poor humanists, too. They do not imagine that all their talk about freedom, potential, actualization, might provide the basis for our new racism, the racism of self-control. Adorno and other critical theorists antedating deconstructionism tried to make the point in reference to existentialism and other philosophical humanisms. Heidegger's freedomism is one of the best; authenticity, said not to be conditioned by anything ontic, becomes a matter of ontological grace, something you are born with or without, strength of character as they say, a concept so central to the vision spun by Hitler. From Adorno's *Negative Dialectics* (1973): 'The more freedom the subject ascribes to itself, the greater its responsibility; and before this responsibility it must fail in a life which in practice has never endowed a subject with unabridged autonomy.' In the end it is not behaviorism, the study of the imposition of law on behavior, that will produce the most law-abiding citizens. The guilty subject, law-abiding, is best manufactured in the offices of humanistic psychology with its reaction-formation insistence on the sovereignty of the subject. Foucault ('The subject and power', 1982):

> This form of power applies itself to immediate everyday life which categorizes the individual, marks him by his own individuality, attaches him to his own identity, imposes a law of truth on him which he must recognize and which others have to recognize in him. It is a form of power which makes individuals subjects. There are two meanings of the word, 'subject': subject to someone else by control and dependence; and tied to his own identity by a conscience of self-knowledge. Both meanings suggest a form of power which subjugates and makes subject to.

Foucault did not claim his own work to be exempt from the power–knowledge dynamic, by the way, and it often maddened him. Fringe academic movements have always been integral to the maintenance of liberal, and therefore nonrevolutionary attitudes in the young. The very fact that he remained successfully employed indicated that he had perfected the art of going just far enough, but not too far, so that students might imagine that they were getting something really new. Foucault would be the instrument of normalization for those wilder graduate students.

The hiddenness of power in knowledge in successful power–knowledge constellations provides deconstructionism with its difficult methodological problems ('The success of power–knowledge mechanisms is proportional to their ability to hide themselves,' Foucault, 1978). We have already rejected the subjectivist method – questioning the subjects who make knowledge about their intentions will get us nowhere. Power–knowledge relations are not produced in or by the subjects who promote the knowledge. The relations are produced elsewhere, so that the question of researchers' intentions is the perfect decoy, deflecting attention from the social field to individual feelings, turning a social question into an introspective one. From *Discipline and Punish*: 'Analysis should not concern itself with power at the level of conscious intention or decision. It should not attempt to consider power from its internal point of view and it should refrain from posing the labyrinthine and unanswerable question: who then has power and what has he in mind?'

How are we to conceive of such determinations of knowledge outside the people who produce knowledge? It is here that deconstructionism is inspired by Saussure's linguistic structuralism and is thereby appropriately termed a poststructuralism. Let us mention just a few of the most relevant Saussurean principles. Here are three.

First, the language system into which any individual is born is a social system, essentially anonymous and not the invention of any one person or group of persons. For language to operate as communication it must be fundamentally nonpersonal, intersubjective rather than subjective, not private.

Second, the intersubjective language field is the product of innumerable historic influences, geographic changes, political shifts, economic developments, and so on, which, taken as a whole, produce arbitrary changes over time. Different sets of historic influences gave rise to the development of the French and Chinese languages, for example, so that they can have different sounds for the same meanings. These differences are products of myriad events outside the intrinsic logic of the language system – from the point of view of the intrinsic workings of the system, they are arbitrary in that no sound is superior to any other. Saussure demonstrated that seemingly logical etymological progressions over time are often more accidental than we would at first imagine, and the etymological logic often breaks down at the most fundamental points, the derivation of roots, which change arbitrarily over time.

Third, at any given time the language field consists of a set of rules determining what can be said and not said. Only certain sounds (signifiers) can be used to designate certain meanings (signifieds). Differences in language rule systems arising over time or across space do not make differences just on the side of sound, but also on the side of meaning. Historic changes are not merely a matter of ever-new sounds for the same old meanings. Thus, the arbitrary changes over time determine not only what can be said and not said, but also what meaning distinctions can be thought and not thought. With Saussure the *cogito* as source of thought is replaced by an anonymous dispersed language field, outside of and determining the knowing subject. Foucault (1979) expressed this Saussurean principle in the following way: 'Power–knowledge relations are to be analyzed not on the basis of a subject of knowledge; on the contrary, the subject of knowledge as well as the objects known and modes of knowing, ought all to be considered effects of power relations.'

Foucault's insight and fecundity were in imagining a whole host of anonymous social structures, which, like language rules, determine what can be said and not said, thought and not thought. Foucault's daring was to reject structuralism's apoliticism, to recognize that structures determining discourse are often structures of social domination. But he also rejected the Marxist politicism which would locate oppression in rather than between subjects, that is, in a ruling class rather than in a social structure. 'Analysis should take power as something which circulates. It is never localized here or there, never in anybody's hands, never appropriated as commodity or piece of wealth. Power is employed and exercised through a net-like organization. Individuals or classes are the vehicles of power, not its source' (Foucault, 1980). Again, Foucault's position is an anti-subjectivism – the question of the 'who' of power relations is a deflection from the field where power operates. Multiple fields of power dynamics – economic, scientific, religious, for example – might temporarily form dominating cohesions, but those are rarely produced by some bad guy a the top of the heap. In fact, Foucault liked to demonstrate that the upper classes are, often as not, the objects of social repression; for example, in *History of Sexuality*, Vol. I, he reminded us that the repressive maneuvers of psychoanalysis were first practiced on the upper classes.

Investigation of power–knowledge mechanisms, instead of aiming at the distant and uppermost bad guys, ought to aim more 'locally', Foucault (1980) insisted.

> Analysis should not concern itself with the regulation and legitimation of power in their uppermost or central locations. Instead it should be concerned with power at its extremities, in its ultimate destinations, with those points where it becomes capillary, that is, in its most regional and local forms and institutions. Its paramount concern, in fact, will be with the point where power surmounts the rules of right, extends itself beyond those limits, invests itself in power techniques, equips itself with instruments and eventually even violent means of material intervention.

Power relations are given most concretely at their margins, in marginal situations, with marginal people. In psychology that is where power applies itself to either exclude or normalize.

Let us go to the margins of psychology for an example. The margins of *History of Sexuality*, Vol. I contain a footnote referring the reader to an even more marginal set of notes, unpublished but safely archived, notes describing events at Charcot's clinic where Freud claimed to have 'discovered' the sex instinct:

> A handwritten note gives an account of the session of November 25, 1877. The female subject exhibits hysterical spasms; Charcot suspends an attack by first placing his hand, then the end of a baton, on the woman's ovaries. He withdraws the baton and there is a fresh attack, which Charcot accelerates by administering inhalations of amyl nitrate [a sexual stimulant now sold in porno shops].

Foucault (1978) wondered about the young Freud in that clinic:

> Freud comes to the clinic. He sees interns giving women inhalations of amyl nitrate, and they bring them, intoxicated, for Charcot to see. The women adopt certain postures, say things. They are listened to and watched and then at a certain moment Charcot declares that this is getting ugly, he whispers to Freud: 'We must not speak of these genital causes.'

The 'discovery' of the sex instinct! Discovery? Have the sex instinct or else. It was a power production. Once produced, this theory of the sex instinct and hysteria has circulated far and wide to exclude both women and homosexuals. Constituted as an instinct, this item called sex ought to be aimed like a phallus, not diffuse like a woman, straight like an arrow, not perverted and inverted like a homosexual. As soon as sex was manufactured as an instinct, a whole set of exclusions, derisions and dominations were set into motion.

Why bring up such unseemly events? Maybe they are in the margins because that is where they belong. Can anything constructive be gotten out of such sordid details? In a way, no. Deconstructionism aims more to destruct than to construct. It aims to loosen systems that otherwise, in their self-satisfaction, in their seriousness, would produce ever more totalizing and totalitarian effects. The principle of deconstruction is anti-totalizing, the principle of 'N-1', as Deleuze and Guattari put it. The totalizing demands of the psychologies of unity are to be countered by stances of multiplicity, but these latter will not be achieved by adding more and more (for this is the very movement of totalization). From Deleuze and Guattari's *On the Line* (1983): 'A multiple must be made, not by continuously adding a higher dimension, but, on the contrary and most simply, by force of restraint, at the level of dimensions already available, by making N-1. Only thus does the one become part of the multiple: by always being subtracted from it.' Foucault (1972): deconstructionism 'is trying to deploy a dispersion that can never be reduced to a single system; a scattering; it is trying to operate a decentering that leaves no privilege to any center'.

The goal is to build up a 'strategic knowledge' in the arena of power plays, which is the arena of surface events, unscientized, unpsychoanalyzed, unhermeneuticized (all techniques of deflection to more 'serious' matters). We evade these deflective maneuvers despite the serious/nonserious ideological coercion, inverting the old adage that it is good (and hard) to build, bad (and easy) to destroy. It was Nietzsche who warned us to look for strategies of domination when we hear talk of virtue. Fortified by Saussure's structuralism, we make the inversion. Anonymous and arbitrary systems of social constraint, such as language rules, are largely impervious to destructive maneuvers by persons or groups of persons. The fact is that deconstruction is a most difficult task. Social systems are characterized by inertia. Change is slow and rarely the result of individual efforts. Social systems are at work to sustain themselves so that the most vigilant deconstructionist movements will never deconstruct to chaos, but at their best, will loosen, create some slight flexibility, some momentary social tolerance. Part of the dynamic of inertia involves our fears regarding not plugging into the system. 'Danger. Watch out. The slightest deviation and everything will go up in smoke' – in *Molecular Revolution* (1984) Guattari parodies the party line. Society is vigilant in its attempt to prevent the introduction of the negative.

Deconstructionism is vigilant in return. 'My point is not that everything is bad, but that everything is dangerous, which is not exactly the same as bad. If everything is dangerous, then we always have something to do. So my position leads not to apathy but to a hyper activitism' (Foucault, 1980). Deconstructionism is a pessimistic activism that expects to find domination and control in the most innocent places, especially in the innocent places. Like the innocent places of the 'reformed' mental health system. Now there is an elaborate exclusionary and normalizing machinery that Foucault treated at length. According to Foucault our present machine had its origins in the Age of Reason: what to do with the unreasonable? Exclude them along with the criminals, it was decided. But soon that exclusion recoded itself. The irrational distinguished themselves from the other prisoners by refusing to take part in the collective work of the prison, no matter how cruel the tortures. Then there were two codings: irrational and unproductive. Moral and economic social machines joined up, and that pairing remains our definition of psychosis today.

Foucault made a melodrama to set the stage for *Madness and Civilization*, his major work on the mental health machine. He made an eerie beginning that is his reaction to the horrifying documents on the treatment of the mad a few centuries ago:

> At the end of the Middle Ages, leprosy disappeared from the Western world. In the margins of the community, at the gates of the cities, there stretched wastelands which sickness had ceased to haunt but had left sterile and long uninhabitable. For centuries these reaches would belong to the nonhuman – dogs, rats. From the fourteenth to the seventeenth century, they would wait, soliciting with strange incantations a new incarnation of disease, another grimace of terror, renewed rites of purification and exclusion. (Foucault, 1973b)

For many years the mad would be locked up, absorbing bizarre tortures, refusing to work no matter what, recalcitrant, catatonic. Then came the great breath of fresh air, the new moral therapy that replaced torture with psychological introspection. Exclusion of the mad would not be for the sake of exclusion; it would be exclusion for the sake of inclusion. Exclude from society in order to rehabilitate into society – the invention of a double-speak that is still popular in psychology today. Foucault (1973b) wrote about this breath of fresh air: 'The sufferer was caught in a relation to himself that was of the order of transgression, and a nonrelation to others that was of the order to shame.' Think here of today's halfway houses, where a requisite shame and contrite attitude is the admission ticket.

Freud, far from divesting himself of this old moralism, scientized it and thereby legitimized it for the twentieth century. The pseudo-family set-up, established in the Quaker hospitals in the age of morality, the importance of therapist as father-figure, the introspective turn, the importance of character (ego) strength – all these continued themselves in psychoanalysis, continued to denigrate and diminish the psychotic individual. 'Apparently this new pseudo-family is supposed to place the patient in a milieu both normal and natural,' Foucault wrote (1973b). The comfort of a strong dad, the comfort of a family. But in reality the situation alienates the patient even more because it is so obviously not a family, only a 'fictitious family decor of signs and attitudes', as Foucault put it. Yet the patient is asked to play the stupid game, to infantize himself. Halfway houses with their stupid rules. Telling a thirty-year-old man who has committed no crime to be good or he will not get TV tonight.

The denigration of psychotic anti-productive desire is not enough. The desire is considered downright dangerous. Guattari's passage from *Molecular Revolutions*, already mentioned above: 'Danger. Watch out. The slightest deviation and everything will go up in smoke. A specially close watch must be kept on those unsavory little groups whose words and turns of phrase and attitudes could easily contaminate whole populations.' Not only labeled with some belittling psycho-term, anti-productive desire must be defused as well as labeled. The defusion is accomplished by a diffusion, splitting the desire up, spreading it out. Like infantization, this maneuver depends first of all on transference, that is, on authority. The desire is split up, part staying where it was, part transferred to the therapist. Once transferred, it is interpreted, split again and again, duplicated and reduplicated, coded, recoded and overcoded, until, exhausted by the weight of interpretation, it deflates. In an interview, Deleuze commented on Foucault: you have taught us the indignity of being represented, of being interpreted. Interpretation is employed to tell people what they should want. The idea that the madman may simply not *want* to be productive is anathema; he must want something else, something hidden.

The new hermeneutic emphasis has done nothing for the politics of psychodynamic theory. In the most strictly humanistic, psychological, demedicalized forms, psychodynamic theory relates to psychosis as the same normalizing mechanism that it has been all along, leveling anti-productive desire with interpretation instead of thorazine. In *Molecular Revolutions*, Guattari characterizes the technique of interpretation as a fundamentally capitalist enterprise, not in the sense that it is economically driven, which it certainly is, but rather in the sense that the principle of exchange is omnipotent: 'capitalism reduces everything to a state of shit, of an amorphous and simplified flux from which everyone must extract his own share in his own private and guilt-ridden way. The keynote is exchange: absolutely anything, in the proper proportions, can be equivalent to anything else.' It is the hermeneutic principle.

In *Anti-Oedipus* (1977), Deleuze and Guattari quote Melanie Klein exercising her billyclub of interpretation:

> The first time Dick came to me he manifested no sort of affect when his nurse handed him over to me. When I showed him the toys I had put ready, he looked at them without the faintest interest. I took a big train and put it beside a smaller one and called them Daddy-train and Dick-train. Thereupon he picked up the train I called Dick and made it roll to the window and said 'station.' I explained: the station is mummy. Dick is going into mummy. He left the train, ran into the space between the outer and inner doors of the room, shutting himself in, saying 'dark' and ran out again directly. He went through this performance several times. I explained to him: it is dark inside mummy. Dick is inside dark mummy. Meantime he picked up the train again, but soon ran back into the space between the doors. While I was saying that he was going into dark mummy, he said twice in a questioning way: 'Nurse?'

The poor kid was scared, and who can blame him? We imagine that by avoiding objectification and medicalization, the hermeneutic, psychodynamic and humanistic trends in psychology somehow transcend the job of social control that is explicit in other forms of psychology. Nothing could be farther from the truth. In the end, the prying interpretations of humanistic and psychodynamic approaches are far more efficient at normalizing than are either the anti-psychotic drugs of the medical approach or the shaping techniques of behaviorism. Psychology – all of it – is a branch of the police; psychodynamic and humanistic psychologies are the secret police.

References

Adorno, T. (1973) *Negative Dialectics*. New York: Continuum.
Deleuze, G. and Guattari, F. (1977) *Anti-Oedipus*. New York: Viking.
Deleuze, G. and Guattari, F. (1983) *On the Line*. New York: Semiotext.
Foucault, M. (1972) *The Archeology of Knowledge*. New York: Harper Colophon.
Foucault, M. (1973a) *The Order of Things*. New York: Random House.
Foucault, M. (1973b) *Madness and Civilization*. New York: Random House.
Foucault, M. (1978) *History of Sexuality*, Vol. I. New York: Random House.
Foucault, M. (1979) *Discipline and Punish*. New York: Random House.
Foucault, M. (1980) *Power/Knowledge*. New York: Pantheon.
Foucault, M. (1982) The subject and power. *Critical Inquiry*, 8 (Summer): 777–95.
Guattari, F. (1984) *Molecular Revolutions*. New York: Penguin.

7

Postmodernism and Subjectivity

Lars Løvlie

Postmodernism – culture as sign

If you asked me 'What is postmodernism?' I would be hard put to answer. We are, of course, used to expecting that the suffix '-ism' denotes either a *Weltanschauung* or a position or an argument. When Jean Baudrillard blots out the difference between illusion and reality by declaring culture a 'limitless proliferation of signs' (Baudrillard, 1988: 22), it is an imaginative *Weltanschauung*. When Jacques Derrida makes 'writing' his critical point of view, it is a philosophical position. When Paul de Man criticizes the rhetoric of romanticism, it is a literary argument. But postmodernism is this and many more things, so the answer is still very much in the open.

Baudrillard is a good read. His *Amérique* (1986) keeps you in suspense by its ironic balance between personal idiosyncrasies and cultural analysis. Derrida's and de Man's texts are heavier going with their often subtle theoretical or philosophical ambitions. What these authors have in common is the rhetorical point of view, which says that reason is determined, not by logic, but by the turns and twists of metaphoric language. We may believe ourselves to be the masters of language. In fact it is more apt to say that language masters us. Language can then be described as a structure of signs which is itself the repository of meaning, independent of reference to the 'facts' of the world or the intentions of a subject.

Instead of being defined by the correspondence between word and world or between sign and its factual referent, meaning is now found in the relation between signs. That is to say, signs do not have meaning in themselves but get their meaning by the distinctive place they occupy in contrast to other signs in the network of language. This, incidentally, makes the traditional search for definitions not only dubious, but futile. A definition fixes the relation between signifier and signified, between word and concept. The postmodernist wants, by contrast, to untie that connection to allow the free play of signs. He does not go for identity but for the manifold and equivocal. Now, why not go along with postmodernism and give up trying to define it? We may still use the word 'postmodernism' as an index term pointing towards a position which is set apart from traditional ones. It is a different position which in fact makes difference itself its point of view. Postmodernism is one voice in the many-faceted discourse of (post)modern times.

Death of the subject

I have established as my first index of postmodernism the idea of culture as a system of signs. My next index is the postmodernist declaration of the 'death of the subject'. This declaration strikes the theme of this chapter, which is about the place of the subject in postmodernism. First of all, the death of the subject is of considerable interest as a critical philosophical statement. Secondly, taken at face value, it seems to eliminate a basic presupposition of psychology and education: the idea of an autonomous and intentional agent. Thirdly, the declaration may provide an avenue to some central problems of postmodernity.

The problem of modern subjectivity may be elucidated by way of three images: the 'thread of life', the 'circle' and the 'core'. As for the first image, tradition will have it that the perfect development of individual life follows a continuous course from origin to end, from birth to death. Even if it allows for the brittleness of life, this is the image of a more or less consistent theme unfolding throughout a life; historical time being the harmonizer. Goethe put the image to literary use in *Wilhelm Meister's Lehrjahre* (1795–6), making a genre of the *Bildungsroman* or 'formation novel', characteristically portraying the formation of a person through stages of life, ending in the reconciliations of ripe adulthood. Hegel's *Phenomenology of Spirit* (1807/1977) made formation the project of the world spirit, marking the apotheosis of formative reason. This is the idea of continuity, linking the origin (*arche*) and the goal (*telos*) of life, as in the romantic vision of the child unfolding its innate abilities and talents towards a final ripening. The postmodernist regards such adventures as the fond delusions of the tradition. He wants to replace it by the image of the severed thread, by the discontinuous and by the fragmentary which never reaches a final fulfilment.

The second image, that of the circle, is the image of a final reconciliation of opposites and contradictions into a harmonious whole. In the history of education, Friedrich Schiller is the great harmonizer. *On the Aesthetic Education of Man* (1795) sets the task for aesthetic education: to join the 'laws of nature' and the 'laws of reason' in the *play* of feeling and thinking. Play frees the subject from both the compulsion of nature and the constraints of reason, bringing the contradictory forces into active harmony.

We are also reminded that Friedrich Froebel, the father of the kindergarten, had the ball or the sphere as one of the 'play gifts' for children. The sphere suggests the harmonious totality of man and world, individual and society, thought and feeling. The postmodernist cracks this totality open, laying bare the fissures and fractures both within and without the subject, ever denying him or her the satisfaction of finally rounding it off. Jean-François Lyotard describes communication in modern society in terms of an 'agonistics', where 'to speak is to fight' (Lyotard, 1984: 10). Agonistics is directed against the idea of discourse and consensus as a totalizing force, an idea Lyotard detects in Habermas's theory of communicative action.[1]

As for the image of a core, that is, the idea of a centre or origin from which things grow or unfold, the Rousseauian idea of 'natural' man is a case in point. In *Émile* (1762) Rousseau traces morality and reason back to their origin in human nature. The idea of a pristine core of natural reason is the special target of the postmodernist. In his or her view it connects with the traditional ideas of an essence or spirit or truth inhering in subjectivity. Worse even, thinking in terms of a centre invites an authority that leaves us defenceless against impostors of every description, be it philosophers, politicians or professors of education. What some readers see as the incoherent literary antics of Derrida may be taken as an attempt to escape the authority of established philosophical discourse, an authority which has its basis in the concepts of reason, logic and truth.

I have turned to the historical roots of the idea of subjectivity, both to hint at the breadth and authority of that notion and to suggest the scope of postmodernist critique. That critique stabs at the heart of the most cherished ideals of Western culture: the traditional view of science as a truth-seeking activity, of universal human rights as a political ideal and personal autonomy as an educational goal. Postmodernism is more than a squabble between contemporaries over intellectual hegemony (even if it is that, too). Intellectually, it is the voice of the modern sceptic, and violently so.

Now, to argue that in the current discourse called postmodernity the issue of subjectivity is the central theme seems paradoxical. As I have already intimated, postmodern writers seem all intent on making an end to the talk about the subject as a locus of reason and autonomy. Instead they invoke writing (Derrida) or power (Foucault) or narrative (Lyotard) as the encompassing and anonymous forces swallowing up individuality, dismissing the idea of self-reflection celebrated as philosophy's main concern from Plato to our own days. Yet, the postmodernist writer seems unable to make his or her points without implying a subject. Any writer denying the existence of the subject does it, of necessity, in the name of the author subject. So the subject paradoxically rears its head by the declaration of its death. We shall see that in the end the death of the 'old' subject engenders a new but less ambitious notion of the subject.

Deconstruction

At stake in the postmodernist discussion is the idea of the subject as an indubitable point of reference for thought and action, and as the locus of freedom and truth. Let us follow the postmodernist argument. To do that I shall narrow my perspective from post-modernism to 'deconstruction', mentioning only some of the issues connected with the deconstruction of the subject. The word is a hybrid between 'destruction' and 'construction', conveying the idea that old and obsolete concepts have to be demolished for new ones to be erected. Norris defines it as the 'vigilant seeking-out of those "aporias", blind-spots or moments of self-contradiction where a text involuntarily betrays the tension between rhetoric and logic, between what it manifestly *means to say* and what it is nonetheless *constrained to mean*' (Norris, 1987: 19). The question is, what is deconstruction aiming to replace? Let me try and answer the question by starting in a somewhat roundabout way.

Self-presence

Most people would agree that the experience of self is an immediate or intuitive act of consciousness. For me to say, for instance, that 'I am trying to find myself' cannot be taken literally. If I did not already know myself in a fundamental way I could not even make the statement. I would not in fact know what I was talking about, unless we imagine the perfect teacher telling me about myself and per-suading me that it was true of me that I actually had a self and therefore could know it. That knowledge could of course, induce me to utter the sentence above and make me start *talking* about my self (which would be the perfect example of indoctrination). But would that amount to a knowledge of self and could it make me *mean* what I said?

Derrida challenges the idea of 'self-presence'. This is not to question the view of the former paragraph: that we grasp our self in an immediate act of self-reflection. It is directed rather against a view that seems to follow naturally from it: that this self is truly described in terms of a centre or essence of personality. This view suggests that our thoughts, intentions and actions issue from an 'I' inside me, being part of my character. When I speak of personal thoughts, honest intentions or authentic choice, I also presuppose a principle of unity holding my life together as *my* life and not the life of anybody else. This may be called the principle of the 'one in the many'. The principle represents the psychological version of the classical idea of unity or *logos*, which gathers, as it were, the particulars of my psyche under a common description.

Authenticity

There is another idea that is closely linked to the principle of the one in the many. It is the idea that what is true of self-present consciousness is also, by extension, true of what I say. We all know the feeling that at the very moment of stating a fact or formulating an insight, what we say is simply and unquestionably true. Especially in the case of a new and maybe radical insight, telling it to somebody else seems to coincide with the truth of the insight. There seems to be an immediate bond between what I say and what I mean, between sound and sense. Truth is tied in a privileged way to the spoken word so that what I say has the full power of authenticity. Derrida's expression 's'entendre parler' conveys this intimate relation between intent and meaning: it means both to hear oneself speak and to grasp the meaning of what one says in one single act. Since this is what characterizes authentic speech we may call it the 'principle of authenticity'.

If we now ask what deconstruction is, we have part of the answer: it is the critique of the two principles of the one in the many and of authenticity. That is, the critique of 'logocentrism' as the idea of a centred reason ordering our universe and of 'phonocentrism', the idea that truth inheres in the spoken word, in listening to the other in dialogue. Or, if you want, it is the critique of the image of the core. The deconstruction of logocentrism is, by implication, a critique of Enlightenment political reason with its belief in universal principles of freedom and equality and a universal political solidarity.

On the other hand, the deconstruction of phonocentrism implies a critique of the Enlightenment belief in truth as centred in autonomous individuals and authentically uttered in statements, judgements and actions. Broadly speaking, both the Hegelian idea of a unifying historical reason and the Kierkegaardian idea of an authentic subject are here scattered to the winds. Instead we get fragments or 'fractals' of reason and an anonymous individual submitted to the play of structure, power or narrativity. The question now is, what is the theoretical step that takes us from the traditional view of rational man to that of postmodern man?

The structure of signs

A clue is found in the work of Ferdinand Saussure, who set out to criticize the idea that what I say refers to some independent and self-sufficient thing or reality. He questioned the view that the relation between signs or between signifier and signified was fixed in logical correspondence. In his theory the units of a system of signs cannot by themselves be positively defined. They are rather the products of relations or differences between signs and therefore in a certain way both arbitrary and as such undecidable.

Consider, for instance, the words 'bed', 'beg' and 'bag'. The point is that these terms cannot be exhaustively defined in themselves. They can, however, be defined 'negatively' by the differences that distinguish them from each other. They are, in Derrida's words, exposed to the play of differences, involving

> syntheses and referrals that prevent there from being at any moment or in any way a simple element that is present in and of itself and refers only to itself. Whether in written or in spoken discourse, no element can function as a sign without relating to another element which itself is not simply present. This linkage means that each 'element' – phoneme or grapheme – is constituted with reference to the trace in it of the other elements of the sequence or system. This linkage, this weaving, is the *text*, which is produced only through the transformation of another text. (Derrida, quoted in Culler, 1982: 99)

Because of the fundamental undecidability of its elements, we cannot pin down the truth of a statement or a text.

The subject as text

Deconstructed, the 'text' is the system of differences, transformations and substitutions. The radical deconstructionist move is to *constitute the subject as text* (or the text as subject), making it impossible for that subject to refer to itself in any consistent way, independent of the world of signs it is enmeshed in. The text replaces the transcendental ego of Kant. In this scheme the subject is doomed to perpetual exile from itself. It is exposed to the endless substitutions of meanings. 'The absence of the transcendental signified [read: self-present subjectivity – L.L.] extends the domain and the play of signification [read: the projection of meaning – L.L.] infinitely' (Derrida, 1981: 278). By letting the subject be swallowed up in the text, the transformation of 'essential' rational man into 'relative' postmodern man is fulfilled.

Anonymous self

Deconstruction may, as I have already said, be taken as an effort to construct by destruction. Let us pursue the idea of the subject as text, that is, submitted to or enmeshed in the ever-changing permutations of its own life. The steps taken are important. First of all, doubt has been thrown on the idea that subjectivity is the essential unity of self or reason. Then the bold move was taken towards describing subjectivity as a structure of signs. By this version of the 'linguistic turn' the idea of a centre as either an origin or an end had to be discarded and replaced by the notion of subjectivity without a centre. A radical interpretation of this turn really seems to do away with individuality in the usual sense and replaces it by the free play of structure itself, throwing the subject into the abyss of anonymity.

We get a sense of this anonymity by reading self-descriptions informed by postmodern sociological parlance. On the day of the Copenhagen Marathon in late May 1989, the Danish newspaper *Informationen* ran an interview with one of the would-be participants. The interview ends by the participant denying that running is a running away from oneself (the old 'centrist' psychological explanation). Instead he rather creates himself with all the roles he plays as a student of cultural sociology, as lover and friend and as a runner. He stages himself as the sportsman who is on top of things or – and here is the ironic twist – who at least looks as if he is. The self as the ensemble of stage performance plays up to the idea of a relative self *that knows it is a relative self.* But this irony does not counter or invalidate the self-description; it does not bring us back to a centre of subjectivity. It only extends the self-description indefinitely in a proliferation *ad infinitum* of social poses, the self captured only in the play of new roles; the reflective 'I' but one of them. The self is this proliferation of roles, the progressive showing of (sur)faces.

The defeat of truth

A philosophical version of the irony of signs is found in the account of Rousseau's inability in the autobiographical *Confessions* to fulfil his pledge on the opening page that he is going to give the reader a portrait of himself 'in every way true to nature'. At this point we are reminded of the argument against phonocentrism. That argument questions the belief that the spoken word is the 'natural' or primal bearer of truth. I adhere to the logic of Derrida's analysis, which has the merit of showing both the productivity of 'postmodern' irony and its plausibility as an argument for the deconstruction of the classical subject.

For Rousseau the question 'Who am I?' is answered by his belief in the immediate access to his own authentic self; he can 'feel his own heart'. The truth about himself is not hidden from him behind a veil of ignorance or buried in the depths of his unconscious. The problem is that although his feelings are written on his face, he remains very much a closed book to other people. What he sets out to do in the *Confessions* is to overcome this tremendous obstacle to truth; he wants everybody to 'read his heart'. He wants this inner truth to become 'transparent to the reader' in order to be justly judged and recognized by others. Truth and justice are to him 'synonymous words'. In the end, then, he hopes to be declared innocent of the charges levelled against him in his encounters with others. 'Rousseau appeals the judgment that has been brought against him, seeking a revision of the verdict in which he will not only be found innocent but also recognized as innocent; he wants both his authenticity and his righteousness confirmed' (Starobinski, 1988: 184).

Since he has not been able to convince his adversaries of his just intentions, Rousseau now feels compelled to give up speech and turn to writing. He does not do it gladly: 'Languages are to be spoken, writing serves only as a supplement to speech. . . . Thus the art of writing is nothing but a mediated representation of thought' (Rousseau, quoted in Derrida, 1976: 144). Writing is only a substitute for the real thing, which is authentic speech.

Nature as supplement

Writing, then, becomes a supplement to speech, a medium for the presentation of the self. But here is where the irony of the project is revealed. There is the double and in the end contradictory meaning of the word 'supplement'. In the first place it denotes addition and enrichment. By turning to the written word conventions, idioms and metaphors help the author express his or her feelings and thoughts in an adequate way. On the other hand, to supplement also means to substitute, to replace. It is an exterior addition and therefore in a certain sense alien to its content. 'It intervenes or insinuates itself *in-the-place-of*.' But as a substitute 'it produces no relief, its place is assigned in the structure by the mark of emptiness' (Derrida, 1976: 145).

This 'emptiness' is an instance of what Derrida calls *différance*, and suggests that meaning is both 'differential' and 'deferred', that is, differentiated in structure and time. *Différance* refers here to the gap between Rousseau's professed intentions and their fulfilment in writing. We have seen that Rousseau thought of speech as natural in the sense of belonging to the nature of the individual Jean-Jacques. But precisely by speaking his heart and communicating the natural in its pristine quality the whole project backlashes; in the process of writing the natural is adulterated and made unnatural. The difference is the fact that the expected satisfaction of the natural impulse is paradoxically deferred.

Writing over speech

The novelty in Derrida's rendering of Rousseau's plight is not found in the contradiction mentioned above. It is an instance of the well-known pragmatic paradox, where my intention is contradicted by the way I try to realize it.[2] The important thing is how it reiterates and implements the linguistic point of view: that language has its own ways with us, that I am not, in a fundamental way, the author (and therefore the *auctoritas*) of my own identity. Rousseau may very well *feel* that he is about to realize the best of intentions, but the moment he tries to communicate the feeling language plays havoc with his project. Communication is brittle and the dissolution of meaning an inherent threat.

Derrida goes on to make the further point that 'writing', as the play of language revealed in rhetoric, is not secondary to speech. Rhetoric is at play in speech as well. It is only the classical aberrant notion of subjectivity as essential self that could persuade Rousseau and his readers to make the mistaken distinction between authentic and inauthentic self-presentation. Writing just demonstrates the vanity of holding on to the distinction between authentic speech and inauthentic writing and by implication to the notion of basic authenticity.

Difference is also manifest in Rousseau's *Émile* in its characteristic way, which repeats the contradictory pattern of an opposition between nature and nurture. The professed aim of *Émile* is to account for an education which listens to nature and redeems nature in the very process of education itself. If, however, nature is to serve as a foundation of education, it has to be essential, original and self-sufficient. But education actually is a cultural and supplementary activity. Giving education the task of making nature more natural only makes nature insufficient and secondary. 'It is indeed culture or cultivation that must supplement a deficient nature, a deficiency that cannot by definition be anything but an accident and a deviation from nature' (Derrida, 1976: 146). Precisely by trying to realize nature as the origin of the educational enterprise, the goal of that enterprise is always one remove from its fulfilment.

Both nature and the kindred notion of something natural or

uncontaminated in individuality turn out to be a presupposition without foundation. Their fictitious character is shown by their always escaping a final grasp. The goal is deferred by the work of a 'spacing' or a time gap that cannot bridge beginning and end. This is why, in the opinion of the postmodernist, we actually have to stop talking of personal life or development in terms of continuous processes. The idea of a *Bildung* or formation running in a more or less straight line from birth to death cannot be sustained. That, incidentally, means a farewell to the most treasured image in the history of education. Instead we are persuaded to think of development in terms of hesitations, reservations and displacements; of disappointments, discontinuities and reversals.

Another feature characterizing the rhetorical point of view is its suspicion of metaphors of inner and outer, the hidden and the revealed, cause and effect. Consider the case of psychoanalysis, with it topology of conscious and unconscious. According to Norris (1987), there are marked similarities between Derrida's deconstructive reading of Rousseau and Jacques Lacan's insistence that the unconscious is structured like a language, dominated by the two figures of speech: metaphor and metonymy. Metaphor is at work in the words and symbols used by the patient as pointers to foci of meaning that escape conscious and logical articulation. Metonymy is the figure of speech that gives the part for the whole, as in expressions like 'All hands on deck' ('hands' being short for men) or 'Believe my heart' ('heart' standing for feelings).

In our context metonymy is by far the most interesting, focusing on desire as a process of displacements, substitutions and deferrals that can never reach its object in authentic being. In the case of Rousseau the desire to tell his reader 'everything that has happened to me, everything that I have done, everything that I have thought, everything that I have felt' (Starobinski, 1988: 189) can never be redeemed. His attempt to grasp the whole of his life is consistently dissolved in fragments of desire and intention. The use of the word 'everything' seduces us into thinking or expecting a unity, a final and rounded version of a life. Trying to *write* it down, however, reveals to us that we can only have 'every thing', that is, particulars and not universals. The project of revealing everything comes to grief in the very process of writing, the vagaries of the text never touching the real or natural Jean-Jacques.

The fiction of the unconscious

Returning to Lacan, his approach questions the Freudian topology, especially the idea that the secret of the psyche is found in the hidden depths of the unconscious:

For such is the delusion . . . encouraged by those versions of psychoanalysis which think to delve deep into the patient's psyche by uncovering the truths of repressed experience *behind* or *beyond* the surface complexities of language. The analyst should rather proceed by attending closely to the logic of the *signifier*, to those detours and swerves in the discourse of the patient which mark the irruption of unconscious desire. (Norris, 1987: 115)

This is to argue that interpretation should not take us outside of or behind writing, but literally stick to the letter of the text.

The critique of the classical metaphor of the unconscious is radicalized by Bert States in his book *The Rhetoric of Dreams*. There he proposes to eliminate the unconscious altogether. By denying the old idea of dreams being the royal road to the unconscious, he challenges the idea of dividing the dream in a latent mental content subsequently made manifest by the dream work. Apart from the dubious invitation to think of unconscious intentions, the metaphor of the unconscious thrives on another 'centrist' idea, the one about a homunculus, literally a 'little man' motivating us from deep within ourselves. States sticks to the view that dreams 'do not *mean* to mean anything, and that the clinical act of retrieval of meaning does not imply that dreams are telling the dreamer something he needs to know about himself or preventing him from finding out something that might disturb his sleep' (States, 1988: 29).

States's argument is epistemological rather than psychological. His view is that there is nothing 'deep' in dreams. So we may as well do away with the 'two-mind system' of the conscious and the unconscious. If this tack is taken, psychoanalysis must rid itself of its pretensions of proceeding by causal explanations and start seeing itself as a purely hermeneutic science. The implications are far-reaching. In one bold move repressions, displacements and transferences are lifted from the inside of the psyche to the 'outside' of the text; the archaeology of the psyche is replaced by a kind of literary analysis, a teasing out of figures of speech in the rhetoric of dreams and action.[3]

We are persuaded to confer meaning on dreams in a creative and constructive act of interpretation. States likens the dream to a *pharmakos*, alluding to the ancient habit of sacrificing individuals to expiate the sins of a city. The dream becomes a kind of *pharmakos* that is sacrificed to a better understanding of a person's world. It has no meaning in itself, but gains its meaning by being put into the network of a person's beliefs. Dreams are not products of (unconscious) meanings, but rather productive of meanings. Dreams are what we make of them. The thrust of interpretation is not regressive, but progressive and even futuristic.

How can this view be sustained? A clue may be found in the

distinction between causes and reasons. States does not say that dreams do not have causes. He only argues that these causes are simply physiological processes in the brain which do not determine the content of a given dream. On this view, dreams are caused by complex neurological and hormonal exchanges in the brain. What is hidden from our introspection is not unconscious mental states like impulses, wishes or wants, but simply brain-states. Physical events may cause feelings, images and thoughts. But mental events are not in the mind the way physical events are in the brain. Confusion follows when mental states are conflated with physical states, making the (unconscious) mental the cause of dream imagery.

This confusion parallels that between causes and reasons. Seeing the green man may *cause* me to cross the street. If, on the other hand, you asked me why I crossed the street, I would give you my *reasons* for doing so (avoiding the risks of jay-walking or being on my way to an important appointment). Reasons, just like intentions, can be hidden from others, but not from myself (*pace* weakness of will and bad faith); they are not unconscious. Now, dreams are like reasons. They are accessible to anyone; they are public in the sense of being open to interpretation. To say, then, that there are unconscious reasons for dreams, implying an under or behind, is a contradiction in terms. While causes of dreams are found in physical events, reasons for dreams are found in the dreams themselves, that is, in the interpretation of the dream as text.[4] Just as there are causes of dreams, and reasons for their retention and interpretation, there are no causes for their truth. The truth of dreams is entirely of our own making.[5]

The implications for education are far reaching. First of all, teachers will have to lay off pretensions of saying anything meaningful by explaining the behaviour of pupils by early trauma or conflict. Behaviour has to be taken at face value in its present context, without invoking behind-the-scenes mechanisms. Secondly, behaviour points beyond its own presence and to its possible or future interpretations. The behaviour of the pupil is not a fact but rather an artefact which awaits its future meaning. That future meaning is inherently dependent on the rhetoric used in its rendering. The postmodern paradigm for education is a rhetoric ironically aware of its own transience.

The contradictory self

Let me return for a moment to the question of the death of the subject. If we take the slogan at face value, it certainly spells the death of an almost indispensable notion. The Kantian idea of a moral subject taking the ultimate responsibility for his or her actions is inextricably linked to that notion. The same holds for the romantic ideas of a self-creative individual transcending the boundaries of social and political restrictions, as well as for the pragmatic belief in a problem-solving individual aiming at the reconstruction of personal and cultural ideals. In fact, declaring the notion of autonomous individuality null and void is to give the Enlightenment idea of a rational human being short shrift. Let us not jump to conclusions, but rather retrace our steps a little, to the crucial problem of the self of the autobiography.

From what has been said about language as a structure of signs and of writing as a self-defeating activity, we should not expect the survival of the self even of the autobiography. In his essay 'Autobiography as de-facement' (1984) Paul de Man bears out our suspicion. There he looks into the distinction between fiction and autobiography, arguing that even if autobiography is rooted in the story of a single subject who is identical with the author on the title page, the distinction between the two is undecidable and cannot be upheld.

We are inclined to believe that while fiction has no reference to an authorial self, autobiography is defined by having a clear reference to the self of the author:

> But are we so certain that autobiography depends on reference, as a photograph depends on its subject or a (realistic) picture on its model? We assume that life *produces* the autobiography as an act produces its consequences, but can we not suggest, with equal justice, that the autobiographical project may itself produce and determine the life and that whatever the writers does is in fact governed by the technical demands of self-portraiture and thus determined, in all its aspects, by the resources of his medium? (de Man, 1984: 69)

De Man's reminder is, of course, that recalling the past is not determined by authorial fiat, but by the author's medium, that is, language. The substantial self is lost in the context and creation of its own metaphors.

More specifically, the author's medium is that of recall and reconstruction of a life in the form of the rhetorical figure of *mimesis* or 'imitation'. The author may believe that he or she uses this form as a *means* to his or her own self-presentation. But again it is rather the other way round; the figure is the medium that takes hold of the author and determines the reconstruction and representations of his or her self, making it a fictional self in the very process. De Man's argument is strikingly like that of Derrida. The person who wants to inscribe his or her authentic self on the pages of a book is caught in a contradictory effort: trying to pin down his or her genuine self in writing exposes the author to the play and perversions of that very writing. The face one wants to present is lost in the strictures of the text, and the loss is self-imposed: 'Autobiography veils a defacement of the mind of which it is itself the cause' (p. 81).

Reconstruction of individuality

There is a common accusation against postmodernism that it is irrationalist to the hilt and irresponsible in the extreme. This characteristic hardly holds for deconstruction. Both Derrida and de Man expound theories and thereby join the common activity of testing and teasing out the positions of their adversaries. They partake in the traditional theoretical discourse, albeit in an innovative and at times bizarre fashion. Their approach is dialectical, not only in the sense that they go for the contradictory, but also in the sense that they work parasitically, as it were, on the philosophical and scientific heritage. When Derrida criticizes the 'metaphysical complicity' of traditional concepts like 'speech', 'structure' and 'sign', he is well aware of the need for this classical legacy, 'for we cannot give up this metaphysical complicity without also giving up the critique we are directing against this complicity' (Derrida, 1981: 281).[6]

De Man is not even interested in pressing the case for language, and by implication 'literariness', as constitutive of critical discourse. In his essay 'The resistance to theory' (1986), that is, to literary theory, he explains that resistance as a defence of vested interests and 'rooted ideologies' in the community of scholars. Then he adds a second kind of resistance, which is theory's 'negative' resistance against its own tendency to fossilize into established scientific canon; for 'theory is itself this resistance' to theory (de Man, 1986: 19).

In the end, then, neither Derrida nor de Man – and here we may include both Lyotard and Foucault – dissolves the *critical* subject. They are rather out to demolish ideological positions built on the idea of an epistemic subject being the centre of the world instead of being part of the text of the world. They are doing away with the 'philosophy of consciousness' without throwing out its baby, which is individuality. For instance when Foucault speaks of the relation between individual subject and anonymous 'power' he does it in view of the 'subjection' of individuality. In 'The subject and power', published in 1982, he speaks against the domination of and subjection by universal ideas and institutions, and concludes: 'We have to promote new forms of subjectivity through the refusal of this kind of individuality which has been imposed on us for centuries' (Foucault, 1982: 216).

The striking fact about the deconstructions of these writers is that they incessantly expose us to the irony of experience, that irony hovering between destruction and construction. The irony is part of their theory. In the name of the death of the subject their blend of contextualism and irony actually recaptures the modern individual in his or her position as reasonable and critical subject.

Notes

1 Habermas dispels any doubt about his anti-totalizing stand in his later writings (Lyotard wrote his book in the late 1970s). 'For the transitory unity . . . of a linguistically mediated consensus does not only support, but even furthers and accelerates, the pluralizing of life-forms and the individualization of lifestyles. The more discourse, the more contradiction and difference' (see Habermas, 1988: 180). Habermas's point is that the more abstract your criteria of truth, the more room for local differences of opinions and values.

2 The paradigm for this paradox was initially worked out in Hegel (1807/1977), especially the famous chapter 4, on the development of 'self-consciousness'. It is the story about spirit arriving at self-consciousness through the successive defeats of its own intentions and acts. In the Hegelian scheme these reversals – the way of 'doubt and despair' – are, however, 'sublated' or resolved into progressive experience, ending in 'absolute knowledge'. Therefore the story of the Hegelian spirit is a prime example of the 'grand narrative' denounced by postmodernism.

3 According to States, dreams are not even intrinsically linguistic; they do not 'speak', they only 'think'. When we choose to treat the dream as text, it 'belongs to no one, it has no intrinsic meaning' (1988: 32).

4 This view gets support from Hans Robert Jauss's 'aesthetic of reception'. The causal explanation of dreams neglects the fact that the meanings of a dream rest on the inherent indeterminacy and arbitrariness of interpretation (see Jauss, 1982).

5 See Richard Rorty (1991). Rorty's 'weak' version of postmodernism is pragmatic, in the tradition of Dewey and Wittgenstein. Rorty depicts himself as an 'ironist' who wants to 'poeticize' culture. His differences with the vehement critic of postmodernism, Jürgen Habermas, are, in his own words 'merely philosophical' (see Rorty, 1989: 61ff). Rorty's writings attest to the fact that the 'classical' pragmatism of Peirce, Mead and Dewey can actually forge a link between European 'rationalists' and 'poets', the Enlightenment tradition and postmodernism.

6 The position is, however, typically ambiguous in the case of Derrida. In an interview with Geoff Bennington he has this to say about postmodernism's 'enemy', the Enlightenment: 'Of course in some situations I am totally on the side of the Enlightenment as rationality, criticism, absolute suspicion against obscurantism, etc. . . . when I say we have to deconstruct a thing, I do not say we are *against* it, or that in any situation I will fight it, be on the other side. I think we should be on the side of the Enlightenment without being too naive, and on some occasions be able to question its philosophy' (quoted in Appignanesi, 1989: 220–1). Now, is Derrida a cool Machiavellian, here speaking as a university teacher, defending the rights of the university, while on other occasions he poses as the renegade critic? I think the answer is no. Derrida seems just consistently to practise the guerrilla-type intellectual tactics that offer themselves when there exists no centre for rationality and truth 'outside of the text'. The paradoxical strategy of defending rationality by defeating it is, of course, self-referentially inconsistent. But this inconsistency is only the premeditated stab at the heart of established rationality. The irony is that through the cracks in the old conception of rationality, rationality sprouts new branches.

References

Appignanesi, L. (ed.) (1989) *Postmodernism*. ICA Documents. London: Free Association Books.

Baudrillard, J. (1986) *Amérique*. Paris: Grasset.

Baudrillard, J. (1988) Transpolitik – transseksuel – transestetik. In *Kunstens og filosofiens værker efter emancipationen*. Copenhagen: Det Kongelige Danske Kunstakademi. pp. 21–35.

Culler, J. (1982) *On Deconstruction: Theory and Criticism after Structuralism*. Ithaca, NY: Cornell University Press.

de Man, P (1984) Autobiography as de-facement. In *The Rhetoric of Romanticism* Ithaca, NY: Cornell University Press. pp. 67–83.

de Man, P. (1986) The resistance to theory. In *The Resistance to Theory*. Minneapolis: University of Minnesota Press. pp. 3–21.

Derrida, J. (1976) *Of Grammatology*. Baltimore, MD: Johns Hopkins University Press.

Derrida, J. (1981) Structure, sign and play in the discourse of the human sciences. In *Writing and Difference*. London: Routledge & Kegan Paul. pp. 278–95.

Foucault, M. (1982) The subject and power. In H.L. Dreyfus and P. Rabinow, *Michel Foucault: Beyond Structuralism and Hermeneutics*. Brighton: Harvester.

Habermas, J. (1988) *Nachmetaphysisches Denken: Philosophische Aufsätze*. Frankfurt am Main: Suhrkamp.

Hegel, G.W.F. (1807/1977) *The Phenomenology of Spirit*. Oxford: Clarendon Press.

Informationen, 27–8 May 1989.

Jauss, H.R. (1982) *Toward an Aesthetic of Reception*. Minneapolis: University of Minnesota Press.

Lyotard, J.-F. (1984) *The Postmodern Condition*. Manchester: Manchester University Press.

Norris, C. (1987) *Derrida*. London: Fontana Modern Masters.

Rorty, R. (1989) *Contingency, Irony, and Solidarity*. Cambridge: Cambridge University Press.

Rorty, R. (1991) Non-reductive physicalism. In his *Objectivity, Relativism and Truth*. Cambridge: Cambridge University Press.

Starobinski, J. (1988) *Jean-Jacques Rousseau, Transparency and Obstruction*. Chicago: Chicago University Press.

States, B.O. (1988) *The Rhetoric of Dreams*. Ithaca, NY: Cornell University Press.

8

Postmodern Self-Psychology Mirrored in Science and the Arts

Neil Young

What if I went as a wandering scholar
To trace the past ages, the greed of mankind?
Yes, that's it! *There's* my place! . . .
I'll follow the course of the human race
I'll float like a feather on history's stream
Relive it all as if in a dream . . .
But as an onlooker safe in thought . . .
In short, I'll skim off history's cream . . .
(Brushing a tear from his eye.)
That's in the spirit of pure research!

(Ibsen, *Peer Gynt*)

Things fall apart; the centre cannot hold; mere
anarchy is loosed upon the world.
(William Butler Yeats, 'The second coming')

Before exploring postmodernism it is best to clarify what premodernism and modernism may mean in a variety of cultural contexts. Premodernist can be conceived as starting with the decline of the Greco-Roman or classical context for comprehending the nature of reality. In the fourth century the Judeo-Christian cultural context became the foundation for all assumptions and speculations about the nature of reality in Europe. All of the assumptions during this stage of the history of human consciousness were essentially theistic. The presence of a Creator was everywhere integral to the nature of reality. As Dante summed it all up in the *Divine Comedy*, reality was alive with the formations, transformations and deformations of 'the Love which moves the sun and the other stars' (1321/1939: 485). The cosmos was coherently, rationally and lovingly in order. Moreover, the world was seen and experienced as saturated with eternal significance. Everything was a clear sign of the Eternal Signifier and Signified; every creature was closely connected to the Eternal Source of all significance. Even space was not experienced as empty but overflowing with significance embodied in angelic intelligences. Angels (from the ancient Greek *angelos*, or messengers) were seen as messengers of meaning from the source of all meaning, and the space of the cosmos was fertile with their flashing communications. All of creation was assumed to be cared for by a transpersonal Creator whose intentions were rich with beauty, goodness, truth and wonder. Within this cultural context all of life was transparently meaningful. All of human experience emerges out of the context of an essential sense of 'being-at-home' in the home built by a cosmically transparent Homemaker.

Several assumptions abided in everyday community life in the Middle Ages (Smith, 1982). First, reality always implied the presence of a transpersonal Person out of whose womb creation appeared. Secondly, the structural dynamics and mechanics of the physical cosmos always exceeded our human comprehension. And thirdly, the source of human happiness was not in conquering nature, but in listening carefully to and living with commitment by the laws of life revealed by the Creator. It was the second of these assumptions which began to be radically questioned by the early Enlightenment scientists and philosophers. The Newtonian worldview assumed that the human mind was equal to the task of comprehending the laws of the physical cosmos. The felt and perceived presence of a personal Creator, who was married to matter, was erased out of the context of everyday experience. Theism was dissolved into deism. The Creator who had been so close and intimate with the human community became the distant cosmic clockmaker, who left creation to its own mechanical devices. With this new assumption modernism emerges as a dominant worldview.

Modernism, conceived by the scientific imagination, had three essential assumptions (Smith, 1982: 7). First, that the personal aspects of reality are decidedly less vital than the fact that reality is carefully structured and orderly. Second, that human reason is capable of comprehending these structures through the orderly laws of nature. Third, that human happiness consists in knowing and using these laws to improve material well-being. One of the first prophetic voices to radically challenge the assumptions of modernism was that of the Danish philosopher Søren Kierkegaard (1846/1962). He questioned the concepts that reality was essentially orderly and rational, or that human consciousness was at all capable of comprehending the laws of creation. Postmodern physics (which also emerged substantially in Denmark with the work of Niels Bohr) presented a cosmos almost completely contradictory to our rational way of imagining things. Modernism had challenged our senses with rational explanations of causality. Postmodern physics describes a cosmos which is increasingly difficult to imagine. Not only are apparently solid objects alive with electrons dancing around at a million times a second, but an electron is said to pass from orbit to orbit without passing through space. The frontiers of human consciousness are not only becoming more extensive, but also more ineffable. If the grounding of our human experience in the sensual and spiritual imagination was dissolved by modernism, then our grounding in the rational imagination was dissolved by post-modernism.

These series of transitions in human consciousness can also be seen graphically depicted in the history of the arts. European art up to and through the Enlightenment was created against a commonly shared context and background of objective values. Ortega y Gassett describes this very clearly, showing that when premodernist painters depicted an object they did so as a convergence on the specific structure of their field of vision. Using Ortega's example, when we look closely at an earthen jar our eyes converge on it and give it clarity. Around the object, in the background, is a vague, inattentive sense of vision. This 'close-up point of view' imposes an 'optical hierarchy; a privileged central nucleus articulated itself against the surrounding area' (Ortega y Gassett, 1925/1956: 102). When we view objects at a distance, free of focus, the hierarchical structure dissolves; the visual field is homogeneous; 'submerged in an optical democracy', boundaries scatter and dissolve.

Velasquez was an innovator in this visual evolution. He stopped the eye's migration from one surface to another. The eyes of the artist become in Copernican fashion the center of a more immediate and ambiguous cosmos, around which revolve the various forms of objects. He looks directly before him without preference for any objects. Each surface simply intercepts his vision spatially and temporally. He has shifted consciousness from a close-up to a distant viewpoint. Between the eye and the object is air and light, that is, empty space. As when we see through half-closed eyes, contours and solids dissolve in a democratic synthesis. His paintings can be viewed at a glance as unified and whole.

The close-up view emphasizes the specificity of shapes in a hierarchy of values; it is the medieval or premodern focus on the *thisness* (*huecitas*) of individual persons and objects. The distant view synthesizes, combines and confuses persons and objects in a demo-cratic display of perceptual experience. In the modernist movement the painting of solid shapes has become transformed into the painting of empty space.

With the emergence of Impressionism and Post-Impressionism the relation of the painter's eyes to the objects they behold continues to retreat along the self–object spectrum of relations farther toward the subjectivity of the painter. The viewpoint is now grounded upon the

actual surface of the eye itself and how light and color interplay
within the very process of perception itself. The locus of the creative
activity shifts from the representation of objects as they are seen
toward the very experience of seeing itself. The creative activity of
consciousness in this way withdraws its psychosocial investments (ca-
thexes) in the world at large and converts them into caring about the
experience of the self. This internalizing of the creative activity of the
artist shatters any attachment to the modernist mentality with the
emergence of Cubism. This matrix shift in the visual eye's evolution
toward postmodernism starts with Cézanne, who discovers cones,
cubes and cylinders in self-object relations. With him the sensation
functions of the artist are surrendered to the primacy of inwardly
generated impulses, ideas and images. The object now painted by the
artist arises more and more from within itself and is not an object dictated by the solidity of the sensate-based or 'common-sensical' social
and natural world of experience.

The shift of viewpoint along the spectrum of self–object relations
represented in the arts corresponds closely to the change in consciousness expressed in postmodern physics. Apparently solid objects which are assumed to behave in a rational way are starting to be
explored as chaotic, irrational and swimming with a subatomic fluid
continuity as well as within a shattered discontinuity. With postmodernism we begin to live in a cubist, and later abstract expression-
ist, cosmos. Both the postmodernist painter and physicist explore the
interiority of object-space, but with differing media. Postmodernism
has evolved out of a shift of values and viewpoints toward inwardness. It has been a Dionysian dissolution of Apollonian boundaries.
It has always been a decentering of attention and authority invested
in the world of external and orderly objects; the world order of
Apollo.

If the movements of Western consciousness throughout history, as
depicted in painting and physics, have destabilized and dissolved the
density of perceived objects, these cultural movements as depicted
by the theatrical arts and philosophy have destabilized and dissolved
the very self of the perceiver. Throughout the history of drama the
pivotal aspects of all plays were the acting persons and their assumed
identities, or roles (Fjelde, 1968: 30). Other aspects of theatrical performances, for example, a stage, an auditorium, scenery, etc.,
evolved slowly over thousands of years. The center of a play was the
living player and their persona. If the relation between the acting individual and their role identity can be envisioned as corresponding to
the changing viewpoint of a painter in the model of Ortega y Gassett,
then a complementarity between theater and painting in the history
of human consciousness can be creatively compared. Premodern

painting concentrated on a world of stable and solid objects in the same way theater concentrated on stable and solid subjects. The most comprehensive poetic drama (though never performed on stage) which depicts this stable solidity of the human self is Dante's *Divine Comedy*. He defined the creation and nature of the substantial subject:

> Open thy breast to the truth that follows and know that as soon as the articulation of the brain is perfected in the embryo, the first Mover turns to it, rejoicing over such handiwork of nature, and breathes into it a new spirit full of power which draws into its own substance that which it finds active there and becomes a single soul that lives and feels and itself revolves around itself. (Dante, 1321/1939: 329)

The human subject was seen as singular. The unity of the Creator was inspired and reduplicated in the unity of the human creature. This unity of the human person was seen as changeable, yet essentially indissoluble.

From the solid structure of the substantial self theatrical techniques accumulated in the form of playful disguises, colorful speeches and elaborate displays of costumes. Theatrical performances from ancient times through Shakespeare to the nineteenth century consisted of 'solid state acting' (Fjelde, 1968: 33). Playwrights could safely toy with disguised identities and dissolve the solidity of 'objective' realities (such as Calderon's *Life Is a Dream*, written in the seventeenth century) because of the underlying unity and solidity of the acting self within the roles. There was always that eternal core of the human self which endured all changes and challenges.

Midway through the nineteenth century the consistency at the core of the human self was radically challenged by a ridiculous, yet prophetic, character in the history of Western consciousness, Henrik Ibsen's *Peer Gynt* (1867/1980). Ibsen wrote *Peer Gynt* in 1867 under the influence of Dante's *Divine Comedy*, Goethe's *Faust* and a lot of Italian wine. The cultural context which carries the play for Ibsen starts with his social outrage at the Prusso-Danish War of 1864. Ibsen was a passionate supporter of Scandinavianism, a political hope for mutually supportive and protective relations between Norway, Sweden and Denmark. The invasion and annexation of the disputed Danish duchies of Schleswig and Holstein by Bismarck's Prussian Army was a scandal to the majority of city dwellers in Sweden and Norway. A unified Scandinavian military response, however, was opposed by the people living in the countryside. As a result of the psychosocial and political preferences of the peasant population in the countryside for an isolationist and 'self-sufficient' perspective, the dual Kingdom of Norway and Sweden followed a policy of 'non-intervention' in the Prusso-Danish War. Ibsen was outraged at what he viewed as an unforgivable betrayal of Scandinavian unity and kinship. Instead of a collective response of compassion for the political and physical suffering of a sister-state, Sweden and Norway stood for a noncommitment to Scandinavian relational loyalties and unity.

This lack of international conscience and abundance of provincial complacence was dramatically embodied by Ibsen in the self-satisfied attitudes and actions of Peer Gynt and the troll-creatures. Peer's slippery stances on any issue prefigure the quicksilver play of perspectives in postmodern cultures. The loose loyalties and fragile commitments among cultures, communities, families and friendships in the postmodern period are already embodied in Peer Gynt's loose ways with the lives and loves of other human persons. The relational interwoven 'loops' constructed between persons, families, communities and cultures founded on firm loyalties and commitments are constantly being deconstructed by Peer Gynt's extravagantly loose loyalties. In Act 5 Peer Gynt's major flaw and weakness is characterized by the Button-moulder as being the 'looseness of the loop' that could connect Peer's personality to the world community, as a 'shining button on the vest of the world' (p. 185).

Josiah Royce describes the construction of a human conscience in personality development as deriving from interpersonal, family, community and cultural loyalties (1982: 273ff.). Peer's only loyalties are to the adventures of experimenting with the labyrinthine stimuli and opportunities of life, and not to a love for any person, place or object.

Ibsen is world famous today as a playwright who, inspired by Emile Zola, depicted a solid and detailed 'objective reality' as dominating his dramatic works. As painting was detaching from the object, Ibsen was strengthening the theatrical bonds with the singular objects of the physical and social worlds of experience. Both painting and theater underwent radical yet complementary revolutions in relation to the self-object. As the solid object dissolves in painting, Ibsen dissolves the solid subject in *Peer Gynt*.

In Act 5, scene 5, Ibsen has Peer Gynt strip himself completely of all the assumed identities, roles and disguises he has accumulated. The episode is generally referred to as the 'Onion Scene' or the 'Onion Self' (pp. 176–7). Peer in despair midway through the last act is depicted as digging in the ground for wild onions to eat. He suddenly declares what his epitaph will be: 'Here lies Peer Gynt, a decent soul, emperor of all the animals – emperor? (laughs silently) You prophet's false companion. You're no emperor, you're an onion. And I'm going to skin you Peer, old top! No blubbering now, you can't escape' (p. 176).

Peer peels the layers off the onion, identifying each one with a social role he played during each stage of his development in the drama. Finally in frustration he pulls the onion apart and declares; 'It's nothing but layers – smaller and smaller – nature is witty! How strange it is, this business – life, as it's called! It has cards up its sleeve; but try to play them, they disappear, and you hold something else – or empty air' (p. 177). Peer discovers at the core of his assumed and accumulated sense of self – 'empty air'. He is one of the earliest existential images of a human being as the history of their actions; a collection of social roles attained and abandoned, of identities discarded or transcended. The empty space at his core is surrounded by a system of 'satellite selves', ungoverned by Dante's 'Love which moves the sun and the other stars'.

Peer also embodies Kierkegaard's category of aesthetic consciousness: an experiential impressionism constituted by shifting surfaces of superficial awareness. Like the structure of the play itself Peer's sense of self is scattered according to the thirty-eight various scenes depicted by Ibsen. Kierkegaard's aesthete shatters the self into a collection of provisional yet controlled relationships. He plays with possibilities, yet dares not take the leaps of self-transcendence called for by the ethical and spiritual spheres of consciousness. Peer's radical confrontation with the structure of his self-awareness discloses a lack of coherence, continuity and any center at all. Like the anthropology of Lacan, Derrida and Foucault in postmodern thought, Peer is *acentric*. He acts out the anxiety of our age: a schizophrenic self lost in a labyrinth of imagined, impulsive identities. His actions and reflections are a prophetic display of the Lacanian labyrinth of the human image lost in a hall of mirrors. Peer appears in the mid-nineteenth century as an anti-heroic herald of a radical transition in Western consciousness. The historical unity of the image of the human self is liquified and lost in an ethereal play of possibilities and momentary selves.

In Act 2, scene 7, 'A voice in the darkness' describes the new disintegrated and shifting self-image of Western cultural life. When asked by Peer Gynt *who* the 'voice' is, it responds that it is 'myself'. This is a contradiction in the play of Peer's constant exclamation that he is also 'myself' when in fact it is clear that he has no core self at all. The 'voice' then calls itself 'The Boyg' or, literally 'The Bender'. It is 'the Boyg that's unhurt, and the Boyg that's in pain. The Boyg that is dead, and the Boyg that's alive' (p. 65). Peer's slippery, ethereal satellite selves are, like the Boyg, 'Slime; gray air, not even a form' (p. 65). When Peer attempts to wrestle with and conquer the Boyg, the 'voice' replies: 'the Great Boyg wins, though no fighting rages' (p. 66). There is, as Peer says, 'nothing at all' (p. 66) to grasp, to get a handle on. In a satirical spirit Ibsen demonstrates the frustrations of our attempts to conquer and control our mysterious labyrinthine selves by his having the 'voice' go to sleep and snore while Peer leaps around attempting to catch hold of the slippery mirrors of himself. After all the 'voice' is the very void within his 'selves', the specter and spectator of his scattered, acentric experience of life.

In Act 2, scene 6, Peer confronts the King of the Trolls, who also challenges the modern image of the unified human self. He tells Peer: 'It's strange about this human nature, just how remarkably deep it goes. I'll make a slit in your left eye, till you see the world slant – then I'll cut out the right windowpane. Vision, don't forget, is the source of tears, and the body's bitter light' (pp. 58–9).

As a troll Peer will lose the balanced binocular vision within which the Western cultures have grounded their unified self-concepts and metaphysics. The one eye, or sense of 'I', loses the other eye, or 'other I, not I', in the self–other dynamic of human relationships and identity. The eyes as 'the source of tears', which arise out of the suffering and compassion of the self–other dialogue, are slit and split into a schizophrenic dynamic. The unified image of the self becomes lost in a labyrinth of self-centeredness, without a 'true self' or a 'true center'. The postmodern self-structure is similar to the classic Cretan maze of the Minotaur, except without an Ariadne's thread to lead an endangered ego through its labyrinthine ways successfully.

The Troll King declared that the difference between the human and the troll, (or subhuman or human subconsciousness) is that the human being has a 'true self' while the troll has a 'sufficient-self': 'Among men, under the shining sky, they say: "Man, to yourself be true!" While here, under our mountain roof, we say: "Troll, to yourself be enough!"' (p. 55).

The trolls can also be seen as embodying the emerging middle-class value system of a self-sufficiency grounded on the shifting standards and self–other deceptions of the nineteenth-century business ethos. The capitalist priorities of seeking any means to get ahead of the competition mirror the self-satisfied ethical confusion and contradictions of the troll kingdom ('vile looks fair, foul looks pure', p. 25). The internal contradictions confronted by Peer within himself can be seen as a reflection of the external contradictions of the emerging economic system. The trolls may be metaphors for a self-destructive psychoeconomic reality: a capitalist deconstruction of continuity in our psychosocial worlds of experience.

In Act 4 Ibsen satirizes academics and scholarship in the scene at the Cairo insane asylum, which he calls 'The Scholar's Club'. The director of the asylum is Professor Begriffenfeldt, or literally translated from the German, 'Field of Concepts'. He embodies a comical attack on Hegelian philosophy, which itself represents the culmination of the modernist attempt to explain everything through reason. The crazed Professor Begriffenfeldt announces the end of the modernist Age of Reason when he confidently declares: 'Absolute reason died last night at 11 o'clock!' (p. 140).

This new art form, as well as the free association method of Freud, took seriously for the first time in the history of consciousness a spontaneous and chaotic source of self-identities which shattered the classical images of a coherent self. The substantial self is dismembered, deconstructed and scattered: 'Things fall apart; the centre cannot hold' (Yeats, 1921/1970: 914).

Peer Gynt was first performed in Norway in 1876. Twenty years later, in 1896, it received its first performance in Paris, France. One of the actors playing a troll was to carry the living corpse of 'Absolute reason' into the radically new theatrical worldviews of the twentieth century. His name was Alfred Jarry, and he often referred to himself as 'Doctor Faustroll' (Valency, 1980: 270). One month after appearing as a troll in *Peer Gynt* he wrote, produced and performed in a play which shook the foundation of modernism more than any play in the nineteenth century. This was *Ubu Roi*, sometimes translated as *King Turd* (Valency, 1980: 208). Jarry's scatological attack on rational worldviews was the primal scream of the birth of surrealism and absurdism in the arts of the twentieth century. Through Jarry the lineage from Peer Gynt's disintegration of the modernist self-concepts to the shattered selves and worlds of Artaud, Beckett and Ionesco is clear. In his comprehensive study of contemporary drama, Maurice Valency (1980) characterizes the coming into being of the postmodernist confused and chaotic experience of the self:

> From the time of Sophocles Western drama was characterized by a more or less realistic appraisal of the external world, governed by a superior power, and rendered comprehensible by the marshalling of events in logical order. Thus the drama affirmed the existence of an orderly universe governed by ineluctable principles of eternal validity which it was disastrous to contravene – The rational design which was the soul of the classical tradition was precisely the element which the Avant-garde rejected. The new world of the theatre was the world of Dr Faustroll. The new drama was set in chaos. Its action transpired amid the primal confusion that preceded the Creation . . . the new drama rejected the normal categories of time and space, as well as causality, and made capital of incoherence and spontaneity in the association of images. (pp. 314–15)

Yet dismembering implies re-membering, and the deconstruction of the concepts of the self as substantial can imply their reconstruction in the future. The 'symphonizing' potentials for centrifugal as well as centripedal interactions between the self and the other are always emerging in the choreographies of interhuman consciousness. At the conclusion of the 'Onion Scene' in Act 5, scene 5, of Ibsen's *Peer Gynt*, Peer sees Solveig, the woman he first loved who has waited for him to return for fifty years. He expresses with anguish the emptiness at the core of his 'Onion self' and refers to Solveig, 'One who remembered – and one who could wait' (p. 178). The reconstruction of the deconstructed self, Ibsen advises, is through compassionate, abiding and deeply rooted relationships with others. In other words, a radical restoration of a reverence for interhuman relations could restore and reconstruct a symphonic sense of self–other realities ('making music together') through a deeply committed respect for and abiding acknowledgment of each other. Following Ibsen's re-creative imagery, the scattered self reconstructs a sense of continuity and wholeness again through intimate loyalties. Solveig can be seen in this sense as the restorative symbol of the centripedal agency and process of re-membering the dis-membered self. At the conclusion of the play she answers Peer's inquiry as to where his 'true self' has been all of the intervening years with the words, 'In my faith, in my hope, and in my love' (p. 208). Perhaps these are prophetic words that point toward a new horizon beyond postmodernism's deconstruction of the rational and substantial self. Our new postmodern view of a relationally defined self may recover some of the stability lost in the radical decentering of the self in contemporary psychology by remembering the anchorage, sanctuary and sanity offered to the relational self by the cultivation of the classical values of faithfulness, hopefulness and lovingness. In this way we may integrate the ancient and the contemporary in the grounding of the current concepts of the self in the ancient values which, when cultivated well, are the surest paths of radical openness to abiding and anchoring relationships.

References

Dante, A. (1939) *The Divine Comedy*, trans. J.D.F. Sinclair. New York: Oxford University Press. (Original work published in approximately 1321.)

Fjelde, R. (1968) Peer Gynt, naturalism and the dissolving self. *Drama Review*, 13.

Ibsen, H. (1980) *Peer Gynt*, trans. R. Fjelde. Minneapolis: University of Minnesota Press. (Original work published in 1867.)

Kierkegaard, S. (1962) *The Present Age*. New York: Harper & Row.

Ortega y Gassett, J. (1956) On point of view in the arts. In *The Dehumanization of Art*. Garden City, NY: Doubleday. (Original work published in 1925.)

Royce, J. (1982) *The Philosophy of Josiah Royce*, ed. John Roth. Cambridge, MA: Hackett.

Smith, H. (1982) *Beyond the Postmodern Mind*. New York: Crossroad.

Valency, M. (1980) *The End of the World: An Introduction to Contemporary Drama*. New York: Oxford University Press.

Yeats, W.B. (1970) The second coming. In *The Norton Anthology of Poetry*. New York: Norton. (Original work published in 1921.)

9

Postmodern Epistemology of Practice

Donald E. Polkinghorne

The story of academic psychology is a subplot within the history of modernism. Psychology as an academic discipline originated as a purposeful effort to apply the epistemological principles of Enlightenment science to the study of human beings. The plot of the story of psychology, according to its orthodox archivist (Boring, 1950), is the progressive accumulation of modernist knowledge about human behavior. For several decades, however, philosophers of science and deconstructivist authors have assailed modernist epistemological assumptions and the narratives based on them. These critics maintain that the modern or Enlightenment period is coming to an end and that a new 'postmodern' period is beginning. If academic psychology is to adapt to the coming postmodern condition, it will need to reconfigure its narrative. The psychology of practice provides a template for this reconfiguration. My thesis is that the psychology of practice, unlike academic psychology, is configured as a postmodern science. A way for academic psychology to reconfigure itself into a postmodern science is to embrace the epistemological characteristics of the psychology of practice. Such a move would also help to bring about a unified 'science-practice' psychology.

The psychology of practice – the second psychology – emerged under the shadow of academic psychology. While academic psychology was focused on the discovery of general laws of human behavior, the psychology of practice was focused on pragmatic action in service of the mental health and personal development of people. The psychology of practice found academic psychology's epistemological commitments and quest for truths of limited relevance to responding to the needs of its clients. In developing its own body of knowledge, the psychology of practice created a fragmented collection of discordant theories and techniques. It was the actual interactions between practitioners and clients that provided the data on which the knowledge of practice was built. Although it is rarely addressed explicitly, underlying the knowledge generation in the psychology of practice is an implicit epistemological stance. The tacit assumptions of this epistemology of practice are: (a) there is no epistemological ground on which the indubitable truth of knowledge statements can be established; (b) a body of knowledge consists of fragments of understanding, not a system of logically integrated statements; (c) knowledge is a construction built out of cognitive schemes and embodied interactions with the environment; and (d) the test of a knowledge statement is its pragmatic usefulness in accomplishing a task, not its derivation from an approved set of methodological rules. I argue that these are postmodernist assumptions and that the psychology of practice provides a forceful illustration of the implementation of a postmodern science.

This chapter is organized into three sections. In the first section, I present a reconstructed postmodern epistemology. In the next section, I sketch the development of the two psychologies – the psychology of the academy and the psychology of practice. In the final section, I make explicit the tacit epistemological assumptions in the psychology of practice and show their affinities to the reconstructed epistemology of postmodernism.

Postmodern epistemology

The term *postmodernism* is often employed to cover a general cultural transformation taking place in Western societies (Huyssen, 1990). Postmodernism is the consequence of the failures of the program of modernism. The grand narrative of the modernist program assumed a logical and ordered universe whose laws could be uncovered by science. As the knowledge of these laws accumulated, it could be used to benefit humankind and eventually lead to the emancipation of humanity from poverty, sickness, and class and political servitude (Lyotard, 1984). Faith in the modernist program has been eroded by the atrocities of two world wars, the awareness of environmental crises, the intractability of the problems of urban ghettos and the continuing possibility of nuclear holocaust. Instead of building a world of prosperity, health and freedom, modernism has produced a civilization fearful of the tools of destruction developed by its science. In addition, the fundamental assumptions of modernism that provided the basis for its scientific program of emancipation were being undercut by philosophers of science. The loss of faith in what appears as a now exhausted modernist enterprise has brought forth the postmodern response.

The postmodern reaction to the loss of faith in modernism has taken two forms: on the one hand, a radical rejection of the possibility of knowledge and a celebration of the diverse and ephemeral; on the other hand, a critical recognition of the limits and excesses of modernism, yet a willingness to continue to seek under-standing without the certainties of modernist assumptions. Madison (1988) has used the term *postmodernist* to refer to the more radical reaction, and the term *postmodernistic* to refer to a reconstructed, but no less critical, response. Harvey (1989) has characterized the postmodern*ist* position as 'the total acceptance of the ephemerality, fragmentation, discontinuity, and the chaotic' (p. 44). Although modernists had recognized the transient, the fleeting and the contin-gent, they understood these forces as obstacles to be overcome in the search for the eternal and immutable. What makes the post-modern*ist* position different is the acceptance, even the sancti-fication, of the diverse. Rather than attempting to transcend or counteract the mutable, postmodern*ist* thought 'swims, even wallows, in the fragmentary and the chaotic currents of change as if that is all there is' (Harvey, 1989: 44).

Although the loss of faith in the modernist program shows itself in diverse ways in the venues of cultural expression – philosophy, politics, architecture, the visual arts, literature, performance, tele-vision, film (Conner, 1989) – my concern in this section is the under-mining of the epistemology of modernism by postmodern philosophers (see Dewes, 1987). One of the tools used by post-modern philosophers to remove the foundation stones of modernist epistemology was deconstruction (see Derrida, 1974). Deconstruc-tion uncovers the unfounded and historically conditioned assump-tions within a discourse. Postmodern authors approach the modernist belief in the discovery of the method by which truth can be found merely as one of the many possible discourses about knowledge generation. Postmodern writers maintain that when they apply deconstructive techniques to the modernist discourse, it is exposed as simply an ungrounded, historically situated conver-sation.

The postmodern epistemology that emerges from the deconstruc-tion of the modernist epistemology emphasizes four basic themes: foundationlessness, fragmentariness, constructivism and neoprag-matism. Relativist postmodernist authors attend only to the first three themes; affirmative postmodern authors, while addressing the first three, also include neopragmatism.

Foundationlessness. Human knowing is the outcome of inter-pretive cognitive schemes that produce a recognizable order in and meaning of experience. We do not have access to pure impressions and sensations, but only to the products of our cognitive operations. Consequently, human awareness does not contain images reflecting an independent reality; instead, it consists of constructions based on human organizing capacities (Rorty, 1979). We cannot escape the confines of our experience to know reality from a 'God's eye' view; hence all knowledge retains the taint of our humanness.

It is as if we were in a virtual reality machine. Virtual reality machines are devices used in pilot training and, more recently, for entertainment. Through use of computers that generate visual, auditory and tactile impressions, the machines simulate the experience of being in an airplane or some other environment. When people are fully engaged with the machines, their experience appears to be real. What is present in experience is assumed to be an accurate representation of an external reality. In the ultimate virtual reality machine, people have no way to determine whether their experiences are 'genuine' or creations of the machine. Our virtual reality machines are created by the biological makeup, cultural assumptions and language games in which we are immersed. We have no way to get out of the machine to test the validity of our experience. Our observations cannot be trusted to represent the real, nor can our rationality be assumed to mirror the order of the real. We have no sure epistemological foundation upon which knowledge can be built. Our experience is always filtered through interpretive schemes.

Fragmentariness. Postmodernism maintains that the real is not a single, integrated system. It is, instead, a disunited, fragmented accumulation of disparate elements and events. Even the self is not a unified whole, but a complex of unintegrated images and events (Gergen, 1991). While modernism attended to regularities and commonalities, postmodernism focuses on differences and uniqueness. Postmodernism holds that discourses that 'totalize' the real as a single, integrated system are impositions that dismiss or distort the essential diversity and indeterminacy. Each movement or change is the consequence of the coming together of a unique set of multiple forces at a particular place and time. Knowledge should be concerned with these local and specific occurrences, not with the search for context-free general laws. Fragmentation is a function of both differences in location and situation and differences in sequence and time. Explanations of a particular event do not necessarily hold for previous or future instances of the event. Reality is not a static system underlying the flux of experience, but is itself a process of continuous change.

Not only does the real express itself differently in diverse locations and times but the repertoire of interpretive schemes used to understand reality vary according to location and time. Various schemes of understanding are used to make sense of and explain phenomena and movements by different cultures and at various times within each culture. A common theme of the postmodern epistemology is that linguistic systems stand between reality and experience (Rorty, 1989). Each language system has its own particular way of distorting, filtering and constructing experience. No one language system, such as the system of formal and computational logic, holds a place of cognitive privilege. Each language system is to be recognized and honored as one among the many systems by which order can be constructed in experience. The explanations produced by the variety of language systems stand side by side, each providing its own distinct understanding. The leveling and acceptance of diverse language and explanatory systems imply that previously discarded systems should be revivified. Progressive discarding of previous systems on the premise that more recent systems are more able to reveal truth is a tidy but misguided leftover from modernism. The reintroduction of formerly cast-off systems will increase our repertoire of ways to encounter and make sense of the real.

Constructivism. Postmodern epistemology attends to the flux and fragmentation of the surface manifestations of the real. It denies the possibility that a philosophic tool can be developed to penetrate these surface manifestations. If such a tool were possible, postmodernism doubts that it would find beneath the surface disarray a universal and permanent structure. The experiential stratum where ordinary human learning is located is below the surface diversity and above ultimate foundations. Human knowledge is not a mirrored reflection of reality, neither the reality of surface chaos nor that of (if they exist) universal structures. Human knowledge is a construction built from the cognitive processes (which mainly operate out of awareness) and embodied interactions with the world of material objects, others and the self.

Rather than reproductions of clear pictures of the real as it is in itself, human experience consists of meaningful interpretations of the real. These interpretations are chiefly characterized by the ways in which the things that make up the real (physical objects, conceptual categories, other people and the self) can contribute to the accomplishment of purposes (Okrent, 1988). Thus, the world appears in human experience as organized and meaningful. Person–world interactions are made by being understood as instances of a category. The repertoire of the cognitive conceptual patterns that serve as the organizing forces for the construction of experience are limited by biological givens. Although there is considerable diversity in the particular patterns that serve any person, some interpretive patterns seem to be common to all people. The diversity results from the different historical, cultural, social and personal environments in which we are located. The communality results from the generic biological inheritance we share with one another (Johnson, 1987: xix).

A culture's or individual's collection of interpretive patterns is not static. If interactions cannot be assimilated by present patterns, the patterns change to accommodate the previously uninterpretable and meaningless interaction. Change proceeds through the imaginative work of metaphoric and metonymic processes to more general or more differentiating patterns (Lakoff, 1987).

The themes of foundationlessness, fragmentariness and constructivism, by themselves, produce a negative epistemology. Any knowledge claim has equal standing with any other. Apart from political power, there is no source of legitimation by which people or institutions can impose their knowledge systems on others (Lyotard, 1984). The fourth theme – neopragmatism – provides criteria for judgments about knowledge claims and human actions.

Neopragmatism. Neopragmatism accepts the postmodern conclusion that there can be no coherent predictive body of knowledge based on a transparent access to an independent reality. It does not, however, accept that a postmodern discipline has to be solipsistic and relativistic (Rorty, 1991). Human beings do make choices, complete projects and accomplish purposes in the world. Their everyday choices of which actions to pursue in order to bring about a desired result are most often informed by previous experiences rather than theoretical predictions. Neopragmatism shifts the focus of knowledge generation from attempts to describe the real as it is in itself (theoretical knowledge and 'knowing that') to programs to collect descriptions of actions that have effectively accomplished intended ends (practical knowledge and 'knowing how'). Pragmatic knowing concentrates on understanding *how* to, for example, ride a bicycle, rather than on knowing *what* laws of nature allow the bicycle to remain upright.

The test for pragmatic knowledge is not whether it produces a picture that corresponds to the real. In the postmodern view, we have no way to ascertain whether there is such a correspondence. Instead, the test for pragmatic knowledge is whether it functions successfully in guiding human action to fulfill intended purposes. One does not ask if a knowledge claim is an accurate depiction of the real – is it true? One asks, rather, does acting on this knowledge claim produce successful results? A pragmatic body of knowledge, thus, consists of a collection of examples of action that have worked to bring about desired ends.

The pragmatic interpretation of constructivism emphasizes the practical success of cognitive patterns. While retaining the notion that cognitive patterns are not necessarily an accurate representation of the patterns of the real, neopragmatism maintains that cognitive interpretive patterns are not completely aberrant and divergent from actually existing regularities. If they were, humans would not have been able to anticipate what response their actions would bring and therefore could not have planned or actively worked toward achieving intended goals. Neopragmatism recognizes the functionality of cognitive processes in understanding responsive regularities of the world. Neopragmatism maintains that our comprehension consists of drawing from our embodied interactions with the world enough of a sense of its regularities to accomplish our purposes. The more open we are to increasing and revising our patterns, and the greater variety of organizing schemes we have at our command, the more likely we are to capture the diversity of organization that exists in the world.

Postmodern pragmatism is termed *neopragmatism* (Margolis, 1986) because, unlike the earlier American pragmatism, it includes the notions of foundationlessness and fragmentariness. Neopragmatism does not give cognitive privilege to formal-computational reasoning, sense-datum theory or other foundational claims in determining which actions are appropriate. Although, through trial and error, some actions are found to be more effective in achieving specific goals, neopragmatism does not hold that the body of knowledge is ultimately progressing toward a final and completed state.

A neopragmatic body of knowledge consists of summary generalizations of which type of action has been successful in prior like situations. These summaries are always unfinished and are in need of continual revision as newly effective actions are discovered. Neopragmatism does not suppose these generalizations to be predictive of what actions will work in new situations; rather, the generalizations have only heuristic value as indicators of what might be tried in similar situations. Because neopragmatism incorporates the postmodern understanding of fragmentariness, it holds that each situation is different and contains the uncertainties of its specific location and time. Neopragmatism also holds to the notion of equifinality – that is, the same end can be accomplished in multiple ways. The determination of the value of an action depends on whether it fulfilled its purpose, not whether it followed a particular recipe. The premise of equifinality entails a respect for the various means used in different language games and by different cultures to effect their goals. It also implies a regard for the differences in the value assigned to particular goals by various individuals and groups.

Neopragmatism allows for scientific effort, although the purpose of science is revised. Instead of being a search for underlying laws and the truths of the universe, science serves to collect, organize and distribute the practices that have produced their intended results.

Scientific work also includes the trial of new practices in safe and controlled situations. The results of these trials become integrated into the larger body of knowledge drawn from actual practice. The controlled trials do not assume priority, and they retain the limitations of locale and time, as do all other knowledge statements.

The two sciences of psychology

The first science: practice and modernism

During the last half of the nineteenth century the principles of modern science were applied to the study of human beings. Psychology was one of the academic disciplines that had its beginnings during that period (Giorgi, 1986). Modern science had served well in developing descriptions of the regularities (governing laws) that held in the natural realm. The application of those methods to the human realm was expected to produce a body of knowledge that would allow for the prediction and control of human behavior. Such knowledge would serve society by providing information about how most efficiently to educate children to their maximum potential, to reform prisoners, to organize the workplace, to cure mental illness, and so on (Danziger, 1979).

Psychology adopted the modernist notion that below the surface of apparent willfulness and unpredictableness of human behavior lay consistent laws that determined how humans would respond to various stimuli. The format of the laws was thought to be identical to the laws of the natural realm; that is, they consisted of formal-computational relationships among variables. The method for uncovering these laws was the modernist method of hypothetical-deductive experimentation (Danziger, 1990). Although *basic* research was carried out without obvious or intended direct application, research intended for application became prominent in psychology, especially in the United States (Peterson, 1991).

Psychology followed the pattern of other disciplines in creating a division of labor in which some (primarily situated in the academy) served as researchers, developing the body of knowledge, and others (primarily working in the field) served as practitioners, applying the developed body of knowledge. Practitioners were to limit their practice to applying the findings developed by the academic researchers. In the modernist notion of professionalism, practitioners were the appliers of knowledge and were considered to have lesser standing than the researchers who actually developed knowledge. The activity of science produced knowledge of laws and general principles that could be translated into techniques for use by practitioners in specific situations. Practitioners were to be trained in research so that, as consumers of research, they could read the research journals and keep themselves up to date on the latest findings produced in the academy. They were not to trust as reliable the experiential understandings that they derived from their practice. Because these understandings, which were derived from trial and error or anecdotal experience, had not yet been tested by the rigorous methods of modernist epistemology, they were not considered appropriate to guide the practitioners' actions and interventions. Practice based on personal experiences was unsystematic and was held to produce unpredictable results. When studies (see Morrow-Bradley and Elliott, 1986) showed that practitioners were guided by personal experiences and consultation with professional colleagues rather than the academy's research findings, the proposed solution was to increase in professional training programs the emphasis on the importance of using research findings to guide professional practice (Peterson, 1991).

The second science: practice and postmodernism

As the role of professional psychologists began to change from one of primarily administering and interpreting psychological tests to one of delivering psychotherapy, practitioners began to turn to a second body of knowledge. The repository for this body was the professional literature and oral traditions rather than the academic literature. A series of survey studies has pointed out that academic research in counseling and clinical psychology is little utilized by practitioners. A recent survey (Morrow-Bradley and Elliott, 1986) produced results that are generally consistent with those of prior studies (see Barlow et al., 1984). Its findings were that the source of information about psychotherapy that practitioners found most useful was their ongoing experience with clients; 'only 10% reported psychotherapy research articles or presentations as their primary source of information' (p. 191). Another article on the use of psychotherapy research by therapists (Cohen et al., 1986) also reported that 'therapists learn about therapy overwhelmingly from practical experience with clients and only rarely consult therapy research to help them with difficult clients' (p. 198).

The modernist notion that psychology professionals were appliers of research findings is not an accurate description of actual practice. Practitioners have developed a separate system of knowledge generation which is based on the direct service of clients (Schön, 1983). Their science reflects postmodern epistemological commitments. There are now two sciences of psychology: the modernistic science primarily engaged in by academic researchers, and the science of practice primarily engaged in by practicing psychologists. One of the consequences of this dichotomy of sciences is the tension within the American Psychological Association, an organization that houses adherents of both psychologies.

The epistemology of practice

An examination of the epistemology that implicitly informs the contemporary practice of psychology in psychotherapy and consultation reveals a temper that is basically postmodern. At the explicit level the professional body of literature is a mixture of modernist and postmodern notions. For example, most of the theoretical systems were conceived prior to the developments of cognitive science and its constructivist implications. Freud and Jung wrote as if they were providing descriptions that accurately reflected the actual inner workings of the psyche; Rogers, as if he were describing the actual operations of a substantial self; and Skinner, as if the mechanisms of learning he presented were precise descriptions of real human dynamics. Within a postmodern epistemology, these systems are reinterpreted as models or metaphors that can serve as heuristic devices or as possible cognitive templates for organizing client experiences.

This mixing of conflicting epistemological beliefs not only shows itself in the early literature but is exhibited by practitioners themselves. For example, in providing explanations of human behavior they often retain the modernist notion that the theory they adhere to is an undistorted reflection of actual psychological reality; yet in making clinical judgments in their work with clients, they evince a postmodern belief in individual differences and the need for particularized understanding. As a means of describing the operating epistemology of practitioners, I first present findings from studies of how expert clinicians direct their activities with clients. I follow this with a description of the operation of postmodern themes in the epistemology of practice.

The knowledge processes of expert practitioners

In recent years, several authors have undertaken studies in the knowledge processes employed in professional practice. One of the findings is that expert practitioners employ knowledge processes different from those of novices. Dreyfus and Dreyfus (1986) have identified five types of cognitive processes used by practitioners; the types correspond to five stages of professional development. In the first type used by novices the source of knowledge is understood to be external to the practitioner. Novice practitioners follow the rules and procedures they were taught in the training. In the fifth type, that used by experts, the chief source of knowledge is the practitioner's own experience. Expert practice involves the accommodation of previous understandings to the uniqueness of a particular clinical situation. Common sense argues that the articulation of an epistemology of practicing knowledge must be based on the processes of expert practitioners, not the deliberative procedures and theoretically derived rules that constitute the practicing knowledge of novices.

According to the Dreyfus and Dreyfus study, expert knowledge is dynamic and generates context-dependent understanding. It is produced by the interaction of the expert's repertoire of cognitive patterns with environmental cues. This type of knowledge production is constructivist; it has recently received considerable attention in the literature of cognitive psychology (Gardner, 1985; Lakoff, 1987; Margolis, 1987). Dreyfus and Dreyfus call the conceptual organizing schemes *patterns*; others have referred to them by terms such as *frames*, *schemata*, *scripts*, *attunements* and *working theories* (Abelson, 1981; Hollon and Kriss, 1984; Taylor and Crocker, 1981; Tomkins, 1979). Margolis (1987) holds that as a person experiences many variations on a given type of case, the person develops a repertoire of patterns that includes expectations, images and techniques. Therapists have the capacity to discern when an interpretive pattern being used in an attempt to understand a particular client situation does not fit all its elements and relations. This capacity allows the therapist to reconfigure, refine or develop new patterns that more closely conform to the specific (local) situation. In this manner the network of interpretive patterns changes and grows, increasing in sensitivity to situational differences and variations. Patterned explanation consists of Gestalt processing in which the meaning of events comes from their part in a whole. In addition, Lakoff (1987) proposes that patterned explanation makes use of a variety of organizational structures, a notion consistent with the postmodern emphasis on multiple rationalities.

Studies by Schön (1983) and Chi et al. (1988) also found that in the knowledge processes of expert practitioners mental patterns are revised and adjusted in the light of their professional experiences and reflective thought. Schön describes practitioners as gradually constructing and revising their cognitive patterns and response routines through trial and error. These patterns not only guide practitioners in how to respond to what they find but also inform them about what to look for in the first place. Schön found that most often reflection is prompted by the unexpected that occurs in the course of practice. He calls this 'reflection-in-the-action'. He understands the capacity to engage in reflection-in-action as a double vision that does not require us to stop and think. It is the capacity to keep alive, in the midst of an action, a multiplicity of views of the situation.

In addition to reflection-in-action, reflection may occur outside the situation of action, as when a practitioner who is away from his or her office imagines a client's response to a different approach. Schön (1983) calls this 'reflection-on-action'. Through the use of reflection-on-action, practitioners make explicit and critique the tacit understandings that have grown up around the repetitive experiences of their specialized practice. They construct a new sense for the situations of uncertainty or uniqueness that they may experience. Reflection-on-action consists of a frame experiment in which the pattern previously used to understand a situation is altered or discarded until a pattern that better fits or matches the complexity of the situation is developed. In reflection-on-action, practitioners change from thinking through patterns to meta-cognitive awareness of their cognitive patterns (Forrest-Pressley et al., 1985). In meta-cognition, practitioners focus on the possibility that the situation may not fit any pattern of understanding in their present repertoire or that they may have tried to make the situation conform to a particularly firmly entrenched pattern.

In summary, experienced and expert practitioners generate a body of knowledge through their clinical experiences. This knowledge primarily takes the form of cognitive patterns or prototypical models derived from the practitioners' tacit understandings of human function, from theories and models learned in training and from exemplary clinical experiences. The models are organized as collections of configurations or patterns, rather than formal, logically linked knowledge statements. In practice, understanding progresses to fit the unique configuration of the situation. This development of a contextually informed, particularized knowledge occurs by adapting and revising previously held general models until all elements of the situation are related into a meaningful whole. The products of this particularized knowledge generation are reported as case studies in the professional literature and are retained in the oral tradition, transmitted by internship supervisors and professional colleagues.

Postmodern themes in the epistemology of practice
To document further the presence of postmodern themes in the epistemology of practice, I gathered additional data to supplement the studies of expert clinicians described in the preceding section. These consisted of twelve interviews I conducted with Los Angeles practitioners, four current representative books on psychological practice (Basch, 1988; Beitman, 1987; Bugental, 1987; Mahoney, 1991) and the prefatory statements in the American Psychiatric

Association's 1987 *Diagnostic and Statistical Manual*, third edition, revised (DSM III-R, 1987).

Foundationlessness. In the main, contemporary practicing psychologists do not believe that there is a particular window that provides an undistorted view of psychological reality. For example, Van Maanen (1988), a consulting psychologist, remarks that 'confident possession of some Grail-like paradigm is at best a passing fancy or at worst a power play' (p. xiv). The large number of theories claiming to have grasped the essentials of psychological functioning provide prima-facie evidence that no one theory is correct. Successful therapy is carried out by practitioners who give allegiance to various theoretical systems. Most therapists are comfortable with the diversity of theories treating them as models and metaphors. The various theories are understood as conceptual systems that call attention to different aspects of the emerging complex that is human existence. The theories assist in constructing cognitive order, but not in overcoming the historical and cultural perspectives present in all human understanding. Therapists do not hold to an Archimedean point outside the human condition from which to judge which among the theoretical systems gives the most accurate account of the psyche. Practitioners do not accept the modernist notion that formal-computational rationality mirrors the structures of human existence. When they take a position toward formal-computational rationality, it is usually that, among the various rationalities, formal logic is especially ill suited for explaining the complex interactive and systemic characteristics of the human realm. Reasoning that incorporates Gestalt interconnections appears more appropriate for understanding the causal relationships within the human realm; for example, the ecological model (Bronfenbrenner, 1979), the transactional model (Sameroff, 1983) and the narrative model (Polkinghorne, 1988).

Therapists use previously effective actions as a guide for their future actions; their clinical experiences are the source of their knowledge. Yet experience is not seen as a foundation for sure knowledge. Experience itself is the repository of previous constructions (Basch, 1988), not independent representations of clients as they are themselves. Experience consists of a collection of previous interpreted interactions with clients. The conceptual categories through which experience is made meaningful are arbitrary. The categories do not represent the 'natural' categories of psychological reality, but are templates imposed over the changing, layered continuum of psychological phenomena. DSM III-R (1987) states: 'There is no assumption that each mental disorder is a discrete entity with sharp boundaries (discontinuity) between it and other mental disorders, or between it and no mental disorder' (p. xxii). Even Kerlinger, in his popular research text, reminds readers that psychological variables are hypothetical constructs that 'have been deliberately and consciously invented or adopted for a special scientific purpose' (1986: 27); they are not descriptions of distinct divisions within reality.

The epistemology of practice recognizes that much of practicing knowledge is tacit, dealing with 'knowing how', rather than theoretical and conceptual, dealing with 'knowing that'. Cashdan (1988) and Mahoney (1991) hold that emotional processes as well as intellectual processes produce the knowledge base that informs clinical actions. The epistemology of practice, like that of postmodernism, does not pretend to have or aspire to achieve a foundation upon which it can build sure and unassailable knowledge.

Fragmentariness. Psychological practice emphasizes the uniqueness of each client. Because the meaning clients experience is a function of their interpretive schemes (Beitman, 1987), and because these schemes are developed in the context of their cultural environments and personal histories, therapists' knowledge of clients is attuned to the particular and diverse. Clients' patterns of constructing meaning are themselves in process, changing from session to session. Therefore, each session with a client brings conditions of uncertainty and requires an openness to a fresh understanding of the client (Bugental, 1987).

The same therapeutic action does not usually produce the same response in all clients. Universal or general laws that would allow the practitioner to predict client responses do not hold. 'For each child [or client], the best fit must be worked out through experience, within some very broad guidelines of basic human needs, and then renegotiated as development proceeds and situations change' (Garbino, 1990: 79). Practicing knowledge is always unfinished; it does not give advance notice of the effect a therapist's action will produce. Theories of practice and past experience only serve as a guide to anticipate clients' responses. In work with clients, therapists guide their actions by trial and error, adjusting them in light of the actual responses of clients. Probabilities are not particularly helpful, for they describe only group indexes and do not provide information about individual members of a group (Turk and Salovey, 1988). The body of knowledge collected by practitioners merely provides an array of grids through which to view clients; knowledge of particular clients results from the actual encounter between them and the therapist.

The epistemology of practice possesses a postmodern awareness of the essential fragmentation of knowledge. It respects the diversity of theory and techniques within its body of knowledge. It does not seek a grand theory that will account for human experience regardless of time and place. It is built from the fragments of understanding developed in each clinical encounter. From these fragments it gathers multiple micro-theories as heuristic indicators of how the process of understanding a local situation might begin. Nevertheless, in the actual encounter with each client the micro-theory recedes into the background as the therapist recognizes the unique configuration of the historically present person. The epistemology of practice maintains that it is a mistake for a therapist to universalize his or her experience as applicable to all clients in all situations.

Constructivism. Contemporary analysts of psychological practice (Basch, 1988; Beitman, 1987; Mahoney, 1991) have incorporated into their view the notions developed by cognitive science; namely, that human experience is a construction. The meaning of events and objects is generated by a cognitive recognition of each as an instance of a mental pattern or scheme. These notions have been used not only to understand how clients give meaning to their experience but to understand how clinicians contribute to their own experiences of clients. The clinician's experience of a client is not a transparent reflection of the client, but a cognitive construction. The clinician's experience of the client is necessarily dependent on the conceptual apparatus the clinician brings to the therapy. For example, a therapist committed to Freudian theory will experience clients as having conflicts between the id and ego, and one committed to behavioral theory will experience clients' behavior as learned response patterns. Exclusive commitments to a particular theory serves to limit a clinician's understanding of the human aspects encompassed by the theory. A therapist who has the facility to make use of multiple conceptual systems can recognize more facets of a client than can another who uses only one theory. The use of a systematic eclectics (Beitman, 1987; Garfield, 1989) or integrated theory serves to increase a therapist's repertoire of interpretive schemes and encourages viewing the client from multiple theoretical perspectives.

The body of knowledge of practicing psychology is not 'true' in the traditional sense of having correspondence to an independent reality. Rather, it is a collection of case studies and micro-generalizations that can serve as sense-making templates for understanding clients. For example Halprin (1990), in discussing early childhood intervention projects, notes: 'Evaluations have . . . begun to focus more on systematic collection of "practice knowledge", from veteran practitioners' (p. 485). These templates have worth in specific instances because they have provided a valuable means to understanding

clients. As new conceptual configurations are developed by therapists, they are added to the collection of templates; others, through
lack of use, recede into the background. The epistemology of
practice is an affirmative, rather than a relativistic, constructivism in
that it allows that some templates have been more generally useful
than others.

Neopragmatism. The goal of professional practice is to help clients
overcome their mental distress and gain personal power and
freedom. The psychology of practice has been successful in achieving
this goal. Smith et al. (1980) conducted a meta-analysis of 475
different studies of psychotherapy. The major findings were that
psychotherapy is beneficial, that different psychotherapies do not
yield benefits of different types or degrees and that differences in how
therapy is conducted (group versus individual, length of treatment,
experience of the therapist) make very little difference in outcome.
Mahoney (1991) reports that more recent research studies produce
similar findings.

Practicality, not theoretical orthodoxy, has guided the actions of
therapists. Successful therapy has been accomplished by therapists
committed to various conceptual networks and practicing a variety of
techniques. The psychology of practice accepts the concept of
equifinality – that the same result can be achieved through a variety of
approaches. As Gitlin (1990) stated: 'Theoretically there may be
many pathways, biological or psychological, towards the same result
– that of clinical improvement' (p. 26). In actual practice therapists
are guided more by their clients' responses to their actions than by the
directives of a theoretical position. Therapists adjust their actions to
meet the specific needs of each client; that is, their actions are
essentially driven by pragmatics rather than theory.

The kind of knowledge essential to the psychology of practice is
knowledge of how to produce beneficial therapeutic results. Therapists need to know how to provide a set of experiences for clients that
result in their positive changes. Garfield (1989) has identified six
client experiences that are common to successful psychotherapy: the
experience of a meaningful relationship with the therapist; an
increased understanding of one's self and one's difficulties; an
emotional release; the experience of the therapist's support for
positive behaviors; the experience of a lessening of the trouble-
someness of the problem; and a confrontation of one's own
problems.

The knowledge of psychological practice is manifest first of all in
the skillful actions of practitioners. Conceptual statements about
practice are derivatives from and explications of the tacit understandings that inform the judgments and decisions made within actual

clinical encounters. The knowledge of how to do therapy is demonstrated in the successful doing of therapy. The training of practitioners to do therapy requires more than passing on descriptions of how it is done. Modeling and demonstration by accomplished practitioners are a requisite for communicating these skills. Finally, as is true in mastering other practical skills, learning to do therapy is accomplished through the successes and failures that follow actual performance.

The psychology of practice is an example of the new pragmatism in action. It has come to understand that the human realm is fragmented and disparate and that knowledge of this realm is a human construction without a sure foundation. Yet this understanding has not led to a retreat into a disparaging skepticism; rather, it has led to an openness to diverse approaches for serving people in distress. The psychology of practices body of knowledge consists of the aggregate of the professional community's experiences of what has been beneficial to clients. The criterion for acceptability of a knowledge claim is the fruitfulness of its implementation. The critical terminology of the epistemology of practice has shifted from metaphors of correctness to those of utility.

Conclusion

Postmodernism and the psychology of practice have been two separate developments, neither having much direct influence on the other. Postmodernism is a reflection of a general feeling of the miscarriage of the modernist project. Postmodern ideas have found expression in cultural productions and philosophic treatises. The psychology of practice is a response to the desire to serve people in mental distress in the most beneficial way. The psychology of practice is expressed in the various performances of skilled practitioners and their communications about what they have found to be helpful therapeutic interventions. Although these two movements have developed independently, they have come to similar understandings about the characteristics of the human realm and about epistemology. The psychology of practice, although not self-consciously postmodern, demonstrates the effectiveness of a discipline using postmodern principles.

Opponents of postmodernism maintain that the thrust of the movement is destructive; that is, it offers no constructive proposals to the Enlightenment vision that it is deconstructing. The psychology of practice, however, does provide postmodernism with an illustration of how a postmodern discipline works effectively. The psychology of practice offers a postmodern alternative to modernist academic psychology. More than that, it provides a model for a positive postmodern transformation of other modernist disciplines.

References

Abelson, R.P. (1981) Psychological status of the script concept. *American Psychologist*, 36: 715–29.

Barlow, D.H., Hayes, S.C. and Nelson, R.O. (1984) *The Scientist Practitioner*. New York: Pergamon Press.

Basch, M.F. (1988) *Understanding Psychotherapy: The Science behind the Art*. New York: Basic Books.

Beitman, B.D. (1987) *The Structure of Individual Psychotherapy*. New York: Guilford.

Bell, D. (1976) *The Cultural Contradictions of Capitalism*. New York: Basic Books.

Boring, E.C. (1950) *A History of Experimental Psychology*. Englewood Cliffs, NJ: Prentice-Hall.

Bronfenbrenner, U. (1979) *The Ecology of Human Development: Experiments by Nature and Design*. Cambridge, MA: Harvard University Press.

Bugental, J.F.T. (1987) *The Art of the Psychotherapist*. New York: Norton.

Cashdan, S. (1988) *Object Relations Therapy*. New York: Norton.

Chi, M.T.H., Glaser, R. and Farr, M. (1988) *The Nature of Expertise*. Hillsdale, NJ: Erlbaum.

Cohen, L.H., Sargent, M.M. and Sechrest, L.B. (1986) Use of psychotherapy research by professional psychologists. *American Psychologist*, 41: 198–206.

Conner, S. (1989) *Postmodern Culture: An Introduction of the Contemporary*. Oxford: Blackwell.

Danziger, K. (1979) The social origins of modern psychology. In A.R. Buss (ed.), *Psychology in Social Context*. Chicago: University of Chicago Press, pp. 27–45.

Danziger, K. (1990) *Constructing the Subject: Historical Origins of Psychological Research*. Cambridge: Cambridge University Press.

Derrida, J. (1974) *Of Grammatology*, trans G.C. Spivak. Balitmore, MD: Johns Hopkins University Press.

Dewes, P. (1987) *Logics of Disintegration*. London: Verso.

DSM III-R (1987) *Diagnostic and Statistical Manual of Mental Disorders*. 3rd edn, revised. Washington, DC: American Psychiatric Association.

Dreyfus, H.L. and Dreyfus, S.E. (1986) *Mind over Machine*. New York: Free Press.

Forrest-Pressley, D., McKinnon, G. and Waller, T. (1985) *Metacognition, Cognition and Human Performance*, vols 1–2. Orlando, FL: Academic Press.

Garbino, J. (1990) The human ecology of early risk. In S. Meisels and J. Shonkoff (eds), *Handbook of Early Intervention*. Cambridge: Cambridge University Press. pp. 78–96.

Gardner, H. (1985) *The Mind's New Science*. New York: Basic Books.

Garfield, S.L. (1989) *The Practice of Brief Psychotherapy*. New York: Pergamon Press.

Gergen, K.J. (1991) *The Saturated Self*. New York: Basic Books.

Gierre, R.N. (1988) *Explaining Science: A Cognitive Approach*. Chicago: University of Chicago Press.

Giorgi, A. (1986) Status of qualitative research in the human sciences. a limited interdisciplinary and international perspective. *Methods*, 1 (1): 29–62.

Gitlin, M.J. (1990) *The Psychotherapist's Guide to Psychopharmacology.* New York: Free Press.

Halprin, R. (1990) Community based early intervention. In S. Meisels and J. Shonkoff (eds), *Handbook of Early Intervention.* Cambridge: Cambridge University Press. pp. 469–98.

Harvey, D. (1989) *The Condition of Postmodernity.* Oxford: Blackwell.

Heidegger, M. (1962) *Being and Time,* trans. J. Macquarrie and E. Robinson. New York: Harper & Row. (Original work published in 1927.)

Hollon, S.D. and Kriss, M. (1984) Cognitive factors in clinical research and practice. *Clinical Psychology Review,* 4: 35–76.

Huyssen, A. (1990) Mapping the Postmodern. In L.J. Nicholson (ed.), *Feminism/Postmodernism.* New York: Routledge. pp. 234–77. (Originally published in 1984.)

Johnson, M. (1987) *The Body in the Mind: The Bodily Basis of Meaning, Imagination, and Reason.* Chicago: University of Chicago Press.

Kerlinger, F.N. (1986) *Foundations of Behavioral Research,* 3rd edn. New York: Holt, Rinehart & Winston.

Kuhn, T.S. (1970) *The Structure of Scientific Revolutions,* 2nd edn. Chicago: University of Chicago Press.

Lakoff, G. (1987) *Women, Fire, and Dangerous Things: What Categories Reveal about the Mind.* Chicago: University of Chicago Press.

Lyotard, J.-F. (1984) *The Postmodern Condition: A Report on Knowledge,* trans. G. Bennington and B. Massumi. Minneapolis: University of Minnesota Press.

Madison, G.B. (1988) *The Hermeneutics of Postmodernity: Figures and Themes.* Bloomington: Indiana University Press.

Mahoney, M.J. (1991) *Human Change Processes: The Scientific Foundations of Psychotherapy.* New York: Basic Books.

Margolis, H. (1987) *Patterns, Thinking, and Cognition.* Chicago: University of Chicago Press.

Margolis, J. (1986) *Pragmaticism without Foundations: Reconciling Realism and Relativism.* Oxford: Blackwell.

Morrow-Bradley, C. and Elliott, R. (1986) Utilization of psychotherapy research by practicing psychotherapists. *American Psychologist,* 41: 188–206.

Okrent, M. (1988) *Heidegger's Pragmatism.* Ithaca, NY: Cornell University Press.

Peterson, D.R. (1991) Connection and disconnection of research and practice in the education of professional psychologists. *American Psychologist,* 46: 422–9.

Polkinghorne, D.E. (1988) *Narrative Knowing and the Human Sciences.* Albany: State University of New York Press.

Rorty, R. (1979) *Philosophy and the Mirror of Nature.* Princeton, NJ: Princeton University Press.

Rorty, R. (1989) *Contingency, Irony, and Solidarity.* Cambridge: Cambridge University Press.

Rorty, R. (1991) *Objectivity, Relativism, and Truth.* Cambridge: Cambridge University Press.

Sameroff, A.J. (1983) Developmental systems: contexts and evolution. In W. Kessen (ed.), *Handbook of Child Psychology: Vol. I. History, Theories, and Methods.* New York: Wiley. pp. 238–94.

Schön, D. (1983) *The Reflective Practitioner: How Professionals Think in Action.* New York: Basic Books.

Smith, M.L., Glass, G.V. and Miller, T. (1980) *The Benefits of Psychotherapy.* Baltimore, MD: Johns Hopkins University Press.

Taylor, S.E. and Crocker, J. (1981) Schematic basis of social information processing.

In E.T. Higgins, A.P. Herman and M.P. Zanna (eds), *Social Cognition: The Ontario Symposium in Personality and Social Psychology*. Hillsdale, NJ: Erlbaum. pp. 89–134.

Tomkins, S.S. (1979) Script theory: differential magnification of affects. In H.E. Howe Jr and R.A. Dienstbier (eds), *Nebraska Symposium on Motivation, 1978* (vol. 26). Lincoln: University of of Nebraska Press. pp. 201–36.

Turk, D.C. and Salovey, P. (eds) (1988) *Reasoning, Inference, and Judgment in Clinical Psychology*. New York: Free Press.

Van Maanen, J. (1988) *Tales of the Field: On Writing Ethnography*. Chicago: University of Chicago Press.

10

The Epic of Disbelief: The Postmodernist Turn in Contemporary Psychoanalysis

Louis A. Sass

The epic of disbelief
Blares oftener and soon, will soon be constant.
(Wallace Stevens, 'Sad strains of a gay waltz')

A sea change is occurring in the way many psychotherapists conceive of their work. Members of what might be considered a psychotherapeutic avant-garde have become disenchanted with traditional positivist and realist assumptions, and prefer to think of their activities on the analogy of poetry, art or rhetoric. There is evidence of the belated influence of the 'philosophy of as-if': the notion, prevalent in philosophy and the arts since around the turn of the century, that human knowledge, including the natural sciences, is not an empirical mirroring but an invention used to bring experience into conformity with various needs and values – and that, given this fact, we might as well exploit the invented, inventive nature of what passes for truth. Many who have adopted such positions argue that, in formulating therapeutic interpretations of a patient, one should strive not primarily for correspondence to external or objective reality but, instead, for the beauty of internal coherence or the efficacy of maximal rhetorical force – or even for encouraging the patient to adopt more relativist, self-consciously fictionalist modes of self-understanding.

These developments can be seen as part of more widespread cultural tendencies sometimes described as 'postmodernist'. They are consistent, for instance, with the views of recent postmodernist novelists and critics who reject the view that literature can provide a privileged view, whether of external reality or of inner experience, and who 'accept that reality is made, not found, and that novels had better draw attention to their own fictive devices, rather than trying to pass themselves off as chunks of real-life experience' (Norris, 1985: 157).[1] In psychotherapy this postmodernist trend, as we might call it, is prevalent across a number of schools and can take a variety of different forms. The Jungian James Hillman, for example, wishes to view psychotherapy as a creative endeavor, akin to the arts rather than to science or engineering. Family therapists such as Jay Haley and Paul Watzlawick have long recognized – and attempted to take advantage of – the ways in which certain construals of human interaction, even entirely fictional ones, can have the effect of transforming these very interactions themselves. Even some behavior therapists, now emphasizing their pragmatist rather than positivistic heritage, have discovered social constructionism.

If the trend is most striking among psychoanalysts, perhaps this is because it is they who, traditionally, have had the deepest commitment to certain realist assumptions, concerning both the existence of deep-lying psychic structures (id, superego, the unconscious, and so on) and the relevance of memories from early childhood.[2] Some sense of the significance of these assumptions is conveyed by Mircea Eliade, the scholar of comparative religion, who has compared the Freudian treatment of early childhood experiences to traditional mythic conceptions of momentous, early events occurring in a primordial era of the gods. By postulating primal happenings of early life, we create a sort of time-out-of-time, an all-important era of essential occurrences that precede our fall into history. This has the effect of creating a set of ultimate referents, a place for our searchings to come to rest and a way to transform a sense of arbitrariness into feelings of destiny or fatedness.

In recent years, the influential works of Roy Schafer and Donald Spence, and the less well-known writings of analysts such as Richard Geha and Serge Viderman, have challenged these realist assumptions, arguing that psychoanalytic interpretations are less discoveries than creations and that memories are more invented than retrieved. In their different ways, all these thinkers emphasize how the demands for linguistic expressibility and narrative coherence that are implicit in the largely verbal psychotherapeutic encounter (as well as in the writing of case histories) tend to impose organization on the raw material of the patient's experience. They believe that, to a large extent, this organization is not already implicit in the material, but that this fact is no bar to its having a profoundly curative effect. The relativistic tone of so much of this writing is apparent in the following statement by Roy Schafer: 'A version of the past can only be a narrative about past narratives. And that past toward which we might adopt a fatalistic attitude is not more than one contemporary historical narrative that, for certain purposes, we take to be true and final' (1980a: 3). And Richard Geha, adopting the most extreme position of all, writes that 'everything is a manifestation of the aesthetic faculty'; to him, the 'psychoanalytic enterprise is totally fictional' and should become 'more decidedly a branch of literature' (1988: 141; 1992: 31, 33).

This transformation of the field's self-understanding might be seen as part of the 'flight from history' which Frank Kermode has discerned in the interpretive disciplines in general. There are many who would hail this flight for its presumably liberating effects, and among them is the French analyst Serge Viderman. Viderman writes that the analyst should give up the vain hope of discovering 'a history nowhere to be found', for this 'elusive reality . . . imposes inconsistencies prejudicial to the coherence of our theoretical formulations'. In his view, the search for historical reality shackles the imagination. It unnecessarily constrains the psychoanalytic encounter, whose true purpose is the active *creation* of meanings, not the discovery of meanings in archaic experiences that, in themselves, 'have no structure, no figurable shape' (1979: 262). Donald Spence takes much the same position in his elegant and widely praised book, *Narrative Truth and Historical Truth* (1982). Insisting on the inherent difficulty, amounting in his view almost to an impossibility, of discovering the factual truth about a patient's past life, Spence proposes that the therapist should understand his interpretations as really involving an 'aesthetic experience', claiming 'artistic truth' (pp. 269–70). It is as if Spence and Viderman were applying to psychoanalysis the defense of artifice which Oscar Wilde once suggested for literature: 'As life has no shape and literature has, literature is throwing away its one distinctive quality when it tries to imitate life' (quoted in Graff, 1979: 52).

There are at least a couple of different ways of evaluating these fashionable positions and claims. The more obvious approach is to ask about the general validity of the versions of relativism, skepticism, fictionalism, etc., which they propound – to probe the internal consistency of these positions and the cogency of their dismissals of alternative conceptions of knowledge. This is not my purpose in this chapter; but I would like to say in passing that most of these postmodernist claims, especially the more extreme ones, depend on the naive acceptance of certain dichotomies which the greatest thinkers of twentieth-century philosophy (Wittgenstein, Heidegger, Merleau-Ponty, as well as more recent figures such as Hilary Putnam) have attempted, in their various ways, to overcome – for example, the dichotomy between subjective and objective views of truth and reason, and between absolute certainty and utter skepticism. Indeed, there is something surprising about the excited, celebratory tone with which these recyclings of familiar forms of relativism, fictionalism or idealism are so often received in psychology and psychoanalysis, as if they were the *ne plus ultra* of up-to-date philosophical speculation. This is not to deny the value of the contributions these postmodernists have made – in challenging the scientism, objectivism and

positivism of mainstream psychology, in laying bare the procrus-
teanism of traditional psychoanalytic interpretation and in calling
attention to the role that subjective projection and narrative smooth-
ing do in fact play in the formation of psychotherapeutic understanding.[3]

My purpose in this brief chapter is, however, to consider these
issues from a second standpoint – concerning myself not with the
validity or truth value of the views in question but with their lived
consequences, especially in the psychotherapeutic situation. The
profound existential implications, in particular the potentially debilitating and anxiety-provoking tendencies that are inherent in modern
forms of relativism and subjectivism, have been a major theme in
both literature and art at least since the time of Dostoevsky and
Nietzsche. Yet despite an avowed interest in the impact or rhetorical
force of psychological interpretation, the psychoanalytic postmodernists have largely ignored what is surely one of the most
important ingredients *of* this force: not the actual truth value of the
narratives or other interpretations, but the nature of the patient's
belief – or lack thereof – in the accuracy of these symbolic
representations. For, even if one accepts that interpretations can be
effective without being veridical, it hardly follows that their effectiveness is independent of the patient's *belief* in their veridicality.

This omission is particularly striking in *Narrative Truth and
Historical Truth*, where Donald Spence never directly addresses the
question of the patient's understanding of the issues discussed in his
book. Spence concentrates almost exclusively on demonstrating the
supposed impossibility of an actual correspondence between the
narrative interpretation and the past historical reality; but he never
explicitly says whether the patient would or should be made aware
of this near-impossibility. Given the extent to which psychology, and
psychoanalysis in particular, has permeated our culture, becoming
part of a kind of general folklore, it would seem naive to expect that
such a fact could be kept secret from analysands or other patients (not
to mention the ethical, as well as psychological, problems of such
dissembling – which would amount to a kind of cynical shamanism).
In any case, Spence's way of describing the impact of psychoanalytic
interpretations suggests that, for him, belief in such a correspondence is not terribly relevant, and perhaps would even be counter-
productive, for effecting a cure.

Borrowing a notion from philosophical aesthetics, Spence tells us
that it is not belief in the interpretation that is curative so much as the
suspension of disbelief in its referential truth (by which he means, I
assume, a bracketing of the whole issue of either belief or disbelief;[4]
supposedly, this suspension will allow the patient to 'make himself

accessible to [the interpretation's] artistic and rhetorical surround' and to appreciate 'a kind of linguistic and narrative closure' (1982: 289, 137). Also, Spence recommends that therapists signal a hypothetical or tentative rather than factual tone by prefacing their interpretations with qualifiers such as 'It seems to me that . . .' or 'I wonder if . . .' (pp. 276, 133); and he says that 'clinical impact' should be understood to mean 'aesthetic experience' – something to which truth (understood as involving referentiality, objectivity or historical factuality) would be quite irrelevant (pp. 269, 273, also p. 12). Carried along by Spence's graceful prose, the reader never stops to ask whether the patient's failure to believe in actual historical veracity might somehow be problematic, perhaps even inimical, to therapeutic improvement.

Spence's aestheticist interpretation of the impact of the psycho-therapeutic encounter is clearly reminiscent of the emphasis, common in twentieth-century aesthetics, on the presumed self-sufficiency of the artwork, on its escape from the vulgarity of reference to things existing beyond itself. The writings of Roy Schafer share elements of this kind of aestheticism; but they also stress another (not unrelated) way in which a postmodernist under-standing of psychotherapy could have a salutary effect – namely, by increasing the patient's self-conscious awareness of the perspectival nature of reality and of his or her own role in creating understanding. Thus Schafer writes that a main effect of psychoanalytic treatment should be to help analysands become 'more versatile, sophisticated, and *relativistic* historians of their lives' (1980a: 43, my emphasis; also 1983: 283). In a reversal of the traditional emphasis on developing insight into the present as a (previously unconscious) repetition of the past, he stresses fostering the analysand's self-conscious awareness of the role of his or her own ongoing interaction in creating an *image* or *conception* of the past. 'More and more the alleged past must be experienced consciously as a mutual interpenetration of past and present,' writes Schafer. 'The time is always present. The event is always an ongoing dialogue' (1980b: 32, 49). Here the emphasis is less on the patient's responding to the pleasing coherency of a narrative or other interpretation, than on appreciating the mallea-bility of what passes for reality, and on the patient's recognition of the constituting role of his or her own story-producing mind.

Richard Geha (forthcoming) gives things a slightly more negative, Derridean twist at the end of a recent article, stressing not the creative so much as the critical – or deconstructive – faculties. Here he imagines psychoanalysis as 'an endless interrogation of mind-made worlds that continually deconstructs – if it chooses to proceed – its antecedents'; and he offers the model of avant-garde fiction

advocated by the postmodernist novelist and critic Raymond Federman – of fiction that will be

> the metaphor of its own narrative progress, and will establish itself as it
> writes itself . . . a kind of writing, a kind of discourse, a kind of reality
> . . . whose shape will be an interrogation, an endless interrogation of
> what it is doing while doing it, an endless denunciation of its own frau-
> dulence, of what IT really is: an illusion, a fiction, just as life is an il-
> lusion, a fiction.

For both Schafer and Geha we could say that, to a very great extent,
what is truly curative in analysis is the awareness of the analytic
process itself, and this amounts to an awareness of its fundamentally
relativist or fictional nature; it is this which reveals the essentially
created nature of *all* of reality, thus liberating the patient from his
rigidities, from the fatedness that comes from taking too literally
what is in fact only the narrative one happens to have been living by.
A progressive subjectivization is apparent in Geha's (forthcoming)
adopting of the common deconstructive idea that any creation, such
as a narrative, is fundamentally self-referential – always telling the
story of its own creation in a kind of narcissistic display of the
fecundity or freedom of the narratizing mind.

This vision of fulfillment through self-knowledge and self-creation
has a powerful appeal, of course, for it resonates with some of the
deepest yearnings of the modern mind. And it seems likely that this
form of enlightenment could indeed be helpful – at least for certain
people, with certain kinds of problems and at certain moments in
their development. Undoubtedly there are many individuals who
suffer from rigidities, from too constraining a conception of themselves or too narrow and impoverished a vision of the past; for them
fictionalism and relativism might well be therapeutic. But what of
those who suffer from problems of a different sort – for example,
from feelings of emptiness, meaninglessness and unrelatedness, from
the inability to form stable relationships or from a lack of sustaining
interests or continuing goals, values and ideals? What effect might
the postmodernist vision have on these schizoid, borderline and
narcissistic problems so characteristic of our age?

What is troubling about the postmodernists is, then, the wholesale
endorsement of aestheticism, relativism or fictionalism as *the* truth
and *the* message of psychotherapy, and their nearly complete failure
to consider the dark and troubling side of such views. It is this which
suggests a certain blindness to the existential ambiguities of human
life – ambiguities that are vividly explored in the modern literary and
philosophical tradition from which these postmodernist ideas actually derive.

Friedrich Nietzsche is, with little doubt, the most important philosophical influence on the various versions of relativism, perspectivism, fictionalism, subjectivism and aestheticism that have recently been gathered together under the umbrella of 'postmodernism' (as Geha, forthcoming, and many others have acknowledged). Yet it is interesting to note how blinkered the postmodernist appropriation of Nietzsche can be, how it tends to ignore certain aspects of this kaleidoscopic thinker.

Certainly there is no doubt about Nietzsche's perspectivist inclinations – clearly stated in his firm and continuing opposition to Platonism and all forms of essentialism, which he defined as the 'idle hypothesis' that 'things possess a constitution in themselves quite apart from interpretation and subjectivity'.[5] At times this did lead him to advocate attitudes that are reminiscent of the kind of relativism and skepticism which Schafer and Geha recommend – for example, to favor 'unbelief as an instinct', and 'an absolute skepticism toward all inherited concepts' and toward the 'anthropomorphic error' whereby the mind identifies its own constructs with reality itself (1901/1968 nos 963, 409; Schwartz, 1985: 18). As Nietzsche says in *The Genealogy of Morals*: 'There is *only* a perspective seeing, only a perspective "knowing"; and therefore 'the *more* eyes, different eyes, we can use to observe', the more complete our vision will be (1887b/1968, III: no.12). In *The Gay Science* he glorifies the free spirit *par excellence* – the person who would 'take leave of all faith and every wish for certainty, being practiced on maintaining himself on insubstantial ropes and possibilities and dancing even near abysses' (1887a/1974 no. 347). Yet despite these polemics and this hyperbole, Nietzsche was far from being a whole-hearted proponent of such relativist tendencies. He may have believed that truth was more created than discovered, but this did not prevent him from recognizing that it is usually necessary to *believe* one is discovering something in order to make the effort of creating it (Nehamas, 1985: 59). As far as I can tell, this point has escaped the advocates of a postmodernist style of psychoanalysis, who simply assume their patients will be as enthused as they are by the prospect of embarking on some kind of aesthetic, relativistic or deconstructive game.

One can certainly understand the appeal these latter approaches might have for a certain kind of psychoanalyst – frustrated, perhaps, with the sedentary and distinctly passive nature of the work, maybe growing bored with the tedium of the Oedipus complex and the no less predictable formulae of the more recent schools. To such a person, donning the mantle of the creative artist or the aesthete might be a welcome, and rather flattering, prospect. But many patients are likely to see things rather differently; it is, after all, their lives that are at issue, and for them the sheer weight of certain feelings – of frustration or grief, of ambivalence or fear – may make the view from these vertiginous Nietzschean heights seem somehow less than relevant. And the brute, undeniable reality of certain memories may make them less attracted to the idea of merely making up stories. We might recall that a narrative, by definition, always refers to events beyond itself; and if it is an historical narrative, as in psychoanalysis, the events in question are assumed to have occurred prior to the telling. The idea of concocting narratives, narratives of one's own life, yet not being particularly worried about their accuracy, or their obsolescence in the face of a myriad of alternative versions, may not be consistent with the essence of the narrative impulse itself (at least as this has existed through most of human history); certainly there are many to whom such an enterprise would seem rather futile and self-indulgent. Similar problems apply to the potentially self-congratulatory skepticism advocated by Richard Geha. To experience life as a sort of endless labyrinth of interpretation might come, in fact, to seem rather tedious – if we know in advance that there is in fact no Ariadne's thread, no hidden center, nor even a real Minotaur waiting there to challenge us.

So far I have been describing reasons why the postmodernist approaches to psychoanalysis might fail to be as compelling to patients as they are to their therapist advocates. Clearly, however, these interpretations *have* gained a certain currency, and one presumes they have had some impact on the actual conduct of exploratory, interpretive psychotherapy (how broad or deep this influence is it is impossible to say). It is therefore worth considering another dimension: the kind of influence on the patient or analysand which this stance toward history and interpretation is likely to have. Obviously, the postmodernist advocates emphasize positive effects – liberation, invigoration, the development of flexibility and sophisticated self-awareness – but we cannot ignore other, more unsettling possibilities. We might look to Nietzsche, for it is he who discerned most clearly the sources of danger and weakness inherent in these forms of skepticism and perspectival fluidity which, in his view, were so central to the dawning modern age. He suggests the potential for confusion or enervation, and for encouraging a kind of self-questioning, even self-cannibalizing involution as well as a certain narcissism of the mind – phenomena that certainly play more than a small part in the neuroses, personality disorders and general miseries of our era.

Nietzsche spoke of a 'madly thoughtless fragmentation and fraying of all foundations, their dissolution into an ever flowing and dispersing becoming' as among the 'remarkable symptoms of our age' (1874/1980: 50, 7). He believed that new forms of historical and cultural awareness had exposed man to too many different views of existence. Modern man had been blinded by a 'hypertrophic virtue' – the presence of 'much too bright, much too sudden, much too changeable light'. As a result, 'the lines of his horizon restlessly shift again and again', rendering him incapable of 'rude willing and desiring' (1874/1980: 8, 41, 11). The fictionalist relativism of Schafer or Geha, in which one would never take the current self-understanding too seriously, remaining ever ready to move on to the next, risks having this kind of corrosive or debilitating effect – especially for people who already suffer from problems of a schizoid or narcissistic type. Schizoid individuals tend to sense that their own perceptions, memories and actions are somehow insubstantial; they feel detached, as if separated from the world by a sheet of glass or a bell jar; and they often become overly preoccupied with theories and abstractions, or with internal thought processes that feel as if they are idling in neutral. Though narcissistic individuals are generally more engaged with the social world, the transience and self-centeredness of their attachments rob them too of a real sense of groundedness and, in the end, leave them also feeling hollow and disgruntled. What such people require is hardly a greater appreciation of the multiplicity of perspectives, or of the element of artifice inherent in all of human existence; this might, in fact, only work to increase the sense of detachment and dissatisfaction that brings them to psychotherapy in the first place.

In one of his most powerful attacks on perspectivism, Nietzsche wrote that 'the basic condition of all life' is to have a *single* perspective:

> And this is a general law: every living thing can become healthy, strong and fruitful only within a horizon; if it is incapable of drawing a horizon around itself or, on the other hand, too selfish to restrict its vision to the limits of a horizon drawn by another, it will wither away feebly or overhastily to its early demise. (1874/1980: 10; 1886/1973: 14)

He criticized those 'given over to a restless cosmopolitan choosing and searching for novelty and ever more novelty', the people of an age in which 'Knowledge, taken in excess without hunger, even contrary to need, no longer acts as a transforming motive impelling to action' (1874/1980: 20, 24). And, in a passage that could be read as a critique of intellectual developments in the contemporary world of postmodernist literature and poststructuralist theory, he writes of the age of the 'Don Juan of cognition', the person who lacks sufficient love for the things he knows yet nevertheless pursues knowledge relentlessly until, finally, 'nothing remains to be hunted but the most agonizing effects of knowing' itself (quoted in Jaspers, 1965/ 1979: 392). This is the brother of his despised 'theoretical man', who is 'bent on the extermination of myth' and 'finds his highest satisfaction in the unveiling process itself, which proves to him his own power' (1872/1956: 137, 92).

Many of the dangers of this kind of relativism are illustrated by the character of 'Ulrich', the antihero protagonist of *The Man without Qualities*, the great modern novel by Robert Musil (an avid reader of Nietzsche, from an early age). Ulrich, who stands for Musil as a sort of representative modern man, is an exceptionally self-conscious being, ever preoccupied with a myriad of alternative possibilities and ways of being. A 'possibilitarian', he has lived since childhood in a subjunctive mood, once arguing in a schoolboy essay that 'even God probably preferred to speak of His world in the subjunctive of potentiality . . . for God makes the world and while doing so thinks that it could just as easily be some other way' (1930/1980: 15). The result of this is a feeling of negative freedom, a constant awareness of the groundlessness of existence. Indeed, Ulrich is so aware of 'the leaps that the attention took, the exertion of the eye muscles, the pendulum-movements of the psyche' occurring at every moment that even the act of keeping one's body vertical in the street seems to him to require a tremendous output of energy (p. 7). He cannot forget the importance of perspectives or horizons, and cannot trust his own, for, as another character in the novel points out, Ulrich knows too well that it is always 'only a possible context that will decide what he thinks of a thing'.

And so it is difficult for Ulrich to make decisions, whether in the matter of furnishing his house or choosing a career; he too easily sees the arguments for all possible choices. Indeed, he looses all sense of reality, for, in his hyperreflexive state, nothing exists 'in-itself' but only as an emanation of the viewing mind – there is nothing but a 'world going in and out, aspects of the world falling into shape inside a head' (p. 129). As a result,

> nothing is stable for him. Everything is fluctuating, a part of a whole, among innumerable wholes that presumably are part of a super-whole, which, however, he does not know the slightest thing about. So every one of his answers is a part-answer, every one of his feelings is only a point of view, and whatever a thing is, it does not matter to him what it is, it is only some accompanying 'way in which it is', some addition or other, that matters to him. (Musil, 1930/1980: 71)

Ulrich's indecisiveness might be considered a symptom of what Heidegger (1977) has called 'the age of the world-view'. This is the era, inaugurated by Descartes in the middle of the seventeenth century but reaching a kind of crescendo in the twentieth, when the world is no longer felt to exist as an encompassing or solid external reality, when it is experienced instead *as* a view – a mere subjective projection whose being derives from the individual human subject, or from whatever human perspective or symbolic system incorporates it.

Ulrich seems to have an acute awareness of his own, personal involvement in these acts of constitution – he senses *his* eye muscles, the movements of *his* psyche, *his* ways of looking at things. Many who have written on the culture and sensibility of last few decades would suggest, however, that this sense of idiosyncratic selfhood and personal subjectivity is rapidly turning passé, and being replaced by the more anonymous sense of irreality carried by the flood of media images which now surround us like an atmosphere. For, as we enter more fully into the postmodern world, all seems to pale before the power of the image, causing old distances and distinctions to waver and collapse. The very idea that something real might preexist the image or simulacrum, and remain beyond its grasp, begins to fall away; and so does the idea of some idiosyncratic or private realm that would be the locus of a true or inner self. Instead of the old pathos of distance, with its sense of inwardness and detachment – the condition of an inner self cut off from some unattainable reality – we enter into a universe devoid of both objects and selves: where there is only a swarming of 'selfobjects', images and simulacra filling us without resistance.

But mutations like this are never sudden, never absolute – so naturally we find both conditions existing side by side; we find the old existentialist alienation along with the new postmodern hysteria, euphoria and malaise. That the aestheticized psychoanalysis of Donald Spence remains largely within the first order is suggested by the fact that he continues to believe in a real past and 'true memories' (1982: 60), even at times to yearn for closer contact with them – though he asserts that, like a kind of Kantian *Ding-an-sich*, this formless, unformulable world is virtually impossible to reach.[6] It seems that Richard Geha, more fully at ease in the postmodern age, perhaps, would dismiss all such yearnings for the solid or the unattainable. There is no past – it was already only a fiction, he tells us; even the mind – what might have seemed to be the origin of all this imagery – turns out to be 'a purely mythical site', with only a 'fictional status' (1988: 143). And this, in Geha's view, should be cause for rejoicing, not frustration or regret. And so instead of the anguished, if rather comical, confusion of Ulrich/Musil, Geha offers us the postmodernist message of the novelist Richard Federman: not to worry – for reality, in any case, 'does not exist, or rather exists only in its fictionalized version' (in Geha, 1988: 146); mimesis is but a dream; there is only poesis.

The difference between Spence and Geha might be compared to a shift between phases in a four-stage progression which Jean Baudrillard postulates in an essay on the postmodern loss of reality, 'The precession of simulacra' (1984: 256). The first of these phases is in a sense *pre* modern, for here the image (which could include a narrative or any other form of representation) is assumed to reflect a basic reality; it is a *good* appearance, as in traditional, realist conceptions in psychoanalysis. In the second the image takes on evil qualities, for now it is assumed to mask and pervert a basic reality with which we cannot have contact – which corresponds to Spence's sense that the smoothness and clarity of narrative necessarily misleads us as to the fundamental and nearly ineffable complexity of the real unconscious or the real past. In the third phase the image (or narrative) only *plays* at being an appearance, while actually masking the complete absence of a basic reality; and this seems to capture Geha's sense of the usual functioning of psychoanalytic interpretations or narratives, which fool us into thinking there is a basic, bedrock reality when in fact there is none. The fourth and final phase, the stage of the simulacrum (the image without an original), is the one Geha would like to foster, for here the image or fiction leaves the order of appearances altogether; interpretations become transparently fictional, laying no claim to truth since it is everywhere recognized that there will be only fictions wherever we look.

There is something disturbing about the homogenization of existence implied in this final phase, when all difference between reality and illusion, truth and error, memory and imagination is dissolved. In a famous remark, Hegel decried Schelling's notion of the Absolute by saying it reminded him of a night in which all cows are black; beneath claims to openness and pluralism, to creativity, diversity and play, postmodernism may conceal something similar – a veiled absolutism that could deprive psychotherapy of its critical edge and life itself of its density, its ontological weight. For how can a person be encouraged to acknowledge truly unpleasant truths, especially those sordid, unflattering facts which may lack the compensation of a tragic dimension, if one assumes that there is no distinction between truth and mere fiction – but only stories about stories about stories? And what is to prevent psychotherapy from turning into an elaborate workshop for rationalization, a place for spinning self-justificatory fantasies and fostering all the subtle complacencies of narcissistic entitlement and self-satisfaction? But beyond this there is the thinning or hollowing-out of existence which aestheticism, relativism and fictionalism can effect, and which may contribute to the 'waning of affect', and the loss of a sense of real historical time (on both the private and the public level) that accompany the era of the simulacrum (Jameson, 1984: 58, 61). After all, toward mere images one cannot feel real affects but only 'intensities' – cold and deracinated affect states such as vertigo, the queasy thrill of déjà vu, uncanniness, awe and amazement, the euphoria and nausea of weightlessness. Truer, more full-blooded emotions – love, hate, sadness and simple joy – are debarred for these require grounding in the lived body, in a feeling of connection with real objects and living human beings and in a sense of finitude, of finality and of risk.

A fanciful, allegorical evocation of the kind of existence which postmodern culture may be bringing out, and which postmodern psychoanalysis may be encouraging, is contained in Jorge Luis Borges's famous short story, 'Tlön, Uqbar, Orbis Tertius' (1940/ 1964). This story has sometimes been viewed as a sort of quintessential postmodernist text, not only as exemplifying the major themes of Borges's own work but as celebrating relativism and fictionalism more generally. Quintessentially Borgesian it may be; but its attitude toward the ideologies associated with postmodernism is certainly more ambivalent than this view suggests.

Borges identifies himself as the narrator of 'Tlön, Uqbar', and in the story he tells of how this individual, the Borges within the fiction, learned, from a volume of a mysterious encyclopedia, about the entire history of an unknown planet – with its architecture and its playing cards, with the dread of its mythologies and murmur of its languages, with its emperors and its seas, with its minerals and its birds and its fish, with its algebra and its fire, with its theological and metaphysical controversy' (p. 7). The planet of Tlön is exotic in a very special way, however, for it is really a kind of solipsistic or Berkeleyan world, a place where there is only one discipline, psychology, and where the inhabitants conceive of the universe as a series of mental processes and of thought as 'a perfect synonym for the cosmos' (p. 9). But not only is this land *inhabited* by subjective idealists, it was also *created* by subjective idealists – since, as the narrator soon learns, the whole world of Tlön was dreamed up by a secret fraternity of hermeticists and nihilists who dedicated themselves to demonstrating 'that mortal man was capable of conceiving a world' (p. 15), and who therefore created the First Encyclopedia of Tlön.

Tlön is, in fact, a sort of extreme instance of the subjectivism central in so much of postmodernism, with its relativist, fictionalist and idealist tendencies. This is the same subjectivism that has come to pervade the contemporary psychoanalytic avant-garde, where storytelling is given primacy over seeking out the past. We find it also in writers such as Thomas Pynchon, Jacques Derrida and their epigones, for whom no philosophy can be more than a dialectical game, a philosophy of as-if that attempts, vainly, to understand all aspects of the universe in the light of a single one. And, in Tlön, reality does in fact seem to depend on mind for its very existence – as can be seen from the case of a doorway that disappeared as soon as it was no longer visited or, conversely, in that of the ruins of an amphitheater that continued to exist only because of the presence of some birds and a horse. In Tlön the only truly scandalous philosophy is that of materialism, whose assumptions about substance and the continuity of existence are found to be incomprehensible if not completely ridiculous. It would seem, in fact, that the people of Tlön accept the deconstruction of causality first carried out by Nietzsche and later taken up by postmodernists such as Paul de Man (see Culler, 1982: 86–8), with its replacement of material by psychological sequence; to them, the 'perception of a cloud of smoke on the horizon and then of the burning field and then of the half-extinguished cigarette that produced the blaze is considered an example of association of ideas' (p. 9).

There can be little doubt that the land of Tlön, where not truth or verisimilitude but only the astounding is respected, and where all philosophy is viewed as a branch of fantastic literature, is a projection of certain attitudes of its real author, Borges – whose own tastes ran to Poe, H.G. Wells and the philosophies of Berkeley and Schopenhauer. But it is a serious mistake to understand this story as a simple celebration of relativism and idealism, as what Derrida once called 'the joyous affirmation . . . of a world . . . without truth, and without origin which is offered to an active interpretation' (1978: 292). The story's ending, which might even be read as a prophecy of the coming ascendancy of postmodernism, makes it clear that Borges maintains critical distance from the subjectivism and fictionalism of Tlön, and that he cannot so easily dispense with his own nostalgic attachment to the certainties of realism and common sense.

Borges describes how, around 1944, discovery of the full set of the encyclopedia of Tlön precipitated such widespread fascination with Tlön and its ways that the world was soon flooded with editions of and commentaries on this 'Greatest Work of Man'. People were enchanted by 'the minute and vast evidence of an orderly planet', entranced by this labyrinth which at least is 'a labyrinth devised by man, a labyrinth destined to be deciphered by men' (p. 18). Indeed, it seems that reality itself yearned to yield and did yield to this new order whose appeal Borges compares, significantly enough, to those very absolutisms with which relativism and fictionalism have been wont to contrast themselves: including dialectical materialism and other totalitarian ideologies. But unlike the postmodern champions of the philosophy of as-if, Borges does not fail to see that fictionalism or self-conscious subjectivism can be as dogmatic and metaphysical as are the more obvious absolutisms – and, perhaps, as likely to offer a potentially dangerous, and ultimately enervating, sense of security. And, in a passage which makes many postmodernist celebrations of freedom and nonpresence seem a bit sophomoric by comparison, Borges describes with the necessary equivocation, but not without a certain wistfulness and poignancy, how 'The contact and the habit of Tlön have disintegrated this world' – how, for example, the teaching of Tlön's harmonious but, of course, purely fictitious history has already effaced the history that governed in his childhood and that had at least the possibility of being true: 'already a fictitious past occupies in our memories the place of another, a past of which we know nothing with certainty – not even that it is false' (p. 18).

Notes

1 Whether such views are truly distinctive of the so-called 'postmodernist' art and thought of recent decades, as opposed to involving hyperbolic repetitions of notions central to earlier forms of modernism, is a question I cannot deal with here; see Eysteinsson, 1990, for a cogent deflation of postmodernist pretensions to originality.

2 These may have been real world events or fantasies entertained during infancy and early childhood; the point is that they are assumed to have actually occurred in the past.

3 I have discussed these issues elsewhere: Sass, 1988 and forthcoming; Sass and Woolfolk, 1988.

4 As I.A. Richards remarks regarding Coleridge's notion of 'a willing suspension of disbelief': 'It is better to say that the question of belief or disbelief, in the intellectual sense, never arises when we are reading well' (Richards, 1929/1952: 581).

5 In this passage from *The Will to Power* (1901/1968: section 560), Nietzsche criticizes the hypothesis that 'interpretation and subjectivity are not essential, that a thing freed from all relationships would still be a thing'. He goes further: 'Conversely, the apparent *objective* character of things: could it not be merely a difference of degree within the subjective? – that perhaps that which changes slowly presents itself to us as "objectively" enduring, being, "in-itself" – that the objective is only a false concept of a genus and an antithesis *within* the subjective?'

6 Spence writes: 'language is always getting in the way between what the patient saw or felt and the way this experience appears (variously transformed) in the

analytic conversation. We never make contact with *the actual memory or dream*; language is always the elusive go-between' (Spence, 1982: 286; my emphasis).

References

Baudrillard, J. (1984) The precession of simulacra. In B. Wallis (ed.), *Art after Modernism: Rethinking Representation*. New York: New Museum of Contemporary Art. pp. 253–81.

Borges, J. (1940/1964) Tlön, Uqbar, Orbis Tertius. In *Labyrinths: Selected Stories and Other Writings*. New York: New Directions. pp. 3–18.

Culler, J. (1982) *On Deconstruction: Theory and Criticism after Structuralism*. Ithaca, NY: Cornell University Press.

Derrida, J. (1978) Structure, sign, and play in the discourse of the human sciences. In *Writing and Difference*. Chicago: University of Chicago Press. pp. 278–93.

Eysteinsson, A. (1990) *The Concept of Modernism*. Ithaca, NY: Cornell University Press.

Geha, R. (1988) Freud as fictionalist: the imaginary worlds of psychoanalysis. In Paul Stepansky (ed.), *Freud: Appraisals and Reappraisals, Contributions to Freud Studies, Vol. 2*. Hillsdale, NJ: Analytic Press. pp. 103–60.

Geha, R. (forthcoming) Transferred fictions. *Pychoanalytic Dialogues*.

Graff, G. (1979) *Literature against Itself*. Chicago: University of Chicago Press.

Heidegger, M. (1977) The age of the world picture. In *The Question Concerning Technology and Other Essays*, trans. W. Lovitt. New York: Harper & Row. pp. 115–54.

Jameson, F. (1984) Postmodernism, or the cultural logic of late capitalism. *New Left Review*, 146: 153–92.

Jaspers, K. (1965/1979) *Nietzsche: An Introduction to the Understanding of his Philosophical Activity*, trans. C.F. Wallraff and F.J. Schmitz. South Bend, IN: Regnery/Gateway.

Musil, R. (1930/1980) *The Man without Qualities, Vol. I*. New York: Perigee/Putnam's.

Nehamas, A. (1985) *Nietzsche: Life as Literature*. Cambridge, MA: Harvard University Press.

Nietzsche, F. (1872/1956) *The Birth of Tragedy* [published with *The Genealogy of Morals*], trans. F. Golffing. New York: Doubleday Anchor.

Nietzsche, F. (1874/1980) *On the Advantage and Disadvantage of History for Life*, trans. P. Preuss. Indianapolis, IN: Hackett.

Nietzsche, F. (1886/1973) *Beyond Good and Evil*, trans. R.J. Hollingdale. Harmondsworth: Penguin.

Nietzsche, F. (1887a/1974) *The Gay Science*, trans. W. Kaufman. New York: Vintage/Random House.

Nietzsche, F. (1887b/1968) *The Genealogy of Morals*, trans. W. Kaufman and R.J. Hollingdale. New York: Vintage.

Nietzsche, F. (1901/1968) *The Will to Power*, trans. W. Kaufman. New York: Vintage/Random House.

Norris, C. (1985) *The Contest of Faculties: Philosophy and Theory after Deconstruction*. London and New York: Methuen.

Richards, I.A. (1929/1952) Excerpt from *Practical Criticism*. In W.J. Bate (ed.), *Criticism: The Major Texts*. New York: Harcourt, Brace & World.

Sass, L. (1988) The self and its vicissitudes: an 'archaeological' study of the psychoanalytic avant-garde. *Social Research*, 55: 551–607.

Sass, L. (forthcoming) Psychoanalysis as 'conversation' and as 'fiction': response to papers by Charles Spezzano and Richard Geha. *Psychoanalytic Dialogues*.

Sass, L. and Woolfolk, R. (1988) Psychoanalysis and the hermeneutic turn: a critique of *Narrative Truth and Historical Truth*. *Journal of the American Psychoanalytic Association*, 36: 429–54.

Schafer, R. (1980a) *Narrative Actions in Psychoanalysis*. Worcester, MA: Clark University Press.

Schafer, R. (1980b) Narration in the psychoanalytic dialogue. In W.J.T. Mitchell (ed.), *On Narrative*. Chicago: University of Chicago Press. pp. 25–49.

Schafer, R. (1983) *The Analytic Attitude*. New York: Basic Books.

Schwartz, S. (1985) *The Matrix of Modernism: Pound, Eliot, and Early 20th-Century Thought*. Princeton, NJ: Princeton University Press.

Spence, D. (1982) *Narrative Truth and Historical Truth*. New York: Norton.

Viderman, S. (1979) The analytic space: meaning and problems. *Psychoanalytic Quarterly*, 48: 257–91.

11

From Mod Mascu-linity to Post-Mod Macho:
A Feminist Re-Play

Mary Gergen

The various strands of thought labeled 'postmodern' stand as a major critical challenge to the prevailing pursuits of knowledge – within psychology and elsewhere. The postmodern critique of the representational nature of language – that is, of the capacity of language to record, picture or accurately represent reality – is at its heart. If language cannot serve in these capacities, then propositions about the world cannot in principle be proven through observation. To paraphrase Gertrude Stein, 'A text is a text is a text'; 'reality' is elsewhere – mute, unspeakable.

For many postmodern scholars this argument suggests that there is little left for the intellectual to do, but to demystify or deconstruct the illusory claims to knowledge made by the uninitiated. The task for the critic is to unmask the pretense behind the propositions – demonstrating the knowledge maker to be a fool after all.

Although there is much to be said for critical unmasking, the present text advocates a feminist a-version to this as the end game. As a self-declared postmodern-feminist, I am sympathetic to much postmodern discourse. Yet, I believe that feminists cannot hold the deconstructive posture (It makes us tense, and mostly past, at that). Indeed, on the contrary feminist poses and priorities can enable the social sciences to move toward what I consider a more positive (do I dare the word?) form of postmodernism – one that is generating rather than de-generative. It is within a social constructionist framework, itself a postmodernist endeavor (cf. Kenneth Gergen, 1985) that this piece is set. Other feminist critiques in more traditional forms tangentially or solidly share these concerns (cf. Jane Flax, 1987, 1990; Nancy Fraser and Linda Nicholson, 1988; Mary Gergen, 1988; Wendy Hollway, 1989; Patti Lather, 1986, and chapter 5 of this volume; Judith Lorber and Susan Farrell, 1991; Toril Moi, 1988; Joyce Nielson, 1990; Helen Roberts, 1981; Chris Weedon, 1987).

The script that follows was designed to be read as a dramatic performance. It was originally performed at the Postmodernity and Psychology Conference held at the Centre for Qualitative

Methodology, the University of Aarhus, Denmark, in June 1989.[1] It is intentionally not 'straight talk' and often difficult to follow. The reasons for this shift in linguistic styling are several and significant. First, as feminist postmodernists have come to realize, most of the forms of intelligible discourse in Western culture are suffused with androcentric biases (Judith Butler, 1990; Mary Gergen, 1991; Carolyn Heilbrun, 1988). Grammar, logic and narrative structures, for example, lend themselves to certain problematic ends (such as hierarchy and separation). For many feminists (cf. Luce Irigaray, 1985; Julia Kristeva, 1980; Toril Moi, 1987), the conclusion argues for a breaking with the prevailing traditions of discourse. Second, to adopt the customary forms of 'straight talk' is, for the postmodern, to invite the reader again into the cul-de-sac of traditionalism – that is, into the belief that language maps the terrain. In order to avoid such objectification, one is invited to play with the traditions, unsettle the words, so that consciousness is never lost that the postmodern's language is itself subject to deconstruction. Finally, from the postmodern standpoint, 'straight talk' (and I hope you have not missed the associative possibilities of this phrase) restricts the signifiers (or the meaning of words) in arbitrary ways, which may pass unnoticed. For the 'postmodern', social science writing should, in principle, be shaken loose from its authorized source. The language should be liberated and allowed to speak more evocatively.

The immediate inspiration for this refrain was a plenary address at the Conference on Critical Anthropology at the University of Amsterdam in December 1989, given by Stephen Tyler, Professor of Anthropology at Rice University, a leading hotrodder in the postmodern turn. Freed from the boundaries of convention, alert to linguistic snares, Tyler pursues a course – similar to other post-modern critics – that roams helter-skelter over those left, disciplined bound, behind. My text is a reaction to the solitary stance (t)he(y) takes. It is a lament couched in ironic teasing, as well as an angry chastisement of his text. It sounds as a yelp of the Mother against her errant sons, against all those who assume ontological freedom, transitivity, solipsistic solitude; it is addressed to those who proclaim the immediacy of one/two/selfness – of separation and dissolution – and who revel in the phallic superfluidity that denies connections, relationships and the possibility of love.

The stage directions

Setting for the original performance

A typical academic auditorium in darkness, with bright lights illuminating the stage. A podium is set upon a desk, which may be used or not by the reader as a chair, table or stand. An overhead projector screen is illuminated behind the area stage left of the desk where the words are projected as they are spoken.

Characters
First Woman, as feminist postmodern critic.
Second Woman, her companion.
PM Man.

Costume
Black turtleneck, pants and heels (optional). 1½ meters of red feather boa flung about the shoulders and neck. A hand mirror, with a broken glass, face out, is strung on a ribbon or string about the neck as a necklace.

Script notes
The performance is in two parts; one may think of it (metaphorically) as a pie, a seafood crepe or perhaps a pregnant woman. Part I is the crust; Part II is the filling.
  [ ] indicate stage directions. The actor may use 'finger snaps' to indicate quotation marks for the audience.
  The prologue of the performance is composed of the introductory
                                                  for
lines from Tyler's written text 'A post-modern ⅄ instance'. It describes Tyler's two mental selves, his mind as the book and his mind as the word processor/computer.

The performance

Prologue

Tyler: 'I'm of two minds about this . . . the unmoved one and the moving continuum, Apollo and Dionysus . . . the mind as a book . . . a passionate attention that . . . joins life and experience in an act of production/reproduction/creativity, a conceit that we call the concept . . . and thus note the role of Eros in the sexual act of conceiving the concept, the perfection of form, the fixed entity of the idea, the achieved whole of the inner psyche that makes the integrity of the private mind and repeats itself in the solitude of the book, in the trance-like stasis of reading and writing.
  '. . . my other mind . . . the mind of the word processor/computer . . . replaces the steadiness of contemplative formulation with an excess of dynamic possibilities, turning my private solitude into the

public network, destroying my authorship by making a totalized textuality in which the text is only ancillary' (p. 1).

Part I: The crust

First Woman: Mille Feuille for the Fruits de Mer. How to make sense of the senses to follow. How many sheets can we layer, to make 'womb' for the filling to fit?

Second Woman: [*aside*] It would be much easier (and more to the point) to talk about hot dogs and hot dog buns.

First Woman: But much less elegant, and much less French. The problem, that is, my problem: How to compos(t)e a postmodernist pose, one that does not crush my feminist folds.

Second Woman: Irigaray speaks of the folds of femininity in perpetual embrace. As women, in a constant caress, caressing ourselves.

First Woman: No wonder we do not come to the point the way men do! My question: Can there be a Re-Union with Difference? Is it possible to conceive of A FEMINIST POSTMODERN/ POSTMODERN FEMINIST/FEMINIST-FEMME/POST-MODERN MODIFIED/??????????

Can we have:	Let go of:	and still retain:
Postmod's	**Modernist**	**A Feminist**
incongruity	insularity	involvement
intertextuality	ego-centrism	interaction
mixed codes	stable orders	free flows
chaos	consistency	community
scatology	asceticism	eroticism
playfulness	policy	pliableness
de-powering	power hungry	em-powering
partiality	totality	multiplicity
freedom	ownership	commitment
difference	opposites	dialogue
construction	coercion	creation
activity	rigidity	passivity
restlessness	reality	fantasy
?	?	?

As Edward Said said: 'transform binary opposition into an economy in which terms circulate'. OR as a chaoticist might insist – let the boiling pot of words break the laminarity and the clarity of orderly flow. Uncongeal categories, Both and And. 'Have your cake and eat it' – two. (There's a Mari-ann'ette, French again, a puppet game for you and me. Let us probe for the Un-said.)

Second Woman: Postmodernism. . . . Is it just another sport to add to the Academic Olympics? Who can deconstruct the fastest and the mostest? Bring on the muscle men, and let them strain. Steroid doses and noselogic poses. GOLD/SILVER/BRONZE [*she sings a phrase of 'La Marseillaise'*] 'Allons enfants de la patrie' . . . [*pause*].

First Woman: Did anybody say anything about anyone who wasn't playing their game?

Second Woman: There was some mention of women, at least of their bodies. They're the supplement, the ex-centrics. Without phALL-USes they can't go very far, especially in this game.

First Woman: No body seemed to notice that all the players are 'IN' the establishment. From the Sorbonne to Santa Cruz, the same old tricks, ruses, disguises, they use them to kick the OLD GUARD OUT of power. Re-Volving door policy – so that they could be INNER. More IN, less OUT. They won't hold a door open for anyone.

Second Woman: Just the same old 'Sexual politics' (the old IN and OUT).

First Woman: Well, that's what got me going! Its a love/hate relationship – postmodernism/feminism. How perfectly PM/PMS. Their endless discourses colliding in one condrumatic phrase. But two isms don't make an are, or do they?

Second Woman: Collapsing the opposition of love and hate. Collapsing the opposition: Femme and them, me and he.

First Woman: Collapsing the opposition (by taking the wind out of their sails?) Co-LAP-SING the (T)OP-POSition. (All missionaries are being recalled for faulty transmissions.) Or is it 'Co-Lapsinging' – a name for conjoining. Let our laps sing together . . . Much better.

Second Woman: No one needs to be 'on top'. We don't have to listen to what those dick-shunaries told us.

First Woman: Then let's start a deconstruction. It can happen anywhere. How about here? Perhaps the Zen master is right. It all/nothing makes sense.

Second Woman: A word about Stephen Tyler to whom this piece is daddy-kated. He's a cover-boy[2] (do you think I'm covering something up?), an under-cover (anthro)-agent; looking to dis-cover; running for cover. But there are no more hiding places. Its all on the surface, now. Nothing can hide under pre-texts any more.

First Woman: Tyler is a PM magician . . . talks and even writes PM-ese. Read *The Unspeakable* (Tyler, 1987) if you don't believe me. I admire him. Yet he is the target. I am after the pack. He is the random one whose number came up. My ode is to and with and through him.

In the intertextuality of things, he is a woof and I am a 'Whorf'. Now I shall spin us together in a centrifuge of text. Come follow me along, over and under we go, shuttles on the shades of weaving words.

[*First Woman reads*]:   ***Part II: 'The filling'***

PM Man: All I ever wanted to do was to stay in my room and 'play with IT'.[3]

First Woman: Behold. S.T. one in a new chain of linguistic magistics . . . U.V.W.X.Y.Z. The end of the line . . . where we all have to get off now. How to 'get off' ah, there's the rub. 'Tis nobler in the minds of men perhaps, but is that enough? That is also the question.

The P-M Man, torn apart . . . full of contra-DICK-shun. Of two minds . . . Platonist, left hemispheric, the 'ur-form of the scribal hand' . . . 'taking in hand' . . . E-Man-cipate . . . 'UNMOVED', AND the other mind, Dionysian, 'the boundless' one (do you anticipate MOVED? yes, why not? We were brought up on opposition). 'Moved . . . E-Moved . . . E-MOTION'. . .

Second Woman: Emotion . . . Now we get to the heart of the matter.

First Woman: Sorry to disappoint you, but it's a wrong spelling; don't forget the hyphen. It's E (hyphen) Motion. His motion is not from the heart; it's from the hardware.

PM Man: Give me SPACE! Keep it all separate. That's where it's comFORT-able. (One, Man, One FORT!) E-MOTION . . . the 'moving continuum'. E-Motion on the screen. 'The mind of the word processor/computer . . . poke at . . . mon-key.' (Get the French connection? Its all in the tongue.) Losing the self-consciousness of the left brain, peeling down the cortex to the electronic core . . . fingering 'mon' key, the magic wand that opens doors, boxes, hidden files . . . mesmerized by the flickering shadow-images, dancing naked on the screen. . . .

First Woman: He's CELL-Eee-Brate-ing alone, total-(itarian)-ly in 'calculative power, total manipulative control, abundant resource, speed, complete management . . . hypnotized by the phos-phorescent glow of moving symbols'. . . Listen to him hum.

PM Man: [*shouting*] 'Power is mine!'
. . . 'I have the instantaneous and total knowledge of god and am ONE with the movement of thought . . . I AM THE MOVING MATRIX!! . . .'

First Woman: CLIMAX, cut, end of paragraph . . . CURTAIN.

Second Woman: [*softly*] Should we pull the shades? Cigarette?

PM Man: [*tired*] It is dawn by now. No one can see in. Everyone is asleep. Besides we are not ashamed. We are scholars. It's the thing now. Left or Right: The Thing Was Always It.

First Woman: PM, Poor Man, just trying to get his head together. Or heads together? Is a Man of two heads or three? It's a trinity . . . three in one . . . indivisible . . . a miracle, the priest said. We should all respect it, even if we can't understand.

Second Woman: And be forgiven if we envy. (Who will forgive us? Our Sigmund who art in heaven?)

First Woman: But it's no fun when they won't let you play. Or when all you can be is the nurse, or the patient, or the ground they measure and inspect. Always peeking, then they say, 'Is that all there is?'

When will they learn? [*forceful*] Don't mess with Mother Nature!

Second Woman: E-movement . . . B-movement . . . Re-movement. 'When the boys came out to play, Georgie Porgie ran away.'

First Woman: Who are they trying to scare off? Full of Power and Manipulative Control, Abundant Resources, Speed, Complete Management. The New Army, complete with portable Zenises.[4] Pulling the rug out from under the OLD GUARD. (Didn't we all want to run out of the stands and CHEER!!!?) Down with the OLD ORDER . . . Foundations of Modernity, split into Gravity's Rainbow/Rules, shredded ribbons adorning the May POLE, wavering in the Breeze of breathtaking words/ABSOLUTE-ly nothinged by the shock-ing PM tropes/smashing icons with iron(ic)s/Wreaking CON-SENSE with NON-SENSE/

PARODYING
  PARADING
    PANDERING
      PARADOXING
        PLAYING

What fun! [*singing*] . . . 'London Bridge is Falling Down [*then shouting*] (DE-CONSTRUCT-ED) [*resumes singing*] MY FAIR LADY.'

Where can WE jump in? Shall we twirl your batons? Can we all form a circle? Dance around the fire? the Pole? the falling bridges? Give us a hand. Give us a hand? Give us a hand . . .

PM Man: All they ever want are hand-outs . . . Give'em an inch they'll take a mile. How many inches do they think we've got? [*a brief pause, then, addressing Women*] Besides can't you see we've got play to do? It's not easy just going off to play each day. It takes practice . . . dedication . . . grace. It's not something you can just join in like that. We've got our formation. Can't you see you'll just muck it up? We're in the wrecking business. What business is that of yours? 'You make, we break': We can write it on the truck. Next thing you'll want us to settle down and play house. We've got to be movin' on. It's part of the code. Girls can't be in combat. Besides John Wayne doesn't talk to them, so adios. Don't call us, we'll call you.

First Woman: That call has a familiar ring to it. The call of the WILD.

PM Man: We aren't animals; and don't call us an army! Better a merry dis-band-ment of (dis) Con-victors;
   (dis)Con-artists;   (dis)co-dandies;
           (dis)iden-ticals;
   (dis)-sent-uals;   (dis)-coursers;
(dis)si-paters;   (dis)contents;   (dis)-ap-pere-ers. . .
               (Dig that French)

  cr
    ac
      king
        up (by any meaning you like)
          c
       rac
      king
  up (whatever other meaning(s) you like) . . .

THE JOINT

First Woman: How many joints you got in mind?

PM Man: Hey, it's not personal. No hard feelings?

First Woman: 'How do you mean that?'

Second Woman: Makes you wonder if she has a 'double entendre' in mind. Those Frenchies are at it again.

PM Man: If you wanna make an omelette, you gotta break some eggs.

First Woman: But we've got the eggs.

PM Man: Which comes first, the chicks or the eggs? Sorry I couldn't help it. Old gag line, part of the new PM ritual: Say whatever comes into your head, especially if it's a dumb 'yoke'. [*laughs at his own joke*]

First Woman: Which head?

Second Woman: Another double entendre?!

PM Man: One for all and all for one. At least for the moment. That's another thing. We don't make promises. Just another word for COMMITMENT (the really big C-word, the one that gets you behind bars, and I don't mean mixing martinis). A rolling stone gathers no moss and no mille-deux.

First Woman: Mick Jagger has children.

PM Man: Babies are phallic. If you need one, get one.

First Woman: But your phallus doesn't need bread.

PM Man: 'Let them eat cake,' as good ol' Marie put it. She had a feel for our rap. French, of course.

First Woman: That doesn't solve the problem.

PM Man: It's not my problem. Postmodern life is, as Deleuze (1978) sez, nomadic. And S.T. added, 'We are all homeless wanderers on the featureless, postindustrial steppe, tentless nomads, home packed up.' And as a NATO tank commander once said, 'What kinda army is it when you gotta bring along the outhouse for the femmes?'

First Woman: Looks like it's going to be a short revolution – about one generation.

PM Man: Au contraire, Baby, we've just begun. I mean the trashing is in dis-progress. Disciplines to dismantle/Methods to maul/Truth to trample/origins to emasculate.

First Woman: Who's on the clean-up committee?

PM Man: You sound like somebody's mother. Whose side are you on anyway? Few minutes ago you wanted to dance in the streets. Down with the old, up with the new. (Never satisfied; always want something ya can't get . . . Bitch, bitch, bitch.)

First Woman: You sound de-fence-ive. Have I got your goat?

PM Man: Now you're getting down to something. Thanks, but no thanks. I get off graphically. Who needs flesh? And I can logoff any time any time any time . . . Let's leave it at that. Stephen Tyler has said: 'Postmodernism accepts the paradoxical CONsequences of . . . irreconcilable ambiguity without attempting to end the CONflict by imposing CLOSURE . . .'

We're a-dispersing . . . 'dis-pursing' . . . we are getting farther and farther away. Space is beautiful.

First Woman: It's gonna be mighty COLD out there . . .

PM Man: 'Earthling, do you read me? . . . do you read me?? . . . do you . . . reeeeead . . .???

First Woman: You're fading Major Tom.'

[*A signal getting weaker and weaker can be heard. No one strains to listen after a while. No one cares. It's perfect.*]

SILENCE

Notes

This work was originally produced while at The Netherlands Institute for Advanced Study, Wassenaar, The Netherlands.

1 I wish to recognize many people who helped me with this presentation. In particular I wish to thank Kenneth Gergen for his enthusiastic and expert editorial and dramatic assistance. I would also thank the wonderful people at Aarhus,

especially the women, who witnessed and gave me support for the first production, and Steinar Kvale, who dared to let me do it. I ask Stephen Tyler's indulgence; without him I couldn't have written it. (He has since given it.) Thanks also to my croquet colleagues at NIAS, who helped me get some of the lines right, especially Gigi Santow, Rene van Rijsselt, Peter Mair, Wojciech Sadurski, Jack Donnelly and Michael Bracher.

2 The front cover photograph of Clifford and Marcus's (1986) book shows a young anthropologist (Stephen Tyler) writing his field notes as an older man of the village looks on.

3 The Lacanian sign transposed as the Word, the Object, PC, the Thing of Things, or 'whatever turns you and it on'.

4 Donna Haraway (1988) has written with similar feelings: 'The further I get in describing . . . postmodernism . . . the more nervous I get. The imagery of force fields, of moves in a fully textualized and coded world . . . is, just for starters, an imagery of high-tech military fields, of automated academic battlefields, where blips of light called players disintegrate (what a metaphor!) each other in order to stay in the knowledge and power game. Technoscience and science fiction collapse into the sun of their radiant (ir)reality-war' (p. 577).

References

Butler, J. (1990) *Gender Trouble: Feminism and the Subversion of Identity*. New York: Routledge.

Clifford, J. and Marcus, G. (eds) (1986) *Writing Cultures: The Poetics and Politics of Ethnography*. Berkeley: University of California Press.

Deleuze, G. (1978) Nomad thought, trans. J. Wallance. *Semiotext(e)*, 3: 12–20.

Flax, J. (1987) Postmodernism and gender relations in feminist theory. *Signs*, 12: 621–43.

Flax, J. (1990) *Thinking Fragments*. Berkeley: University of California Press.

Fraser, N. and Nicholson, L. (1988) Social criticism without philosophy: an encounter between feminism and postmodernism. In A. Ross (eds), *Universal Abandon: The Politics of Postmodernism*. Minneapolis: University of Minnesota Press. pp. 83–104.

Gergen, K. (1985) The social constructionist movement in psychology. *American Psychologist*, 40: 266–75.

Gergen, M. (ed.) (1988) *Feminist Thought and the Structure of Knowledge*. New York: New York University Press.

Gergen, M. (1991) Life stories: pieces of a dream. In G. Rosenwald and R. Ochberg (eds), *Storied Lives*. New Haven, CT: Yale University Press.

Haraway, D. (1988) Situated knowledges: the science question in feminism and the privilege of partial perspective. *Feminist Studies*, 14: 575–99.

Heilbrun, C. (1988) *Writing a Woman's Life*. San Francisco: The Woman's Press.

Hollway, W. (1989) *Subjectivity and Method in Psychology: Gender, Meaning and Science*. London: Sage.

Irigaray, L. (1985) *Speculum of the Other Woman*, trans. G. Gill. Ithaca, NY: Cornell University Press.

Kristeva, J. (1980) *Desire in Language: A Semiotic Approach to Literature and Art*, trans. T. Gora, A. Jardine and L. Roudiez, ed. L. Roudiez. New York: Columbia University Press.

Lather, P. (1986) Research as praxis. *Harvard Educational Review*, 56: 257–77.

Lorber, J. and Farrell, S.A. (1991) *The Social Construction of Gender*. Newbury Park, CA: Sage.

Moi, T. (ed.) (1987) *French Feminist Thought: A Reader*. Oxford: Blackwell.

Moi, T. (1988) Feminism, postmodernism, and style: recent feminist criticism in the United States. *Cultural Critique*, 9: 3–22.

Nielsen, J.M. (ed.) (1990) *Feminist Research Methods*. Boulder, CO: Westview Press.

Roberts, H. (ed.) (1981) *Doing Feminist Research*. London: Routledge.

Tyler, S. (1987) *The Unspeakable: Discourse, Dialogue, and Rhetoric in the Postmodern World*. Madison: University of Wisconsin Press.

Weedon, C. (1987) *Feminist Practice and Poststructuralist Theory*. Oxford: Blackwell.

12

From Theory to Practice and Back Again: What does Postmodern Philosophy Contribute to Psychological Science?

Seth Chaiklin

'Postmodernism' is primarily a movement of philosophical thought. As psychologists, we are not usually concerned with developing and analyzing philosophical questions. So why should one, as a psychologist, bother to enter into the description and analysis of philosophical questions? What do we go to philosophy for? What do we expect to get out of it?

The main value of philosophical reflections is ideological. These reflections are used to motivate arguments about which problems are valuable to solve, what kinds of knowledge we should be trying to get and what expectations, goals, hopes and ideals to have for our scientific activities. I would expect that the application of postmodern philosophy to psychology will be most productive at this ideological level. I would find the application of this philosophy compelling if it raised new points about the goals of psychology or interesting directions in which to achieve these goals. As Ken Gergen writes: 'the postmodern turn begins to offer psychology new ways of conceptualizing itself and its potentials. And, if properly understood, postmodern thought opens vistas of untold significance for the discipline' (this volume, p. 25).

The ideological use of postmodern philosophy characterizes several recent attempts to apply postmodern philosophy to psychology (see chapters by Gergen, Polkinghorne and Kvale in this volume). Unlike other chapters in this volume, these three are directly concerned with using concepts claimed by postmodern philosophy in order to criticize existing psychological science, and to offer views for the future practice and development of psychology based on or inspired by postmodern philosophical principles. The present chapter examines these three chapters with the expectation that one would be particularly likely to find some insight into and arguments for what postmodern philosophy can contribute to psychological science.

The main conclusions will be that (a) applications of postmodern philosophy to psychological questions have not been particularly compelling, and have been marked by numerous contradictions or confusions; (b) these applications have tended to overdraw the differences between a 'postmodern' and a 'modern' psychology to the point that it becomes necessary to make some historical analysis of the content of these concepts; and (c) more productive paths are available for addressing problems raised in these chapters. For example, the positive criteria offered in these chapters reflect interests and accomplishments of cultural-historical psychology.

Brief review of applications of the 'postmodern' concept to psychology

Let us suspend the postmodern question for a moment, and first ask what is the main positive interest expressed in the chapters by Gergen, Polkinghorne and Kvale, as well as the 'psychologist' who is implicitly addressed in these chapters. My purpose here is to establish some common vision of the nature and goals of psychology as expressed in these chapters, independently of whatever contribution postmodern thinking might provide to the development of these goals. We can then come back and evaluate the contribution of postmodern concepts for developing the main interest.

The primary concern in Gergen's chapter is to advocate that psychologists become active and engaged participants in the cultural process. He writes that 'Postmodernism asks the scientist to join in the hurly-burly of cultural life', 'to tell it as it may become', 'to break the barriers of common sense', 'to open new alternatives for thought and action' (this volume, p. 27). An important part of this process is for the psychologist to be self-reflective about the values that are being used and 'to develop new intelligibilities that present new options to the culture'. The 'psychologist' to whom Gergen is directing his comments is probably an 'experimental psychologist' because Gergen often refers to the experimental method, laboratory studies and such psychological processes as learning, perception, memory, cognition, motivation and emotion.

The main concern in Polkinghorne's chapter can be described in two ways. The most immediate concern is to describe some epistemological principles that can serve to elucidate a psychological science of practice. His main thesis is that 'the psychology of practice . . . is configured as a postmodern science' (this volume, p. 146) and the 'epistemology that implicitly informs contemporary practice of psychology in psychotherapy and consultation reveals a temper that is basically postmodern'. The more general concern is that this epistemology might be a part of a self-standing science of the practice of psychology: a unified 'science-practice' psychology. His psychologist is focused on pragmatic action in service of the health and development of persons. More specifically, Polkinghorne's discussion is focused on psychotherapy of clients, perhaps of several varieties (that is, family, group, couples, individual), though this is not specified.

The principal concern of Kvale's chapter is to identify the main task of psychology, where it could contribute a core of concepts (to other disciplines or to society) that could not be offered by other disciplines. 'Except for the theoretical contributions of that marginal school of scientific psychology – psychoanalysis – and the current popularizations in the therapeutic market, psychology has today little to tell other sciences or the public at large' (this volume, p. 40). He further posits that the current emptiness and irrelevance of a psychological science to culture at large may be due to psychology being a product of modernity, the study of the logic of an abstracted 'psyche' out of touch with a postmodern world. Kvale's 'psychologist' is harder to discern though he does mention a dichotomy between research and professional psychology.

Despite the differences in the immediate concerns of these chapters and in the 'psychologist' to whom each chapter is directed, there is an obvious commonality among them; each chapter is seeking to find a psychology that can make some positive contributions (dare we say improvements?!) to spheres of human activity. Moreover, the emphasis is on the idea that psychologists should be engaged in significant societal institutions or practices and developing ideas or practices that would be useful to these institutions.

At first glance, one does not need to employ postmodern philosophy to have the goal of a societally useful psychology. Such values have been expressed from the early days of psychology. Why have these authors taken up postmodern philosophy in service of that goal? How does it help them realize this goal?

A common theme among all three chapters is that psychology (as it is commonly conducted) is a product of modernity ('the vast share of contemporary psychology is conducted within a modernist framework' – Gergen; 'The story of academic psychology is a subplot within the history of modernism' – Polkinghorne; 'Psychology is a project of modernity' – Kvale) and that intellectual and cultural developments in the late twentieth century have undermined this psychology and its epistemological justification ('How are these [modernist] presumptions [of psychological inquiry] challenged by lines of argument in the postmodern sphere?' – Gergen; 'If academic psychology is to adapt to the coming postmodern condition, it will need to reconfigure its narrative' – Polkinghorne; 'If . . . modernity has come to an end, this may also involve the end of psychology as a science' – Kvale). In short, these authors are arguing that it is necessary to reconsider psychology in light of the general intellectual developments that are called postmodern philosophy. Presumably it will not be possible to develop a societally useful psychology if we continue with psychologies that are motivated by modernist assumptions (as construed by these writers).

What is 'modernist' psychology?

If one considers some common themes in these three chapters, it is easy to project what might be called a 'received' view of the characteristics of modernist psychology. In particular, a modernist psychology is grounded in the assumptions that there is a formally structured universe that can be discovered through methods, particularly experimental ones, that will reveal true, universal laws, preferably of 'formal-computational' or 'hypothetical-deductive' variety, that are true for all times, places and persons. Gergen and Polkinghorne also refer to the idea that the modern view expects that the results of knowledge acquisition should be cumulative, resulting in a progressive increase in our knowledge about the world.

These kinds of assumptions are presumably what motivates most university-based psychologists in the late twentieth century, while practicing or 'borderline' psychologists are involved in practical work with a different epistemology. 'There are now two sciences of psychology: the modernistic science primarily engaged in by academic researchers, and the science of practice primarily engaged in by practicing psychologists' (Polkinghorne, this volume, pp. 154–5). 'Whereas academic psychology is becoming a museum of modern thought, professional psychologists encounter human beings in their current world' (Kvale, this volume, p. 48). Both Polkinghorne and Kvale refer to the tensions in the American Psychological Association between researchers and practitioners as evidence of a gap between theory and practice.

What should we aim for?

To this point we can see that these three chapters argue that university-based psychology has a drive toward universal theories, and this will not be adequate to realize the general goals these postmodern critics describe for psychology. It is possible to construct a fairly common view of specific positive criteria that these chapters propose for how psychological research should be conducted in light of the postmodern themes raised by their authors.

Our knowledge is constructed, not built on an independent reality, but rather is constructed through language games and conceptual schemes (see Polkinghorne's discussion of 'foundationlessness' and 'constructivism' and Gergen's discussion of 'vanishing subject matter'). No single method is going to guarantee successful results (cf. Gergen on the 'marginalization of method'; Polkinghorne on 'fragmentariness'; Kvale on multi-method). Moreover, we can no longer be certain that our efforts will actually result in progressive improvement of the human condition (cf. Gergen on 'the grand narrative of progress').

Instead, guided by principles claimed by postmodern philosophers, these three chapters place more emphasis on developing knowledge that is societally located in particular societally relevant practices. Knowledge should be concerned with these local and specific occurrences, not with the search for context-free general laws. Kvale maintains there is an inherent affinity of anthropological understanding with its focus on local knowledge and central themes of postmodern thought. Moreover, this knowledge should be timely, taking into account the particular historical and cultural conditions of the investigation. 'Postmodern thought invites the investigator to take account of the historical circumstances of his/her inquiry' (Gergen, this volume, p. 24). 'It does not seek a grand theory that will account for human experience regardless of time and place' (Polkinghorne, this volume, p. 160). 'In order to understand human activity, it is necessary to know the culture, the social and historical situation, in which the activity takes place' (Kvale, this volume, p. 31).

Based on these principles, Gergen sketches three possible lines of development for a postmodern psychology: technological advance; cultural critique; and construction of new worlds. The first, and least important in his view, is to develop our ability to do things such as aimed at by psychological tests or educational programs. The second is for the scholar to de-objectify the existing realities, to demonstrate their social and historical embeddedness. The third, referred to before, is to 'open new alternatives for action'.

In Polkinghorne's view, a psychology of practice, based on postmodern epistemological principles, should develop a pragmatic body of knowledge which consists of a collection of examples of actions that have worked to bring about desired ends. 'A neopragmatic body of knowledge consists of summary generalizations of which type of action has been successful in prior like situations' (this volume, p. 152). In the case of psychotherapy, this knowledge is generated from the clinical experiences of experienced and expert practitioners and takes the form of patterns or prototypical models and exemplary clinical experiences.

Kvale proposes the improvement of practice as the aim of research as a replacement for the quest for scientific legitimation, the search for universal knowledge, and the use of method as truth guarantee.

How are we to gain this knowledge?

Now that we know a little about the goals of psychological science from a postmodern perspective, we would like to consider what procedures should be used to achieve these goals.

Gergen does not seem to hold much hope for the concept of 'method'. 'Under postmodernism, however, methodology loses its coveted position' (this volume, p. 24). Unfortunately, he does not say what position method should take, if any. He underplays the possibility and value of technological innovations, and puts more emphasis on the need for cultural critique and construction of new worlds. Taking up the narrative emphasis in postmodern thought, Gergen suggests that cultural critique can be accomplished through examining discourse and that new alternatives can be created by scholars willing to break the barriers of common sense by offering new forms of theory, of interpretation, of intelligibility; it is through the well-formed word that psychological scholars are positioned to transform culture.

Kvale suggests that system evaluation and qualitative methodology appear congenial to a postmodern understanding of the world. He recognizes a serious problem that researchers encounter who want to work with a focus on timely problems: professional practitioners encounter man in his world, though often without an adequate conceptual grasp of the relation of man to his cultural context. He does not offer any suggestions about how we can achieve this conceptual grasp, beyond the fact that, in line with Polkinghorne's epistemology of practice, it does not advocate a practice devoid of theory. It is an argument to take professional practice seriously, to conceptualize and reflect upon the many philosophical and political issues raised by this practice.

Polkinghorne wrote that 'The epistemology of practice recognizes that much of practicing knowledge is tacit, dealing with "knowing how", rather than theoretical and conceptual, dealing with "knowing that"' (this volume, p. 159). He further maintains that common sense argues that the articulation of an epistemology of practicing knowledge must be based on the processes of expert practitioners, not the deliberative procedures and theoretically derived rules that constitute the practicing knowledge of novices. Neopragmatism shifts the focus of knowledge generation to programs to collect descriptions of actions that have effectively accomplished intended ends. Science serves to collect, organize and distribute the practices that have produced their intended results.

What are the procedures by which we shall come to this knowledge? One method includes controlled experiments of new methods which can be integrated into knowledge that is drawn from practice. Another method is to develop 'cognitive interpretive patterns' of actions that produce successful results. Expert practitioners reflect on and articulate their repetitive experiences in their specialized practices in the form of cognitive patterns. These patterns are, according to Polkinghorne, derived from the practitioners' tacit understandings of human function, from theories and models learned in training and from exemplary clinical experiences. Trial and error seem to be particularly important.[1] Theoretical views can be used as a source of ideas, but theoretical development does not seem to be an important goal in the epistemology of practice.

Does postmodern philosophy help?

I have tried to show that a primary concern of these three chapters is that psychology should be oriented more toward addressing societally significant matters in a local, historically grounded manner. I am sympathetic with this vision for psychological research and practice. If I am going to work toward that goal, then I will have limited time for reading and applying postmodern philosophy in my psychological work. Therefore, one reason to read these three chapters, by psychologists who have clearly devoted some time to reading and formulating their ideas about postmodern philosophy in relation to psychology, is to find out if I should spend more time studying postmodern philosophy.

On the basis of this reading, I am not encouraged by the prospects of postmodern philosophy opening untold vistas for psychology. I will take up two major problems in the applications found in these chapters. First, I will make some general comments about the application of postmodern philosophy to psychology found in these chapters, using some postmodern principles as part of the evaluation. My basic conclusion is that the ideological use of postmodern philosophy found there is not particularly interesting or insightful. Second, I will turn to the positive methodological ideas offered in these chapters, concluding that they do not seem to offer any advantages or insights over existing ideas, and may even be regressive.

The prefix 'post-' implies syntactically that the modern has been transcended. In practice, however, an 'anti-modern' stance is usually held or implied (cf. Habermas, 1981). The psychological applications of postmodern concepts found in these chapters follow this tradition: postmodernism undermines modernist psychology (Gergen); the characteristics of the postmodern epistemology are the antitheses of the modernist epistemology (Polkinghorne); a postmodern psychology is a contradiction in terms (Kvale).

These chapters have used a construal of 'modern psychology' as a foil against which to put forward their positive proposals for psychology. Why is so much energy devoted to formulating a 'modernist' dragon to be slain by a postmodern knight? There are several reasons to doubt the utility of this rhetorical approach.

First, if a psychology grounded in postmodern principles is worthy of attention, then I would think these arguments could be put forward in their own terms rather than as a negation of existing (or in some cases unjustifiably overdrawn – cf. Polkinghorne's discussion of 'modern' view of the universe as a single, unified logical system) traditions. Why should psychologists who want to apply postmodern philosophy let their analyses of psychological issues be initially defined as a negation of issues and questions that come out of needs and problems of intellectual traditions they want to reject? Along these lines Shotter's chapter (this volume) starts more directly from some assumptions that he characterizes as postmodern, and does not really formulate a 'modern' opponent.

Second, taking a tip from Lyotard (1984), one of the central tenets of a postmodern view of knowledge is the unnecessity of consensus as a method of scientific development (Lyotard, 1984: 63–5). A shifting to a philosophical pragmatism that says why not 'both/and' instead of 'either/or' – or what Polkinghorne referred to as a principle of equifinality. On this view, there is little need to devote so much effort to a view that is deemed insufficient.

Third, if knowledge is local and contextual as the postmodern view holds, then I would expect that philosophical principles would have this status as well and that their application to psychology will have to be worked out in relation to substantive psychological problems that are being investigated (unless of course this postmodern view is going to be used as another grand narrative with some universal epistemological principles). For example, it might have been more interesting for Polkinghorne to start with and discuss some specific principles of practice developed from his experience and growing out of specific needs and problems that confront the aspect of psychology he is concerned with.

Fourth, it gives the impression that a postmodern-inspired psychology will be able to 'wipe the slate clean' and 'start from scratch' without need to take into account the history of psychology that has preceded. Toulmin (1990) describes a similar kind of dream from the modernist Cartesian tradition, and suggests, instead, that we should acknowledge and refine our conceptual inheritance rather than think that we can cut free from it (cf. pp. 178–9). Polkinghorne acknowledges the possible contribution of existing theoretical schemes, but is ambivalent about their value.

Fifth, the concepts of 'postmodern' and 'modern' are thoroughly polysemous, and refer to complicated, historical conditions. Several scholars have noted that it is impossible to define 'postmodernity' in a singular, unambiguous way (for instance, Kvale, this volume; Løvlie, this volume; Lyotard, 1986). Similarly, it may be questionable to try to characterize a 'postmodern age' (Feher, 1987: 195; Kolakowski, 1986: 9). The same point can be made about the term 'modern', which has a long and complicated history that has been used to refer to several historical periods, starting in the late fifth century when the term first appeared in Latin in response to the decline of the Roman empire, through to periods in the sixteenth, seventeenth, eighteenth and even nineteenth centuries (Habermas, 1981; Kolakowski, 1986; Madsen, this volume; Toulmin, 1990).

It should be clear that (a) the labels 'modern' and 'postmodern' do not communicate very much by themselves; (b) it is probably impossible to formulate clearly whether psychology is 'modern' or 'postmodern'; (c) the diversity of meanings should remind and encourage psychologists not to dismiss immediately a tradition labeled as 'modern' or 'postmodern' without closer investigation of the substantive goals and principles involved (or in other words, not to assume that one writer's definition of 'modern' or 'postmodern' encompasses another's).

Turning now to the subject matter of psychology, I have tried to address these chapters at the level of the goals expressed for psychology and the criteria for worthwhile psychological research and practice. If knowledge should be handled more locally and historically as these chapters have asserted, then it would make more sense when analyzing psychology to be more local and historical. 'Psychology', like 'modern' and 'postmodern', is a complicated, historical development. It is difficult to talk about it as a monolithic subject (Koch, 1976).

To put it mildly, I find the characterizations of 'modernist psychology' and its equation with contemporary practice in university psychology departments to be a little overdrawn. It is hard to find specific examples of psychology, particularly as practiced today, described in these chapters. Gergen referred to controlled experiments in laboratories and some general topics as described above, but it would have been nice to have one contemporary, mainstream example, drawn say from *Psychological Review*, to illustrate his point. Polkinghorne did not refer to specific examples of psychological studies that fall into the modernist tradition, yet draws support for his epistemology from research traditions (Chi et al., 1988, on expertise; the 'schemata' concept and probably a lot of 'constructivism') that have worked literally in the formal-computational tradition he criticized (that is, constructing computer simulation models as part of the research program). Kvale listed some recent developments in psychology such as 'psycholinguistics and cognitive science' (which I would call 'mainstream' or even 'modernist'), but he dismissed them as being questionably within the subject matter of psychology. He mentioned recent research on parallel distributed processing as having some aspects close to a postmodern understanding, but overlooked the fact that this tradition is continuing to try to find universal laws. It is a little disconcerting to find such an ahistorical, nonspecific treatment of psychology by writers who are working with the postmodern principles of local, contextually bound knowledge.

In sum, if the purpose of applying postmodern philosophy in the present context is to articulate and legitimate new forms of psychological practice or new questions and problems for investigation, then these chapters are not convincing. The inaccurate characterization of the 'modern' philosophical and 'academic' psychological traditions makes it impossible to engage in a serious ideological debate about existing forms and methods in relation to a postmodern-inspired psychology.

Nonetheless, we can set the ideological problem aside, and start from the positive goals for psychology set forth by these chapters. As I suggested, these positive goals do not seem to depend on postmodern philosophy. As research psychologists, we would like to believe that one consequence of our discipline's efforts to systematically study spheres of human experience and practice is the development of societally useful knowledge. This view is not original, of course, with a postmodern tradition. One of Francis Bacon's arguments for using scientific methods was the possibility of developing knowledge for human improvement. One of the goals in creating the *Encyclopédie* during the French Enlightenment was to make knowledge freely available to the public. The burgeoning area of research on eyewitness memory for natural events and its application in court trials (for instance, Ceci et al., 1987; Fiske et al., 1991) and the development of training programs for amnesics (for instance, Glisky and Schacter, 1989) are two of the many examples that could be cited where psychological research and researchers, inspired in part by an interest to find universal laws, have become involved in the 'hurly-burly life of cultural life-culture'. We do not even have to have the high aspirations ascribed to Enlightenment thinking: mastering Nature, emancipating Humanity or finding a rational and certain Truth. I suspect most psychologists would be happy if we could understand human practices and conditions in a way that would make a modest contribution to creating humane societal conditions. Toulmin (1990) described this more modest humanist version of modernity that developed in the sixteenth century. Thus, the question is whether conscious attention to postmodern philosophy can provide some guidance in achieving those goals. I will focus in particular on the proposals for how knowledge should be generated in a postmodern psychology, and the relation between theory and practice in those procedures.

One part of approaching these goals is to develop our knowledge about human practices and institutions. Whether called a method or not, we have to have some procedures for developing this knowledge. It can be described as an issue of 'fixing belief' (Peirce, 1877/1966). Peirce described four general methods that historically have been used to establish knowledge. Gergen, Polkinghorne and Kvale do not seem to advocate the first three methods described by Peirce: tenacity (for instance, religious faith), authority (for instance, the Pope) or a priori (for instance, metaphysical philosophy). However, there is more ambiguity about their position toward the fourth and final method Peirce describes, the scientific method.[2]

There is a clear critique against the idea of using a method as a generator of truth (Gergen, Polkinghorne), so it is not so clear what the procedures of knowledge generation should be. Gergen does not seem to acknowledge that empirical processes could have any role in the development of psychological knowledge. I find Gergen's emphasis on 'well-formed words' to be puzzling. If that is to be the main criterion of psychological science, then I personally would look to Dostoevsky (1864/1972: especially the second half of chapter 1) and Tolstoy (1899/1961) for inspiration. Perhaps others would look to newspaper columnists and filmmakers. All these sources have their value, but does Gergen mean to imply that there is no serious and essential role for empirical work in a postmodern, psychological science? Also, I do not understand how someone who emphasizes the importance of understanding historical conditions of inquiry would then propose that psychologists can construct tests for psychological deficits 'So long as one does not objectify terms such as "performance", "deficits", "evaluation" and "psychotherapy"' (this volume p. 26). Does Gergen expect that if psychologists are sensitive to the valuational implications of mental tests the rest of society will be as well? We already have too many counter-examples starting with Binet's test, which was originally developed for socially useful purposes to identify children who were having trouble in French schools, and which became objectified by others. In short, the positive methodological guidance that Gergen extracts from postmodern philosophy seems unpromising for addressing societally relevant psychological problems.

Polkinghorne is more sanguine about the role of empirical processes, noting that clinicians' experiences should be the source of knowledge generation. He acknowledges that we should hope for more than a method of authority (or power) and offers his epistemological analysis as a basis for developing a useful psychology.

Polkinghorne's focus is on psychotherapy with clients, but it is possible to generalize his argument to other spheres of practice that are interested in the mental health and personal development of individuals, such as education and work. In these areas, one could make similar arguments that schoolteachers, office managers and shop foremen should develop their own science based on their practical experiences.

It is a little difficult to establish Polkinghorne's views about the relation between the psychology of practice that he describes and research psychology. On the one hand, one could read his chapter as offering some views about how persons should be trained as psychotherapists. Here one finds sensible suggestions: descriptions of how to practice are not sufficient; it is necessary to practice; it helps to see skilled practitioners at work; and so forth. On the other hand, he sometimes counterposes his epistemological proposals as a general research strategy for developing knowledge about practice (for instance, suggesting that if academic psychology were to reconfigure itself along the lines of his epistemological analysis, then we could start to have a 'science-practice' psychology). Therefore, one could read Polkinghorne's epistemological principles as offering a more general set of guidelines for how psychological knowledge should be developed. From this point of view, his proposals are inadequate as a basis for research development.

Polkinghorne's arguments for knowledge development focus primarily on the recording and refining of tacit understandings derived from the practical experience of experts, and expressed as summary generalizations of experience that are effective in practice. The psychology of practice's body of knowledge consists of the aggregate of the professional community's experiences of what has been beneficial to clients. Theoretical conceptions are not considered an important objective of development in an epistemology of practice.

As noted before, Kvale acknowledges that there should be a place for theoretical development, but does not elaborate on its role. Both Polkinghorne and Kvale note a tension or dichotomy between research psychology and practical or professional application of psychology. Polkinghorne seems to resolve the tension by accepting the dichotomy, but voting for the other side, giving primacy to the practical, thereby simply reinforcing the dichotomy.

Polkinghorne's chapter seems to have confused the relation between theory and practice. Just because a theory is inadequate as a complete prescription of action while one is sitting with a client in a psychotherapy session, this does not mean that theoretical concepts and analysis should not have a central role in developing knowledge about a practice. No science, human or natural, has a complete theory of practice that provides guidance about what to do in every single practical case. More critical is the question of whether a science of practice can be developed without a theoretical foundation.

Polkinghorne's chapter cites Thomas Kuhn as a postmodern philosopher, but does not seem to acknowledge a central point developed by Kuhn (among many others), that scientific terms are theory laden. Does Polkinghorne expect that his scientific practitioners will be able to develop concepts to express their clinical experiences that are not embedded in a general theoretical scheme? Similarly, does he expect that these generalizations will be meaningful to others if there is not a theoretical scheme from which to interpret them? Unfortunately, Polkinghorne's chapter does not offer any examples of summary generalizations or cognitive patterns, so it is difficult to offer any answers here. If it turns out that theoretical schemes are needed to interpret summary generalizations, then we are back to the problem of how to develop a theoretically grounded practice.

In the long history of analysis about the relation between theory and practice, it is generally recognized that theoretical developments are an important part of developing a more effective practice (Kant, 1793/1983). In Kurt Lewin's well-known words, there is 'nothing so practical as a good theory' (Lewin, 1951: 169); or in Lévy-Leboyer's (1988) reversal, 'There is nothing so theoretical as a good application' (p. 785). Is it still necessary to make arguments about the importance of theory for helping us to formulate and evaluate ideas?

Where do we go from here?

In reviewing these applications of postmodern philosophy to psychology, I have come to see that the primary line of argument is to oppose a 'modernist' psychology with a 'postmodernist' alternative. However, the collective image that emerges from these chapters is that postmodern psychology, at best, has an ambivalent relation to the role of theory in knowledge development. Another possibility is to work toward a more theoretically informed practice and a practically informed theory as part of the same practice. These are explicit goals of the cultural-historical psychology and critical psychology. Both these traditions are grounded in dialectical philosophy, and emphasize the importance of understanding human practices as societally embedded practices within ongoing historical traditions. Rather than seeing theoretical development and practical applications as naturally opposed, they argue for the importance of theoretical formulation as a way of understanding and further developing experience. Research in this tradition has been done on psychotherapy (for instance, Dreier, 1992), education (for instance, Davydov, 1988; Moll, 1990) and work (for instance, Bødker, 1990; Engeström, 1992).

I mention these cultural-historical approaches because they have the kinds of positive characteristics that these chapters call for, but were inspired by a philosophy that is not particularly postmodernist. I would not expect the cultural-historical traditions to be ill received by psychologists who are interested in postmodern principles, but psychologists who write from a conscious postmodern perspective do not acknowledge these traditions either.

To conclude, I have not tried to argue that postmodern philosophy is useless for achieving the kinds of goals expressed in the chapters by Gergen, Polkinghorne and Kvale. Rather, I have argued that these chapters do not offer much hope that postmodern philosophy will help achieve the goals for psychology that they set forth. Psychologists with interests in a societally oriented psychology might find that the cultural-historical traditions provide a more promising philosophical basis for developing their scientific work.

Notes

I thank Mariane Hedegaard and Steinar Kvale for critical comments on various drafts of this chapter.

1 Gradually constructing and revising their cognitive patterns and response routines through trial and error: 'Theories of practice and past experience only serve as a guide to anticipate clients' responses. In work with clients, therapists guide their actions by trial and error, adjusting them in light of the actual responses of clients' (p. 159).
2 I do not endorse all that Peirce wrote about the scientific method in his article, but fuller discussion is not relevant here. The main point is only to note these global methods for establishing knowledge.

References

Bødker, S. (1990) *Through the Interface*. Hillsdale, NJ: Erlbaum.
Ceci, S.J., Ross, D.R. and Toglia, M.P. (eds) (1987) *Children's Eyewitness Memories*. New York: Springer.

Chi, M.T.H., Glaser, R. and Farr, M.J. (eds) (1988) *The Nature of Expertise.* Hillsdale, NJ: Erlbaum.

Davydov, V.V. (1988) Problems of developmental teaching. *Soviet Education,* 30 (8): 6–97.

Dostoevsky, F. (1972) *Notes from Underground,* trans. J. Coulson. New York: Penguin. (Original work published in 1864.)

Dreier, O. (1992) Re-searching psychotherapeutic practice. In S. Chaiklin and J. Lave (eds), *Understanding Practice: Perspectives on Activity and Context.* New York: Cambridge University Press.

Engeström, Y. (1992) Developmental studies of work as a testbench of activity theory: the case of primary care medical practice. In S. Chaiklin and J. Lave (eds), *Understanding Practice: Perspectives on Activity and Context.* New York: Cambridge University Press.

Feher, F. (1987) The status of postmodernity. *Philosophy and Social Criticism* 13: 195–206.

Fiske, S. T., Bersoff, D. N., Borgida, E., Deaux, K. and Heilman, M. E. (1991) Social science research on trial: use of sex stereotyping research in Price Waterhouse v. Hopkins. *American Psychologist,* 46: 1049–60.

Glisky, E.L. and Schacter, D.L. (1989) Extending the limits of complex learning in organic amnensia: computer training in a vocational domain. *Neuropsychologia,* 27: 107–20.

Habermas, J. (1981) Modernity versus postmodernity. *New German Critique,* 22: 3–14.

Kant, I. (1983) On the proverb: That may be true in theory but is of no practical use. In *Perpetual Peace and Other Essays,* trans T. Humphrey. Indianapolis, IN: Hackett. pp. 61–92. (Original work published in 1793.)

Koch, S. (1976) Language communities, search cells, and the psychological studies. In W.J. Arnold (ed.), *Nebraska Symposium on Motivation, 1975* (vol. 23). Lincoln: University of Nebraska Press. pp. 477–559.

Kolakowski, L. (1986) Modernity on endless trial. *Encounter,* 12: 8–12.

Lévy-Leboyer, C. (1988) Success and failure in applying psychology. *American Psychologist,* 43: 779–85.

Lewin, K. (1951) *Field Theory in Social Science.* Chicago: University of Chicago Press.

Lyotard, J.-F. (1984) *The Postmodern Condition: A Report on Knowledge,* trans. G. Bennington and B. Massumi. Minneapolis: University of Minnesota Press. (Original work published in 1979.)

Lyotard, J.-F. (1986) Defining the postmodern. *Postmodernism ICA Documents,* 4: 6–7.

Moll, L. (ed.) (1990) *Vygotsky and Education: Instructional Implications and Applications of Sociohistorical Psychology.* New York: Cambridge University Press.

Peirce, C.S. (1966) The fixation of belief. In P.P. Weiner (ed.), *Charles S. Peirce: Selected Writings.* New York: Dover. (pp. 91–112). (Original work published in 1877.)

Tolstoy, L. (1961) *Resurrection,* trans. V. Traill. New York: New American Library. (Original work published in 1899.)

Toulmin, S. (1990) *Cosmopolis: The Hidden Agenda of Modernity.* New York: Free Press.

13

'Postmodernism' and 'Late Capitalism': On Terms and Realities

Peter Madsen

A postmodern period?

I have been asked to talk about 'postmodernism', 'late capitalism' and 'ideology'. None of these terms are very clear. The last mentioned, ideology, was the centre of an intense debate some twenty years ago. You could not say that the debate ended up with a clear result; the term was rather dropped as somehow obsolete, even if the subject matter did not disappear. In a way the opposite is the case when it comes to 'postmodernism', since the term is persistently used, even if it is not at all clear that there is any corresponding subject matter. The term 'late capitalism' – finally – is today something like a nostalgic reminiscence of the days when the left imagined that capitalism would disappear fairly soon.

Where are we, then? I guess that everyone would agree that we are currently witnessing the reproduction and even expansion of capitalist social and economic relations. But that is a fairly weak characterization of our social and economic surroundings. Let us say that the first question to raise in relation to the theme I was asked to discuss – that is, 'postmodernism as late capitalist ideology' – would be: what are the characteristic features of the present state of capitalism? The subsequent question could then be: in what sense – if any – does it make sense to characterize these features as 'postmodern'? It becomes obvious, then, that 'postmodernism' is used in two ways: to characterize a certain situation or condition, let us call it *postmodernity*; and to characterize a certain cultural tendency (or ideology), and let us reserve the term *postmodernism* for this tendency. Which brings us to a reformulation of the first question: could the dominant features of the present state of capitalism be characterized as 'postmodernity'? And further: is it possible to characterize certain cultural trends as in some sense related to these dominant features, as 'postmodernism'?

Let me now, at this stage of my reasoning, formulate a thesis for discussion that would relate to the Marxian concept of ideology. The term 'ideology' was, of course, used in a variety of contexts in the writings of Marx. The version I am referring to is the concept of reification in *Capital* – that is, ideology understood as *the repro-duction at the level of consciousness, symbolization or discourse of the way in which the form of capital presents itself for a social agent located in a specific situation in relation to the social process in as far as it is determined by the form of capital*. The fundamental point here is that ideology in this sense is related to the forms of capital – for instance, the commodity form, fixed capital, the realization of value in the sphere of circulation, etc. Somewhere in *Capital*, Marx talks about the form of capital related to interest, the capital that engenders more capital – apparently out of nowhere. This is, to Marx, the most concept-deprived (*begriffslose* in German) form of capital, precisely because it in no way makes apparent or represents how the increment of value is engendered. That a phenomenon is deprived of concept means in plain English that it is mystifying, that it engenders ideology at a high level of mystification (if it is not counterbalanced by analysis, by conceptual tools). But Marx was living in relatively innocent days in this respect. Since then forms of capital that are even more deprived of concept have developed – that is, forms of capital that are even more distant from the real foundations of the values.

Now, what in this frame of reasoning would be the form of capital that at present dominates the public sphere of reference, the phantasmagoria of today? It is not fixed capital, the accumulation of means of production; nor is the entrepreneur, the man who produces or at least organizes production, building the foundations for providing goods of some kind, the hero of the cultural industry. Until autumn 1987 the cultural hero was for some years the guy who was able to predict the rise and fall of stocks and bonds at the stock exchange. The calculation in relation to the movements of value relates to forms of capital that are even less conceptual than interest capital. The manipulations that created and destroyed fortunes overnight were only very distantly related to any kind of production of value. These forms of capital had – to put it in other terms – *no referent*; they were *pure signifieds*. The whole game was played at an immanent level, at least apparently. No wonder that the Reagan era provided the frame for this game. Reaganomics itself had a very weak foundation in real production, and was to a considerable extent based on a mixture of foreign debts and orders from the Pentagon – pure decision-making, that is. And this is the other aspect of the cultural hero; he is smart and alert, imposes himself, is determined. *Will and immanence* – that is, absence of reference to real foundations – then, might be the characteristics of some in a sense dominant features of, if not the present state of capitalism (since the crisis at the New York stock exchange in October 1987 changed the picture a bit), then at least those years that witnessed the expansion of the discourse of postmodernism as a cultural ideology. Some versions of postmodernism – or, rather, some cultural trends that among others were termed postmodernist (or poststructuralist) – were precisely marked by (the idea of) the absence of reference, the affirmation of will, or both. Absence of concept in the form of capital would thus correspond to absence of referent at the cultural level, according to this version of the analysis of ideology in the Marxian sense. And according to the same thesis, October 1987 would be the beginning of the end of this ideology: the beginning of a return to reality in economics and the public sphere – and accordingly in the cultural sphere. This may even be true to some extent; not only is the discourse on economics still more concerned with real production, but it also seems as though cultural discourses are approaching reality again. (For a detailed and eminent discussion of postmodernism and postructuralism, see 'Mapping the postmodern', in Huyssen, 1987.)[1]

Modernization and the inner conflicts in developed capitalism

But there is a fundamental problem involved in that kind of analysis, namely the level of generalization. That is why I have used formulations like 'the dominant feature'. One of the widely discussed contributions to the controversy over late capitalism and postmodernism is Fredric Jameson's essay 'Postmodernism or the cultural logic of late capitalism' (1984). The general frame of reference in his (in many respects very stimulating) essay is a historical scheme that delineates a development from competitive capitalism through monopoly capitalism to multinational capitalism. The cultural forms would correspondingly develop from realism through modernism to postmodernism. If it was not for the modifications introduced by Jameson with the concept of the 'dominant', this would be *Geistesgeschichte* in Marxian shoes – that is, an attempt to give a materialist version of the well-known desire to periodize that is so characteristic of the tradition of histories of the arts (cf. Madsen, 1989). It may tend to paper over the fact that a given society is heterogeneous and hence the cultural forms manifold. Even if the analysis of dominant features of a given situation may give important hints (and this is in principle what Jameson is aiming at), it is no less important to stress that in the real world the interaction of heterogeneous factors is the background for the articulation of ideology – or perceptions and conceptions of the situation in general. It is not least the clash between new and old forms of social and economic organization that engenders the cultural forms (and this is what is often forgotten in discussions of these matters).

Let me in this vein formulate another thesis on the relation between 'late capitalism' and 'postmodernism' for discussion. Postmodernism is according to the term something that follows after modernism. The characterization of postmodernism depends in this sense on the concept of modernism involved. Here again we encounter the double sense of the terms, and again it might be useful to split the term 'modernism' in two: that is, *modernity* and *modernism* (cf. Berman, 1982).

But a third term might be useful in order to avoid the pitfalls of periodization. Let us call the process that engenders the experience of modernity *modernization*. Classical German sociology was fond of the dichotomy between *community* and *society* (in German: *Gemeinschaft* and *Gesellschaft*). *Community* (or 'traditional society') meant close personal relationships based on perpetuated norms and patterns of interpretation as well as relatively stable social relations and forms of production, whereas *society* meant the kind of modern, urbanized, abstract and more fluid social relations and corresponding changes in norms and cultural patterns of interpretation. This is not a scheme of periodization, but a characterization of simultaneous features of society during the process of modernization.

'Modernism', then, in the arts (and in philosophy) may be regarded as *a common denominator for a variety of trends related to the process of modernization*. What is commonly called modernism in the arts is an extremely heterogeneous field. But you might say that all of these trends in one way or the other represent *answers* to the questions raised by the process of modernization understood as – among other things – the conflict between *Gemeinschaft* and *Gesellschaft* in the direction of the dominance of *Gesellschaft*.

The process of modernization is – at least apparently – penetrated by *rationality* and *technology*. The reactions to these features are not homogeneous. The 'constructivist' and 'functionalist' trends embraced rationality and technology, whereas surrealism and what we call 'high modernism' (like T.S. Eliot) reacted against rationality. Several trends, among them 'high modernism', demonstrated a certain nostalgia for *Gemeinschaft*-like social relations and hierarchical social structures; whereas other trends, not only constructivism, but also surrealism, endorsed the communist idea of a future society based on equality. My point is that even if the field of modernism is so heterogeneous, all of these trends represent reactions to the process of modernization; *the common denominator is, so to say, external to the cultural field*. This fact makes it obvious *how false the idea of a homogeneous, rational, progressive modernism is*. This idea has nevertheless been widely accepted in the discussion on 'postmodernism'.

But it would be worthwhile to ask if a similar analysis might work in relation to 'postmodernity' and 'postmodernism'. If it is true that 'modernism' in its different versions represents reactions to the process of modernization understood as the conflict between *Gemeinschaft* and *Gesellschaft* – that is, reactions to the experience of modernity – it then follows that postmodernity must be the experience of a situation in which *Gesellschaft* is predominant; or rather, a situation where the inner conflicts in *Gesellschaft* are predominant. Translated into the terms of Marxian analysis this means – at the socioeconomic level – *a situation where capitalist relations and their inner transformations dominate the conflict between pre-capitalist and capitalist social and economic relations*. I want – as Jameson does – to stress the term *dominate*, since the conflicts between pre-capitalist and capitalist social relations do not disappear; the participation in the labour market by large numbers of women who previously were housewives is one important example of these 'earlier' conflicts.

Looking back at the attitudes dominating 'the modern tradition', it is easy to register a certain change as far as rationality and technology are concerned. Even if the anti-rationalist and anti-technological attitudes so characteristic of certain modernist trends may still be around, it is obvious that a qualitative change has in many ways taken place in the background of the experience with rationality and technology since the heyday of classical modernism. Ecological awareness is perhaps the most important factor, but behind that lie nuclear weapons and the annihilation rationality of the Third Reich. In the perspective just outlined this means that critical attitudes are no longer engendered by the conflicts between pre-capitalist and capitalist forms or between *Gemeinschaft* and *Gesellschaft* (to put it bluntly), but by *the ways in which capitalism itself creates problems*. A similar clear-cut distinction between the two sources of critique is of course a preliminary fiction; in real life the two may very well be mixed up, as the experience behind them is.

Architecture as paradigm: from production to consumption

My point may be demonstrated at another level as well, if we look back at the first phase of conflicts between modernism and postmodernism – that is, around 1960 (cf. Huyssen, 1987). What was at stake in those days was not least the opposition between high and low culture. The modernist critics maintained an idea of high modernist culture as a kind of cutting edge of experience, as an avant-garde in that sense; whereas the new attitude, named postmodernism, was characterized by *a mixture of high and low culture*. A typical exponent of this attitude was Susan Sontag with her book *Against Interpretation*, where the last essay was entitled 'One culture and the new sensibility' (1966).

What literature (or the movies) was for the first phase of the debate, architecture became later, and thereby the whole question of surpassing modernism got a more political twist. But in both cases the question of popular culture against some kind of avant-garde was at stake. And this is precisely an inner conflict in developed capitalism, *a conflict engendered by the expansion of the cultural industry*. It was, in other words, a conflict between on the one hand the modernist articulation of different attitudes towards the process of modernization and on the other the cultural effects of a fully developed capitalist society. Many themes that have been taken up in the arts and in art criticism under the label 'postmodernism' have to do with the way in which the cultural industry and advertising capture the production of images and interpretative patterns. The theme was, of course, present in 'modernism' too, in for instance *Ulysses*, but never predominant as in for instance Warhol.

Robert Venturi's well-known formula is illustrative: 'Main Street is almost all right' (1966). This runs of course counter to the typical modernist critical attitude towards the popular frame of mind and the way in which people themselves arrange their surroundings.

But, before I enter the discussion of more recent architecture and architectural critique, I want to go back some decades. In 1908, the Austrian architect Adolf Loos wrote a famous essay called 'Ornament and crime' (Loos, 1908/1962). His main point was that things made for use should get rid of all kinds of ornament, and this included architecture. Loos's polemics were directed against the historicist architecture that had dominated the new buildings in Vienna during the last part of the nineteenth century. Following Otto Wagner in this respect (cf. Schorske, 1980), he wanted a kind of architecture that corresponded to the modern age. This architecture should first and foremost be devoid of ornament. His own works did not altogether conform to this point of view, but the main trend in functionalist architectural endeavours had one of its starting points here. It is today a commonplace to associate this kind of architecture with the progressive movements in politics, as was indeed – in some respects at least – the case with the German Bauhaus.

But it is interesting to read the radical left-wing criticism of functionalism formulated by Ernst Bloch in the middle of the 1930s.

I quote from his essay 'Berlin, Funktionen im Hohlraum' ('Berlin, functions in vacuum'):

> To be objective (*sachlich*) means to make life and its things as light as cool. Initially nothing else is formulated by this than *emptiness* created through exclusion. Immediately afterwards the deceit is demonstrated in as far as the emptiness becomes nickelled in order to glisten and dazzle. The inanimation of life, polished as the commodification of men and things, as if it was in order, yes order itself. Here is the new objectivity, the highest but also most indiscernible form of distraction; it is realized through 'honest' form. But it is only the honesty of the foreground, and it does not provide anything palpable, not the slightest scroll as further proof; a smooth appearance hides crooked ways. . . . with the contempt for fantasy a *further* motive was added to the deceit, that is the *hypocrisy* of the new objectivity (*neue Sachlichkeit*), its puritan aspect amidst of the fancy appearance. A repetition of classical serenity and severity passed through the world, through that life of noble simplicity and tranquil grandeur the capitalists were living. Whereas the simple deceit worked through gaiety (*Heiterkeit*), this deeper, classicist deceit parades through severity, absence of ornaments, simply puritanism; this objectivity is ornamented through the absence of ornaments. A long time ago it was a form determined by use; it is rather coated with technoid ornaments. Its mechanic model was a long time ago transformed into its own aim; it is working as a substitute for ornament. . . . The same aim has the *last* motive of objectivity, namely the elaborated but nevertheless broken, that is *abstract*, rationality; it corresponds in its abstract guise simultaneously to the capitalist style of reasoning. It corresponds to the 'capitalist plan-economy' and similar anomalies that the capitalist is trying to use in order to grasp the forms of tomorrow in an attempt to keep yesterday's forms alive. This kind of objectivity stays – in economy as in architecture – at the surface; behind the build-in rationality the complete anarchy of the profit-economy carries on. (Bloch, 1935/1977: 216; my translation)

This kind of critique points out that functionalism on the one hand anticipates a rationally organized society (and that meant to Bloch a communist society), but on the other hand is a piece of ideology inasmuch as it papers over the fact that capitalism is fundamentally irrational. This is a type of critique that might be labelled *critique of ideology*; functionalism is, so to speak, concretely built ideology, and it manifests the two sides of ideology in *this* sense: affirmation and anticipation.

After the Second World War the original impetus in functionalist architecture was taken over by the building industry and integrated into the construction of cheap and unimaginative urban structures. At the same time advanced functionalism became the dominant representative building form for big business. It is tempting to say that the postmodern critique of functionalism is after all a critique of the industrialized depraved functionalism of the postwar period and the compromised representative design of the same period. But things are more complicated, since the representative role of functionalism or the international style was already the target for Ernst Bloch's critique. And it was indeed the argument put forward by Philip Johnson, when he prepared the ground for Mies van der Rohe in the USA, that bankers and similar people in Germany appreciated Mies's work. And further, whatever the grandeur of Le Corbusier's plan for the renewal of Paris and similar projects, their inhuman character is obvious.

Versions of 'postmodern' critique of modernism in architecture

What was then the critique directed against modernism in architecture from the *postmodernist* critics? Against Mies's dictum 'Less is more' Venturi formulated his 'Less is a bore' (1966), implying a standard taken from a completely different sphere – that is, *the sphere of consumption and entertainment*, the sphere of low culture. In lieu of the rationalization from above proposed by the spokesmen of the international style, Venturi and others re-evaluated the spontaneous results of 'bad taste'. This may sound democratic, but it is a kind of democracy that has a certain cynical twist (as pointed out by Kenneth Frampton, 1982), when Venturi writes that Americans should not hang around on public squares but stay at home around the TV set. And it became even more problematic when Las Vegas was taken as a kind of model in *Learning from Las Vegas* (Venturi et al., 1972).

As I proposed in the case of the heroes of the cultural industry, we may take the models for architectural style as an indication of the changes in culture or ideology. The Viennese historicism Loos reacted against involved on several occasions models that had ideological implications. The public buildings along Vienna's new boulevard, the Ringstrasse, were meant as representations of the emerging liberal bourgeoisie (cf. Schorske, 1980). The parliament was in Greek classicism (implying the democracy of Athens); the university was in Florentine Renaissance style (implying Renaissance humanism); and the town hall was in Gothic style (implying the free city-state). It was thus the political and cultural self-representation of the progressive bourgeoisie that was at stake.

Functionalist architecture had other models – the factory, storage buildings and means of transportation such as the ocean steamer. It is thus *the sphere of production* that sets the norm for the architectural style, and it is further the more abstract side of this sphere of production – that is, rationality and technology as such – that seems to dominate the imagination. This already implies two fundamental problems involved in 'the international style'; it is not concerned with the public sphere beyond the mere representation of rationality, and its dominating frame of reference is pure rationality: precisely the kind of rationality emancipated from any other guideline that created or rather lent its hand to such disasters during this century. From the point of view of what Horkheimer and Adorno baptized the 'dialectics of enlightenment' (1947/1971), the international style was – to the contrary of its self-representation – part of the problem rather than part of the solution.

What then are the implications of the postmodern critique of the international style in relation to these questions? The statement that it is 'boring' is not very illuminating, nor is the simple reference to the sphere of consumption and entertainment. Against this background the conclusion lies at hand that the shift from the international style and rationality to postmodern consumption and mixtures of style represents a shift in ideology corresponding to the shift in the public focus from production to consumption. To the extent that this critique is valid, 'postmodernism' might thus be regarded as the adequate ideology of consumer society. That is why it is important to remember that the postmodern critique of aristocratic modernism emerged simultaneously with postwar consumerism. The cutting out of the questions of the public sphere and politics corresponds to the postwar development of the holy trinity of suburban housing, cars and TV sets, significantly enough exactly what Venturi refers to in his formulations of an alternative to the international style. One of his statements from *Learning from Las Vegas* sounds like this:

> Most critics have slighted a continuing iconology in popular art, the persuasive heraldry that pervades our environment from the advertising pages of the *New Yorker* to the superbillboards of Houston. And their theory of the 'debasement' of symbolic architecture in the nineteenth-century eclecticism has blinded them to the value of the representational architecture along the highways. Those who acknowledge this roadside eclecticism denigrate it, because it flaunts the cliche of a decade ago as well as the style of a century ago. But why not? Time travels fast today. (Venturi et al., 1972: 2)

So: 'Billboards are almost all right.' Modern architecture is dissatisfied with the existing conditions, writes Venturi, but 'Analysis of the existing American urbanism is a socially desirable activity to the extent that it teaches us architects to be more understanding and less authoritarian.'

But this aspect of Venturi's position is not the only postmodern attitude towards architecture, nor are the positions labelled postmodern the only possible critical attitudes towards the international style. One of the points of departure for Venturi was the question of urban context. Quoting T.S. Eliot on the way in which each new literary work changes world literature, Venturi insisted on the demand to take the context into consideration when new buildings are designed (1966). This is exactly what the international style tended not to do; in the extreme case of Le Corbusier the context should be destroyed in order to give room for the new and splendid urban structure. At this point there is no doubt that aspects of the postmodern critique have represented a return to reality – and not necessarily in an affirmative sense.

Nor is the interest in the actual users of architecture necessarily identical with some kind of acceptance of consumer society as it is. The architectural critic Charles Jencks, probably the other most important ideologue of the 'movement', includes in his account of *The Language of Postmodern Architecture* a description of the way in which the architect Ralph Erskine involved the actual habitants in a renewal project in England. This is the story as told by Jencks:

> his office became immersed in the Byker community by setting up shop in a disused funeral parlour, selling plants and flowers (an obvious popular activity in England), acting as the local 'lost and found', that is, doing countless non-architectural things as he got to know the people, and they his team. Then the slow process of design and construction took place, endless discussions and rather small decisions, so that landscape, 'doorway', colour, history, idiosyncrasy and other non-commensurables could find a place. The success of the result, both as an amusing and humane environment, makes this a key postmodern project in theory if not in precise coding. (1977/1984: 104)

In this process the architect is involved with the people in question; he just does not accept the immediate result of their adaptation of consumer culture. In many ways this corresponds to the idea of grass-roots democracy that was widespread during the 1960s and has been since then.

An alternative to postmodernism

But the question of the relation between architecture, culture in general, politics and the local situation has perhaps most fully been explored by Kenneth Frampton (1980, 1982). In an essay called 'The isms of contemporary architecture' the present problem for a committed architecture is stated like this: 'Ultimately the challenge surely resides in the question: what strategies may be employed by architects to achieve "rootedness" in an essentially uprooted and dislocated age?' (1982: 77). This is a question that emerges in the context of a critique of the kind of 'populism' which is involved in certain postmodern endeavours like Venturi's, but the perspective is broader. Frampton stresses that 'a recourse to superficial historicism can only result in consumerist iconography masquerading as culture' (1982:77). And this is a recurrent theme: the main degrading contemporary impulse stems from consumerism. As a consequence, Frampton must express a severe critique of the kind of complicity with consumerism that has been proposed as an alternative to the shortcomings of the modern tradition. The movement from Venturi's 'Main Street is almost all right' to the unqualified acceptance of the superficial Mafia opulence of the Las Vegas strip is criticized as a contribution to the liquidation of critical consciousness: 'ideology in its purest form'. Nevertheless, the evaluation of the rational tradition itself remains a crucial task.

Architecture is an exemplary field for cultural studies inasmuch as artistic, cultural and social concerns are so obviously bound up with political and economic power. This fact provides an easy legitimation for the shortcomings of the postwar versions of the international style; the artistic concerns, etc., were not realizable for political or economic reasons. But Frampton – in his essay 'Place, production and architecture' – has explicitly stated the more complicated problem: 'the exact manner in which this impoverishment has come about however – the extent to which it is due to abstract tendencies present in Cartesian rationality itself or alternatively to ruthless economic exploitation – is a complex and critical issue which has yet to be judiciously decided' (1982: 37). This is an aspect of the dialectics of Enlightenment taken in its full significance – that is, not only as the immanent dialectics of reason, but as the dialectics of the interaction of this reason with its human, social and natural contexts, to put it bluntly. Whereas it is easy enough in the more spiritual field of the humanities to stick to an idea of mainly intellectual contradictions, in the field of architecture the interaction with technology, economics and politics cannot be overlooked. Hence the importance of the retrospective considerations in Frampton's writings on modern architecture.

Time and again the clash between the medieval city and the classical ideals of the Renaissance is mentioned: 'that extraordinary moment when the "classic" monument became the representation and hence the projection of values which were generally absent in the urban fabric of the medieval town' (Frampton, 1982: 67). Bringing this clash several centuries up towards the present we can recognize a similar conflict in the confrontation towards the end of the last century between Otto Wagner's ideal of an architecture corresponding to the modern era and Camillo Sitte's concern for the qualities inherited from the medieval structure of the city (cf. Schorske, 1980);

and Frampton refers with approval, as far as the present is concerned, to 'the emphasis that the "postmodernist" critique has placed on respecting the existing urban context' (1982: 37). But 'Instead of a balanced critique of the modern tradition we are now being subjected to an indiscriminate reaction against the entire evolution of modernist culture.' The result is a 'combination of kitsch imagery with operational efficiency' (1982: 37).

The question is thus how a kind of local identity can be upheld without a relapse into some kind of kitschy sentimental nostalgia. And this question has to be put in another manner today than in earlier stages of the expansion of rationalism and modernization, since we are now, as I have stressed earlier, living with an acute consciousness of the disastrous potentialities of pure reason that tends to put itself in the service of all kinds of inhuman activities. Whereas the progressive optimism of the nineteenth century to a certain extent could rely on reason and modernization as means of overcoming backwardness, ignorance and misery, the late twentieth century does not provide that kind of horizon, since the process of modernization has proven in many ways disastrous to nature, society and human beings. But the same century has witnessed a proliferation of anti-rationalist and anti-modernist attitudes that no less than pure or instrumental reason have lent their hand to inhumanity.

The solution does thus not seem to be located at the level of opposition between rationalization or 'modernism' on the one hand and tradition or local specificity on the other. In his essay 'The status of man and the status of his objects', Frampton thus stresses 'the dependency of political power on its social and physical constitution; that is to say, on its derivation from *the living proximity of men and from the physical manifestation of their public being in terms of build form*' (1982: 19; my emphasis). To the extent that the question of modern architecture is stated in this manner, the perspective goes beyond the opposition between rationality and locality; it will then be concerned with the conditions for what Oscar Negt and Alexander Kluge termed *the production of social relations* (1972; cf. Madsen, 1982). If we, as I have suggested, take the dominant 'reference' in classical modernist architecture as the rationality of *production*, and the anti-modernist (or postmodernist) trend as fundamentally related to *consumption*, then the question of 'public being in terms of building form' emerges as a concern for *social relations*. But social relations have at least two dimensions added: first the relation to *privacy*, and second the relation to *the public sphere and politics*.

The classical bourgeois model for the interaction between privacy and politics was based on the public sphere as a mediation between specific subjectivity as it developed in the intimacy of the private sphere and general consensus as developed through public debate (cf. Habermas, 1962). The *ideal* was thus the fusion of specificity and generality. The parody of this ideal is as a tendency realized in consumer society where the TV set is the mediator of the general consensus among isolated individuals whose social contact is reduced to driving on the same highways in the pursuit of adequate consumption. The decisive contribution to the organization of 'public being in terms of building form' that has been developed since the Second World War, especially in the USA, is the combination of cars, highways, suburban 'dwellings' (so to say) and TV sets. And this has been a contribution to the destruction of the kind of social relations, 'the living proximity of men', that are the precondition for the collective mastering of the objects of man – that is, society in its metabolism with nature.

This is the context in which it seems adequate to evaluate the question of the local, obviously not by way of an abstract negation of human reason as a means of organizing social relations and human collaboration, nor by way of destroying all kinds of specific conditions and cultural references, since 'the living proximity of men' would loose all flavour and all potentials for further development to the same extent as specific identities would wither away.

But it is precisely at this point that several writers who are generally considered as spokesmen for postmodern positions have called into question political *engagement* itself, the idea of an interaction between individual subjects and the public sphere as a forum for consensus. In this respect 'postmodernism' seems to be an *ideology of resignation* in relation to political problems that have not in any way become less urgent since the days when intellectuals in general were concerned with the real world and not only with the play of significations or simulations.

The idea of a public sphere and – as a tendency at least – rational discourse and consensus-building has as its necessary counterpart the idea of an individual self that is able to reason, form opinions and make decisions on its own – without the guidance of others, as Kant wrote. But the postmodernist idea of the self runs counter to this idea of autonomy. The self is not only decentred – this fact has been well known since Freud at least – but it is supposed to be a pure effect of conditioning factors to the extent that the idea of emancipation that was inherent in the project of the Enlightenment and in the democratic project has become obsolete. This (postmodern) frame of mind is presented as radical and critical, but it is emphatically ideological since it represents as real knowledge the preformation attempted by the public sphere in its consumerist and conformist aspects.

In Kantian terms this ideology might be characterized as self-imposed dependency. To the extent that psychology as a theory aims at human emancipation it will have to contradict the ideology of 'postmodernism' – against the background of a thorough examination of the conditions for emancipation and development of autonomy in a social and cultural situation that is marked by postmodernity.

This does not imply a pragmatic return to some ideological concept of a unified, coherent self – an idea that usually implies all kinds of repression of self and others (as stressed by Horkheimer and Adorno). But the jubilatory farewell, in the name of desire, of heterogeneity, of the body, of otherness, of the sublime or whatever, to all attempts to support an autonomous development of the self is an abdication of the individual subject. It may be sad to recognize to what an extent the supposedly autonomous self is conditioned and fragmented (and this sadness is part of the cultural history of this century); but the joyfulness engendered by embracing the absence of autonomy cannot last for a lifetime – and it represents an extreme version of consumerist liberalism. The fact that something similar to this critique of postmodern ideology has been stated by conservative cultural critics (like Daniel Bell) should not provoke progressive intellectuals to stop thinking.

Note

1   In August 1990 this expectation seemed to be confirmed by the plans to cut the US military budget, but the Gulf war came between. The breakdown of communism in the USSR in August 1991 may of course change the picture once more. In general it is most likely that the rapid changes in the political scenario will bring even intellectuals to the point of recognizing something like reality.

References

Berman, M. (1982) *All that is Solid Melts into Air: The Experience of Modernity*. London: Verso.

Bloch, E. (1935/1977) *Erbschaft dieser Zeit* (Gesamtausgabe 4). Frankfurt am Main: Suhrkamp.

Frampton, K. (1980) *Modern Architecture: A Critical History*. London: Thames & Hudson.

Frampton, K. (1982) *Modern Architecture and the Critical Present*. Architectural Design Profile. London: Architectural Design.

Habermas, J. (1962) *Strukturwandel der Öffentlichkeit*. Frankfurt am Main: Suhrkamp.

Horkheimer, M. and Adorno, T.A. (1947/1971) *Dialektik der Aufklärung*. Frankfurt am Main: Fischer.

Huyssen, A. (1987) *After the Great Divide*. Bloomington: Indiana University Press.

Jameson, F. (1984) Postmodernism, or the cultural logic of late capitalism. *New Left Review*, 146: 53–92.

Jencks, C. (1977/1984) *The Language of Postmodern Architecture*. New York: Rizzoli.

Loos, A. (1908/1962) Ornament und Verbrechen. In *Sämtliche Schriften*, vol. 1. Vienna and Munich: Franz Gluck.

Madsen, P. (1982) History and consciousness: cultural studies between reification and hegemony. In *Thesis Eleven 5/6*. London: Merlin.

Madsen, P. (1989) In search of homogeneity: Wilhelm Dilthey and the humanities, In M. Harbsmeier and M. Trolle Larsen (eds), *The Humanities between Art and Science*. Copenhagen: Akademisk Forlag.

Negt, O. and Kluge, A. (1972) *Öffentlichkeit und Erfahrung*. Frankfurt am Main: Suhrkamp.

Schorske, C.E. (1980) *Fin-de-siècle Vienna*. New York: Vintage.

Sontag, S. (1966) *Against Interpretation*. New York: Dell.

Venturi, R. (1966) *Complexity and Contradiction in Architecture*. New York: Museum of Modern Art.

Venturi, R., Brown, D.S. and Izenour, S. (1972) *Learning from Las Vegas*. Cambridge, MA: MIT Press.

Index

Aanstoos, C., 7
absolutism, 177, 180
academic psychology, 146, 153, 154,
    197, 205–6
activity theory, 46
actor-network theory, 10, 15, 79–81,
    83–4
actor-world, 80, 81
Adorno, T., 21, 111, 217, 222
advertising, 54, 55, 214
aesthetic consciousness, 141
aestheticism, 170, 178
Age of Theory, 40–2, 44
agency, human, 101, 102, 103, 104
Althusser, L., 89, 111
American Psychological Association, 48
amnesia, social, 68
androcentrism, 21
anonymous self, 125
anthropology, 23, 47–8
architecture, 19, 37, 39, 213–20
Aronowitz, S., 10, 94
art, 19, 36–7, 44; and human conscious-
    ness, 137–8; and mathematics, 36
artificial intelligence, 46
Atkinson, P., 93
authenticity, principle of, 123–4
autobiography, 131–2
autonomous self, 101, 102, 111–12, 221,
    222
Averill, J., 28, 67

Bacon, F., 39, 203
Bakhtin, M., 91, 97, 100
Barnes, B., 21, 59
Barthes, R., 95, 98
Bartlett, Sir F.C., 68
Basch, M.F., 157, 158, 160
Baudrillard, J., 2, 7, 32, 33, 48, 77, 89,
    119, 177
behaviourism, 9, 42–5

Beitman, B.D., 157, 159, 160
beliefs, 'closed' system of, 64–6
Bellah, R.N., 43
Benton, T., 79
Bernstein, R., 8, 59, 98
Bhaskar, R., 70
Billig, M., 28, 63, 66, 67
bioregional narrative, 83
Bloch, E., 214–15
Bloom, A., 45, 98
Borges, J.L., 2, 32, 178–80
Bourdieu, P., 21, 84
Bramwell, A., 84
Byrne, D., 103, 105n

Callon, M., 79, 80, 81, 82
capital, forms of, 210
capitalism: consumer, 9, 39; phases of,
    7; see also late capitalism
Caputo, U., 93, 99
Cézanne, P., 138
Chaiklin, S., 194–207
Charcot, J.-M., 114
Cheney, J., 82, 83, 84
Cherryholmes, C., 92, 97, 99
Chi, M.T.H., 156, 208
Chomsky, N., 111
chronology, idea of, 7
Clifford, J., 10, 23, 96
cognitive psychology, 41
Cohen, L.H., 154
collage as artistic technique, 36–7
commensurability, 41, 44
Common Ground, 83
Comte, A., 54, 89–90
Confrey, J., 46
conscience, 140
consciousness, 94, 135–8, 141; aesthetic,
    141; ecological, 82–3, 213; false, 96,
    103; phenomenology of, 46, 94; self-,
    133n

constructivism, 150–1, 160–1, 212
consumer capitalism, 9, 39
consumer society, 54–5, 217
consumerism, 219
consumption, logic of, 7
contextuality, 41; in architecture, 218, 220
critical ethnography, 94
critical social science, 93–5
Cubism, 138
Culler, J., 124, 179
cultural critique, 26–7, 47, 198, 199
cultural hero, 210
cultural-historical psychology, 47, 207
cultural industry, 214
cultural pluralism, 9
culture: and language, 47; as a system of signs, 118–19

Dante, A., 135, 139
Davidov, V.V., 46
'death of the subject', 13–14, 52, 103, 120–2, 130–1
deconstruction, 13, 53, 61, 102, 123, 132; literary, 22, 110, 132, 148; of self, 14, 122, 143, 144
deconstructionist psychology, 46, 110–18
de-individualization, 15
Deleuze, G., 77, 115, 117, 118
de Man, P., 119, 131, 132, 179
Derrida, J., 2, 22, 62, 90, 97, 102, 119, 121, 122, 124, 125–6, 127, 128, 132, 133n, 148, 179
Diagnostic and Statistical Manual of Mental Disorders, 158–9
dialectical materialism, 46
différance, 126–7
displacement, 80
Divine Comedy (Dante), 135, 139
Dostoevsky, F., 204
dreams, 15, 129–30, 133n
Dreyfus, H., 46, 92, 155, 156
Dreyfus, S.E., 46, 155, 156
Dubiel, H., 93, 95
Durkheim, E., 47

Ebbinghaus, H., 44
Ebert, T., 96
Eco, U., 2, 37
ecological consciousness, 82–3, 213
education, 10, 127

Edwards, D., 28, 68
electronic media, 8, 33
Eliade, M., 167
Elliott, R., 154
Ellsworth, E., 100, 104
Émile (Rousseau), 121, 127
emotion, 67
empirical method, 20, 60–1, 204–5
empiricism, logical, 18–19
enrolment, 80
ensembled individualism, 43
entrapping systems, 63–6
environmental ethics, 82–4
epistemic relativity, 70
epistemology: of practice of psychology, 155–62, 195–6, 199–200, 205; *see also* knowledge
equifinality, principle of, 161, 201
Erskine, R., 218
ethics, 44; environmental, 82–4
ethnography, 23, 94
existentialism, 42, 46
externalization of the person, 15
eyewitness memory, 203

facts, genesis of, 65
false consciousness, 96, 103
Fay, B., 94, 95, 102
Featherstone, M., 10, 75
Federman, R., 171, 177
Feher, F., 10, 202
Fekete, J., 100
feminism, 100, 104, 111
feminist theory, 43
Feyerabend, P.K., 21
fictionalism, 167, 168, 171, 177, 178, 180
Fischer, R., 93, 96, 100, 102
Fish, S., 22
Fjelde, R., 138, 139
Flax, J., 21, 94, 102, 183
Fleck, L., 65
Foster, H., 103
Foucault, M., 2, 9, 23, 39, 88–9, 92, 95, 96, 101, 110–17 *passim*, 121, 132
foundationalism, 20–1
foundationlessness, 148–9, 152, 158–9
fragmentariness, 149, 152, 159–60
Frampton, K., 216, 218–20
Frankfurt School, 94, 95
Fraser, N., 100, 183
Freud, S., 43, 114, 117, 155

Froebel, F., 121
functionalist architecture, 214–16; *see also* International Style
fundamentalism, 54

Garbino, J., 159
Garfield, S.L., 160, 161
Geha, R., 170–1, 174, 176–7
Gemeinschaft–Gesellschaft dichotomy, 212, 213
gender, social construction of, 46
generality, limits of, 41
generative theory, 27
Gergen, K.J., 17–28, 46, 59, 60, 66, 76, 78, 79, 81, 149, 183, 194–204 *passim*
Gergen, M., 27, 78, 183–91
Gibson, J.J., 58, 68
Gilligan, C., 28
Giorgi, A., 42, 153
Giroux, H.A., 10, 94
Gitlin, M.J., 161
Goethe, J.W. von, 120
Gonzalvez, L., 91, 93
grammatical illusions, 64
Gramsci, A., 96
Grenness, C.E., 42, 47
Grossberg, L., 98, 102
Grosz, E., 98
Guattari, F., 77, 115, 116, 117, 118

Habermas, J., 7, 21, 33, 90, 93, 94, 133n, 200, 202, 221
Haley, J., 167
Hall, S., 93, 96, 103, 104
Halprin, R., 160
Haraway, D., 100, 102
Harding, S., 21, 99, 102
Harland, R., 88, 89, 90
Harré, R., 66, 67, 81
Hartsock, N., 98–9
Harvey, D., 75, 84, 148
health science, 53
Hegel, G.W.F., 120, 133n, 177
Heidegger, M., 46, 84, 111, 175
hermeneutics, 42, 60–1, 62, 117–18
high modernism, 212
Hillman, J., 166–7
historical writing, 22–3
Hollway, W., 27, 183
Horigan, S., 79
Horkheimer, M., 21, 217, 222

human agency, 101, 102, 103, 104
human sciences, 88–105
humanism, 14–15
humanistic psychology, 41, 42–5, 111–12
humanistic subjectivism, 14
Hundertwasser, F., 37
Husserl, E., 46
Hutcheon, L., 89, 90
Huyssen, A., 147, 211, 213
hypothetical-deductive experimentation, 153

Ibsen, H., 14, 135, 139–43, 144
idealism, 168
identity, 101–2; social construction of, 46, 75–6, 81–4
identity politics, 103–4
ideology, 21, 94–5, 96, 209–10, 215
Impressionism, 137–8
individual and the universal, 33–4, 42–3
individualism, 43
individualist/anti-individualist dichotomies, 76–7
individuality, reconstruction of, 132–3
intellectuals, transformative, 94
intéressement, 80
International Style, 216–18, 219; *see also* functionalist architecture
interpretation, technique of, 117–18; *see also* hermeneutics
intertextuality in the media, 37–8
interview methods, 51, 97, 298

Jackson Lears, T.J., 54, 55
Jameson, F., 2, 7, 39, 211
Jarry, A., 143
Jencks, C., 218
Johnson, P., 216
Johnson, R., 102
judgemental relativity, 70
Jung, C., 155
justice, 9, 71

Kant, I., 206
Kermode, F., 168
Kierkegaard, S., 6, 136, 141
Klein, M., 118
Klix, F., 41
Kluge, A., 220

knowledge, 12; generation of, 20–1, 197–200, 204–6; local, 34, 47, 49, 198; and power, 39, 90, 96, 99, 101, 111, 112, 113, 114; practical, 12–13, 48–52, 198; *see also* epistemology
Koch, S., 40–2, 202
Kuhn, T.S., 21–2, 66, 90, 91, 206
Kvale, S., 31–55, 196–203

Lacan, J., 2, 128
Lakoff, G., 151, 156
language, 35–6, 47, 90, 95–6; and construction of reality, 35; conventions of, 22; and culture, 47; descriptive adequacy of, 92; formative function of, 68; and pathology, 49; 'picture' theory of, 64; and social psychology, 76; as a structure of signs, 119; and understanding, 149–50
language games, 34–5
language systems, 113, 149–50
Lash, S., 75, 76, 77
late capitalism, 209, 211, 212–13
Lather, P., 88–105, 183
Latour, B., 21, 48, 76, 78, 79, 80, 81
Leahey, T.H., 43, 54
learning, 68
Le Corbusier, 216, 218
Lecourt, D., 94
legitimacy, 100; crisis of, 94
legitimation, 32, 33, 40–1, 42, 48, 98, 99
Lenin, V.I., 46
Leontiev, A.N., 46
Lerner, G., 104
lesbianism, 104
Lévy-Leboyer, C., 206
Lewin, K., 206
Lincoln, Y., 92, 98
literary theory, 19, 22
literature, 44, 166; use of collage in, 37
local identity and architectural style, 218, 220, 221
local knowledge, 34, 47, 49, 198
logical empiricism, 18–19
logocentrism, 123
Longino, H., 99
Loos, A., 214, 216
Løvlie, L., 119–33
Lugones, M., 104

Lyotard, J.-F., 2, 7, 18, 25, 31, 33, 34, 35, 39, 50, 58, 59, 67, 77, 98, 121, 147, 151, 201, 202

McLaren, P., 96
Madison, G.B., 35, 148
Madsen, P., 209–22
Mahoney, M.J., 157, 159, 160, 161
Man without Qualities, The (Musil), 175–6
Marcus, G., 23, 93, 96, 102
Margolis, H., 156
Martin, B., 77, 104
Martineau, H., 90
Marx, K., 210
Marxism, 96, 111
mathematics and art, 36
May, R., 14, 42
meaning, 119
measurability, 41, 44
media, 44; electronic, 8, 33; inter-textuality in, 37–8
Melanchthon, P., 39
memory, 68, 167, 203
mental health machine, 116–17
Merleau-Ponty, M., 35, 47
meta-cognition, 157
meta-methodology, 60
metaphor, 128
meta-theory, 59–60
methodology and method, 24–5, 199; empirical, 20, 60–1, 204–5; marginalization of, 24–5; multi-, 51; political nature of, 94–5
metonymy, 128
Miami Vice, 37–8
Michael, M., 74–85
Middleton, D., 28, 68
Mies van der Rohe, L., 216
Mills, C.W., 67, 68
modern vs postmodern, 7–8
modernism, 18–20, 147, 212; in architecture, 214–18, 219; and human consciousness, 136–7; and practical psychology, 153–4
modernist psychology, 197
modernization, 211–13, 220
Moi, T., 183, 184
Morrow-Bradley, C., 154
Morton, D., 97
motivation, 67

multi-method, 51
Musil, R., 175–6
myth, 47

Name of the Rose, The (Eco), 37
Namenwirth, M., 91
narcissism, 174
narrative, 34, 66–7, 167, 173, 177;
    bioregional, 83
natural, status of the, 79
naturalism, 14–15
nature and construction of identity, 81–4
Negt, O., 220
Nelson, J.S., 67, 89
neo-modernism, 7
neopragmatism, 151–3, 161–2, 198, 199
neural networks, 46
New Age relativism, 54
Nicholson, L., 90, 100, 183
Nietzsche, F., 32, 53, 77, 115, 172,
    173–5, 179, 180n
nihilism, 38, 100
nonsense behaviour, 44
nonsense syllable, 44
Norris, C., 122, 128, 129, 166

objectivism: behaviourist, 14; vs
    relativism, 8–9
objectivity, 43, 90; poststructuralist view
    of, 97
one in the many, principle of, 123
ontological discourse, 70
Ortega y Gasset, J., 137
Ossorio, P.G., 65

paradigm shifts, discourse of, 91–3
parallel distributed processing, 46, 203
paranoia, 38
Parker, I., 27, 46, 76
pastiche, 36
pathology and language, 49
Patton, M.Q., 49, 51
Peer Gynt (Ibsen), 14, 135, 139–43, 144
Peirce, C.S., 204
perception, 63, 68
periodization, 7
perspectivism, 35, 47, 174
Peterson, D.R., 153, 154
phenomenology, 42, 46, 47, 94
philosophy of science, 20–1
phonocentrism, 123, 125

physics, 138
pluralism, cultural, 9
politics: and postmodernity, 9–10; and
    privacy, 220–1; and science, 92
Polkinghorne, D., 49, 146–63, 158,
    195–206 *passim*
Popper, K., 20
positivism, 89–90
Post-Impressionism, 137–8
postmodern: meanings of, 1–3; vs
    modern, 7–8
postmodern thought, 2–3
postmodernism as cultural expression,
    2
postmodernity: as description of an age,
    2; concept of, 31–2; and politics, 9–10
poststructuralism, 95–8, 101
Potter, J., 27, 76
power and knowledge, 39, 90, 96, 99,
    101, 111, 112, 113, 114
power structures, 111, 114
practical knowledge, 12–13, 48–52, 198;
    see also epistemology of practice
practice of psychology, 197, 205–6
premodernism, 135–6
privacy and politics, 220–1
production, logic of, 7
professional psychology *see* practice of
    psychology
progress, scientific, 25
psychoanalysis, 9, 40, 43, 44–6, 128, 129,
    166–80
psychodynamic theory, 117
psychosis, 116, 117
public sphere, idea of, 220, 221
Pynchon, T., 179

qualitative research, 51, 53, 199

radical constructivism, 10
Rajchman, J., 95, 102
rationality, 212, 213; in the Age of
    Theory, 41, 44; and architecture, 217;
    expansion of, 36, 220; technical, 44,
    48, 49
reality, 135–6, 149–50; construction of,
    32–3, 35, 46, 53; loss of, 177
reductionism, 111
reflection-in-action, 156–7
reflection-on-action, 157
reflexive texts, 77–8

relativism, 43, 54, 98–101, 167, 168, 171, 178, 180; vs objectivism, 8–9
relativity: epistemic, 70; judgemental, 70
religion, 53–4
research: as generator of psychological knowledge, 13, 51; interactive approaches to, 95; poststructuralist view of, 97; and practical psychology, 153–4, 205–6; progressive nature of, 20; qualitative, 51, 53, 199
research psychology *see* academic psychology
resignation, ideology of, 221
rhetoric, study of, 23
rhetoric of inquiry movement, 67
Richards, I.A., 180n
Richer, P., 110–18
Riley, D., 90, 104
Rogers, C., 42, 155
Rorty, R., 2, 18, 32, 33, 51, 58, 59, 61, 133n, 150, 151
Ross, A., 104
Rousseau, J.-J., 121, 125, 126, 127, 128
Royce, J., 140

Said, E., 88
Sampson, E.E., 27, 43, 76
Sass, L.A., 166–81
Saussure, F. de, 112–13, 124
Schafer, R., 167, 170, 174
Schiller, F., 120
schizophrenia, 174
Schön, D., 49, 50, 154, 156–7
Schorske, C.E., 214, 216, 219
science, 88–91; advances in, 18, 25–6; culture of, 21; philosophy of, 20–1; and politics, 92
scientific change, 91
Scott, J., 101
Scriven, M., 49, 50
self: anonymous, 125; autonomous, 101, 102, 111–12, 221, 222; deconstruction of, 14, 122, 143, 144
self-actualization, 43, 54
self-consciousness, 133n
self-presence, 122–3
self-psychology, 135–44
self-realization, 54–5
semiotics, 94; *see also* signs
sex instinct, 114–15
sexual orientation, 104

Shotter, J., 26, 27, 46, 58–71, 76, 81
signs: culture as system of, 118–19; structure of, 124; *see also* semiotics
simulacrum, era of, 177, 178
Sitte, C., 219
skepticism, 168, 172, 173
Skinner, B.F., 42, 155
Smith, M.L., 161
Smith, P., 95, 104
social constructionism, 46, 53
social control, psychology as, 9–10, 118
social identity formation, 46, 75–6, 81–4
social psychology, 10, 46; transgressive potential of, 74–85
social relations, production of, 220–1
social science, critical, 93–5
Sociology of Scientific Knowledge (SSK), 77
Socrates, 39
Sontag, S., 214
Spence, D., 23, 167, 168, 169–70, 176, 177, 180–1n
Spivak, G., 95, 103
Starobinski, J., 126, 128
States, B., 129
Stephanson, A., 104
Stevens, W., 166
Stolzenberg, G., 64, 65
subject: 'death' of the, 13–14, 103, 120–2, 130–1; poststructuralist theory of the, 101; self-determining *see* autonomous self; as text, 124–5; theories of the, 101–2
subject matter of psychology, 19, 23–4
subject position, postmodern, 74–85
subjectivism, 8, 179, 180; humanistic, 14
subjectivity, 14, 52, 94, 119–33
surface, focus on the, 37–8
surrealism, 212
system evaluation, 12, 49–50, 51, 199
systemic therapy, 10, 12, 49

technological advance, 8, 18, 25–6, 33, 198, 199, 212, 213
teleology, 90
television, 37–8
theatre, 138–44
theism, 135–6
theoretical psychology *see* academic psychology
thought, 'closed' systems of, 64–6

'Tlön, Uqbar, Orbis Tertius'
    (Borges), 178–80
Tolstoy, L., 204
Toulmin, S., 7, 58, 69, 71, 201, 202, 204
transformative intellectuals, 94
transgressive potential of social
    psychology, 74–85
truth, 9, 25, 71, 125–6
Tyler, S., 89

Ubu Roi (Jarry), 143
unconscious, 128–30
understanding, 149–50
universal and the individual, 33–4, 42–3
universal properties, 19–20, 24
universality, 41, 43
Urry, J., 75, 76, 77

Valency, M., 143
value issues, 21, 90
Van Maanen, J., 88, 96, 158
Velasquez, D., 137
Venturi, R., 37, 214, 216, 217, 218, 219

Viderman, S., 167, 168
virtual reality machines, 149
Vygotsky, L.S., 46, 47, 59, 68

Wagner, O., 214, 219
Warhol, A., 2, 214
Watson, J.B., 54, 55
Watzlawick, P., 167
Weedon, C., 100, 101, 104, 183
West, C., 98, 104
Wetherell, M., 27, 76
Wilde, O., 168
Willis, P., 92
Wittgenstein, L., 64, 68, 70
Wolff, C., 40
Woolgar, S., 21, 48, 76, 77
writing, 126–7
Wundt, W.M., 40, 47

Yeats, W.B., 135, 143
Young, N., 135–44

Zavarzdeh, M., 97